July, 2014

*To Lorna and Richard —
Hope you enjoy the journey!
And that your personal journey is
blessed —*

MARIA'S JOURNEY

RAMÓN ARREDONDO & TRISHA (HULL) ARREDONDO

Trisha Hull Arredondo

Foreword by James B. Lane
Introduction by John Bodnar

Indiana Historical Society Press | Indianapolis, 2010

Printed in the United States of America

This book is a publication of the
Indiana Historical Society Press
Eugene and Marilyn Glick Indiana History Center
450 West Ohio Street
Indianapolis, Indiana 46202-3269 USA
www.indianahistory.org
Telephone orders 1-800-447-1830
Fax orders 317-234-0562
Online orders @ http://shop.indianahistory.org

Photo credits for front cover: Courtesy of the Arredondo family

The paper in this publication meets the minimum requirements of American National Standard
for Information Sciences—Permanence of Paper for Printed Library materials, ANSI Z39.48-
1984

Library of Congress Cataloging-in-Publication Data

Arredondo, Ramón.
  Maria's journey / Ramón and Trisha (Hull) Arredondo ; foreword by James B. Lane ; introduc-
tion by John Bodnar.
     p. cm.
ISBN 978-0-87195-286-8 (pbk. : alk. paper)
1. Arredondo, Maria, 1907-2004. 2. Mexican American women—Illinois—Chicago—
Biography. 3. Mexican Americans—Illinois—Chicago—Social life and customs. 4. Immi-
grants—Illinois—Chicago—Biography. 5. Immigrants—Mexico—Biography. 6. Chicago (Ill.)—
Biography. I. Arredondo, Trisha. II. Title.
F548.9.M5A78 2010
305.8968'72073077311—dc22
[B]
                                  2010018209

Publication of this book was made possible by the generous support of the following donors:
Indiana Society of Washington, DC, Gary and Shar L. Miller, Gary and Sandra Neale, and
Joseph and Patricia Turner.

This book is dedicated to Maria (Perez) Arredondo
and all the other mothers who, like her, live their lives
with exceptional strength, sacrifice, faith, and courage
to ensure a better future for their children.

Contents

Foreword

The immigrant experience is a topic of endless fascination to historians and of enduring importance to a full understanding of America's heritage. In 1951 Harvard professor Oscar Handlin published *The Uprooted: The Epic Story of the Great Migrations that Made the American People*, a moving saga of newcomers buffeted by conditions threatening ethnic solidarity and at times rendering families dysfunctional. In 1985 John Bodnar of Indiana University countered with *The Transplanted: A History of Immigrants in Urban America*, which focused on life strategies and adjustments of individuals banding together in the face of economic hardships and nativistic prejudices. Some beat the odds, sprouted strong, lasting roots, and obtained a measure of security and happiness. While neither Handlin nor Bodnar focuses closely on the more than one million Mexicans who migrated north between 1900 and 1930, a new generation of Latino scholars has documented the struggles and triumphs of people once dubbed "invisible Americans."

The Mexican American presence in Northwest Indiana stretches back almost a century to a time of heavy industry. For those settling in the Indiana Harbor section of East Chicago and a similar *colonia* (colony) in nearby Gary, steel manufacturing provided steady, albeit dangerous, work. Some hired in during a traumatic strike in 1919. A steady stream followed during the twenties. Led by Inland Steel, East Chicago factories produced two million tons of steel annually plus such ancillary products as valves, firebricks, cement, oxygen, and petroleum derivatives. In an article in the *Indiana Magazine of History* in December 1981, historians Francisco A. Rosales and Daniel T. Simon compared the Arredondos' neighborhood, located in Inland's shadow, to a frontier town, replete with inadequate housing but no shortage of brothels, speakeasies, gambling dens, cockfighting rings, and billiard halls. Yet there was vibrancy and a sense of *Mexicanidad* or cultural kinship with the homeland. In his book *Barrios Norteños: St. Paul and Midwestern Mexican Communities in the Twentieth Century* (2000), Dionicio Nodín Valdés writes of Latino barbers, tailors, restaurateurs, and merchants offering Harbor residents suits, dresses, confections, *pan dulce* (sweetened bread), *chorizo* (seasoned sausage), and tortillas. Civic leaders such as Miguel Arredondo put on public lectures, sporting events, and celebrations of *Día de Independencia* (Mexican Independence Day, September 16).

Then the Great Depression struck. Steel production dropped precipitously, and government agencies, under prodding from superpatriotic groups, took repressive measures against unemployed aliens. *La Colonia del Harbor* suffered as the result of a nefarious program euphemistically labeled repatriation, in which nearly half a millon Mexicans were either deported or were persuaded to return to Mexico. More than half of those repatriated were legal citizens of the United States. Nascent small businesses and mutual-aid organizations vanished. According to economist Paul S. Taylor, expert on Mexican labor in the United States, the fortunate ones who managed to stay retained a "strong emotional attachment to Mexico, a patriotism heightened . . . by their expatriation and by the attitude of superiority to which they frequently feel themselves subjected." Police harassment was common. Survival skills were at a premium. Margarita Ruiz Maravilla's family, for example, moved a dozen times and sometimes could not afford the fifteen dollar monthly rent. Other times, as Maravilla recalled in a history of the Indiana Harbor by the Señoras of Yesteryear organization (1992), "we found a cheaper or better apartment, one with a bathtub or steam heat." Juanita (Jenny) Arredondo remembered sharing living quarters with other tenants and Maria being forced to do extra chores.

World War II and postwar prosperity reinvigorated Harbor institutions, often under the leadership of returning veterans. Overt forms of discrimination abated. Now one could run successfully for high union office or move into East Chicago's previously all-Anglo neighborhoods (fittingly separated from the Harbor section of the "Twin City" by an industrial canal). Their home a victim of urban renewal, the Arredondos relocated to a more spacious residence. By the 1970s Maria had time to watch her favorite TV soap operas in Spanish while crocheting.

How does *Maria's Journey* fit within the framework of Latino scholarship? It serves as a reliable case study of Mexican family dynamics and of the experiences of Mexicans who immigrated to the Calumet Region of Northwest Indiana nearly a century ago. Mexican family dynamics traditionally were patriarchal, with wives submissive but providing emotional sustenance for household members. Self-sacrificing but with an iron resolve, Maria was nobody's pushover. A practical woman, she believed that God helped those who helped themselves ("*A quien madruga, Dios le ayuda*"). Home was her domain. Husband Miguel administered corporal punishment with his belt, but she was quietly in charge and could wield a broom when necessary. If Maria favored the sons, the motive was to instill them with self-confidence. Upon the birth of a boy, celebrants would exclaim, "How nice, another work check for you!" ("*Qué bueno, otro cheque para ustedes!*"). Daughters accepted the house rules until they got married and moved out. As powerful as were the forces of assimilation, the Arredondos, in the words of youngest son Lorenzo, preferred "the spicy seasoning" to "the melting pot" and retained a strong ethnic identity.

Though unique, Maria's life story exemplifies the resilience strangers in a new land needed to confront successfully life's vicissitudes. Indeed, she represents women in all stations and situations in life who have provided the determination, courage, and persistence needed to hold their families together. Maria emerged strong as the steel forged in the mills that provided employment for Miguel and several of their children. Demanding but devoted, she nurtured a large brood on the tenets of hard work and discipline. They spoke Spanish at home and pulled their weight when they got out of school or even before. Her children's remarkable accomplishments included athletic achievement, high union office, political ascendance, business success, and academic distinction. Whenever they left town, they would solicit Maria's blessing for a safe trip. As Ramón recalled, "We'd kneel before my mom and my grandmother when she was alive, and they'd say some prayers and bless us." The second youngest, Ramón was a keen observer of household dynamics, as was his wife Trisha, who was welcomed without reservation into the family circle. With rare candor, they have recorded for posterity the life journey of an unflappable Mexican American.

James B. Lane

Department of History
Indiana University Northwest

Introduction

The story of immigration is now firmly established in the larger narrative of America. The experiences of newcomers from all corners of the globe currently form a vital part of the very fabric of the nation's history and have become familiar to all. The entire immigration saga is even closely associated with one of the most famous images of America itself—the Statue of Liberty. When citizens celebrated the centennial of the dedication of the monument in 1986, numerous speeches and articles referred to the statue and the nearby immigrant processing station at Ellis Island as beacons that drew millions of newcomers to America and as symbols of the promise the nation represented to many from abroad. In this celebration and in numerous stories told over decades, the point is made repeatedly that individuals seeking political freedom and unprecedented opportunity elected to move to America to realize their dreams.

There can be no question that many people who came to the United States were able to find a life that was more rewarding for themselves and their offspring than the one left behind in some distant homeland. Yet, the idea that immigrant history, or any history for that matter, is simply an account of steady progress, is a myth. Reality can disrupt the storybook version of any experience and render it more confusing—and sometimes more tragic. Thus, any serious retelling of the immigrant experience in America is often filled with all sorts of contradictions. To begin with, American citizens have not always been enthusiastic about the prospect of allowing newcomers to enter the nation. In the 1920s Congress passed a series of bills, severely limiting the arrival of people from southern and eastern Europe and excluding Asians. Chinese immigrants had already been barred in 1882. In the 1960s the pendulum of public opinion became more welcoming again. Federal legislation abolished some of the restrictions enacted in the twenties and made it easier for new arrivals to come from Asia and Latin America. In the present day fierce debates among Americans have once again marked the issue of immigration. On one side critics hostile to contemporary waves of illegal immigrants have called for mass deportations and tighter security at the Mexican border. Those Americans recognizing the historic contributions that newcomers have made to the nation have called for more leniency or at least the creation of a path to citizenship for undocumented workers residing in the United States. Indiana has not escaped some of this controversy. Towns such as Longansport have witnessed controversies in their schools that were sparked by the arrival of Mexicans at a local meatpacking plant. In 2008 the Indiana General Assembly adjourned after being unable to act on a controversial bill that would have cracked down on Indiana companies that hired illegal immigrants.

Underneath the glow of public myths and the glare of political disputes, however, ordinary immigrants have always had to meet the realities of daily life and existence. They have not been able to dwell on fables of success or fears that they were unwanted. They were forced, instead, to find ways to make ends meet, find jobs, and feed their families. The truth is that at the level of daily life the process of settling in America was arduous and not always fulfilling—regardless of how many improvements were being realized over the course of several generations. This story of Maria Arredondo—a woman who struggled against seemingly insurmountable odds just to raise her ten children—is a graphic example of the point that becoming American is often more of an ordeal than the realization of a dream.

Not unlike many immigrants from around the world at various times, Maria lived a life of hardship and turmoil. At key moments in her life decisions were forced upon her. As a child she had to follow relatives to Texas, living the life of a migrant in a boxcar. Her mother coerced her into marrying at age fourteen a man from a higher social station in the vague hope that she could improve the family's fortunes. Throughout her adult life, her spouse, Miguel, was generally insensitive to her needs and insisted she remain confined to her domestic duties. But Maria did not always let others shape the course of her life. In the early years of the Great Depression, when the United States sought to return Mexicans to their homeland so that they would not compete with natives for jobs, Maria—scarred by her early years of deprivation in Mexico—refused to leave. She only returned to Mexico with her children to care for her mother when the elder woman was deported. Soon she brought her family back to America, despite her husband's objections that he could not afford to support them. Faced with countless forces that tried to run her life, Maria retained the ability to fight back and to seek what she thought was best for her children—traits that earned her their everlasting love. When a Catholic priest once asked her to confess her sins, she retorted that with all the cooking, washing, and caring she did for a husband and ten children "do you really think I've got time to sin?"

Maria's Journey is more than an immigrant tale; it is a woman's story that peels back the layers of legend, revealing a life that was marked by a fervent desire to sustain her family in a world and a nation that was intent upon treating her callously. Miguel, of course, played a role and is portrayed not only as a domineering husband but also as a man who was sympathetic to the plight of workers at Inland Steel in East Chicago and worked tirelessly for the advancement of a union. In the end, however, he became a tragic figure who drank heavily, sank into depression, and deprived Maria of the love and affection she needed. She was much loved, however, by her children who remained the center of her life until she died in 2004 at the age of ninety-seven. It is the mix of the tragic and heroic elements that makes her story so compelling. Maria's life was a series of forward and backward steps. Slowly her children moved into the mainstream of American life—into schools, the military, and jobs. Perhaps Maria felt their adjustment to a new country justified all the sacrifices and struggles she made. Her story makes it clear that Maria's life in her adopted country was not simply a happy one. For her, as for many immigrants, America is not merely a land of opportunity—it is a place of mixed blessings and of unpredictable twists and turns.

John Bodnar

Department of History
Indiana University, Bloomington

Arredondo Family Tree

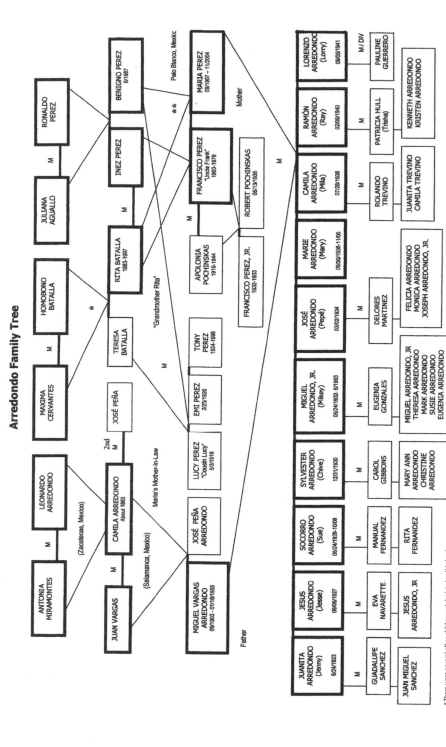

* There were several other children not depicted in this book.
** Rita and Benigno lived together for 11 years after her husband, Inez, died.

1

The Revolution

For centuries Mexico had been divided into two separate classes: those who ruled and those who labored for the rulers. Much like the feudal system of Europe, the wealthy garnered the major part of any profits, while the workers eked out a meager existence. With time the laborers grew weary of the inequities and injustices of the system. They rebelled in an effort to gain at least the beginnings of equality. By 1911 a popular uprising, which became known as the Mexican Revolution, had forced dictator Porfirio Díaz to resign, but his successor, Francisco Madero, displeased revolutionary leaders Pancho Villa and Emiliano Zapata. When Victoriano Huerta deposed Madero two years later, the revolution intensified, affecting peasants living in the state of Guanajuato in south-central Mexico.

"Be quiet *mija*," whispered Rita Batalla Perez, shushing her daughter as they hid from the soldiers. Times were hard in the state of Guanajuato, Mexico, in 1911, as the revolution ravaged the land. Women and young girls took care to keep away from the troops of soldiers who marched through the farms and villages. Raping and pillaging were not just rumors, but a reality many had witnessed. The women were especially vulnerable, but men, too, were at risk of being forcefully conscripted into whichever army was tramping through.

From their position in the bushes, Rita and Maria watched as young boys hidden high in the treetops taunted the marching troops with their slingshots. Pebbles whizzed through the air giving the boys momentary satisfaction as the soldiers looked around trying to discover the source of the missiles. Such devilment was usually ignored, but with enough provocation the men could turn angry. The single-file line of soldiers had been marching through since dawn. It was now late afternoon, and no end to the procession was in sight.

"Those boys should stop that foolishness and lay low until the men pass," Rita hissed. "They'll only cause trouble for themselves."

Maria's huge brown eyes got even wider. The four-year-old shivered with fear at her mother's words. Her ears were filled with warnings: "Stay close," "Don't wander away," "Keep away from the troops, don't draw their attention." Fear was everywhere, and her mother and others like her walked around with stern and worried expressions, their lips moving silently as they prayed, rosary beads passing through fingers hardened by the work of the fields.

Though Maria was too young to understand the nuances of the conflict, she understood all too well the dangers it precipitated. A minority of politicians and businessmen controlled Mexico, while a majority of the population lived and labored in poverty. The schism between the two gradually had flamed the anger of generations; like a drug, the rage of the people infused the blood of men such as Pancho Villa and Emiliano Zapata and inspired them to lead a revolution against the elitist government. In the wake of war the very ones for whom the battles were waged suffered the most. Both sides inflicted further hardships.

"You can trust no one, *mija*," Rita instructed her daughter, using a loving term for "daughter."

"Try to remain invisible. These men will take what they want and there is nothing we can do. At least the rebels will pay something for what they take. The government? Ha! They will steal and ride away. No one in the government cares. They will capture or kill our men and leave the women and children to starve!"

Those in power changed daily. Farmers, peasants, and villagers simply complied with the wishes of whoever was in control at the moment. There was no help to be had from the government unless one was a landowner. Subsidies were unheard of—those who had money ate; those who did not went hungry. The local population was so fearful of the soldiers that when one was shot and lay dead by the road for days, no one came close to him. His money pouch was visible, but despite the peasants' poverty, no one chanced removing it. Fear outweighed even starvation.

Life was a continual struggle. For those like Rita and Maria, each day was a quest for survival. Maria had a vague memory of her father, Benigno. When he was with the family, things had been somewhat easier, but Benigno was gone. Maria scarcely remembered him, though her eight-year-old brother Francisco held some memories of the handsome man who had cared for his mother and then disappeared from their lives. Rita did not speak of him. Her face grew tight if Francisco inquired about his father, and she would turn away in silence. Francisco stopped asking. Maria and her older brother had learned to accept the fact that it was just the three of them in a world where no one offered help or solace.

Hunger became an unwelcome visitor. Rita worked the fields of their tenant land barefoot, picking what crops were in season. If the year brought good crops, life was somewhat bearable, but a bad year meant even more deprivation. The troops were an ever-present factor that could turn any day into a deadly serious game of hide and seek. With no father the family was at a huge disadvantage. In those times a man's presence at least brought some security and respect. A single mother and her children had little status.

Francisco brought home what money he could, taking work where he could find it. For a while he herded sheep, other times he took odd jobs, no matter how difficult or low paying. As the older brother, he bore the responsibility of the man of the house.

"It is so cold at night, mother," he would teasingly complain when he returned from the fields. "I wish I had the coats of the sheep. Then I could lie under the stars and talk to the moon without shivering!"

Rita tried to make light of their situation, pretending to scold Francisco all the while using a loving term for "son." "Talk all you want, *mijo*. The moon will still shine down on you whether you are warm or cold, rich or poor. But though his face may smile, he won't put food in your mouth. You must do that, son, for free meals aren't for the poor."

Maria would smile at her mother and brother's easy banter. She knew she and her brother were loved, no matter how hungry they might be. She willingly helped her mother in the fields, working alongside the other women and children.

In her younger years she sang with the rest of the children as she worked in the fields beside her mother. Her clear, sweet voice happily rose in the words of traditional Mexican songs. She never worried that their "house" was little more than a shanty and meals so meager that a tortilla with salt often carried her through the day. Youth carries its own optimism, and even their squalid conditions couldn't dampen her belief that a better future awaited her.

Rita gave her children a strong faith in God and His goodness, teaching them to pray to statues of the saints that stood on a small kitchen shelf. Each night Maria begged these little wooden icons to watch over her and her family.

Palo Blanco, Salamanca, in the 1950s—where Rita, Frank, and Maria Perez lived during the Mexican Revolution (1910–20)

"Please," she whispered before falling asleep on the lumpy blanket that was her bed. "Please, God, help us to find enough food. Help me to stop worrying and give my brother work. Please, God, give us a better life."

With those words the young girl would close her tired eyes and sleep until the morning brought another day. Though she often awoke with a growling stomach and feet cut and bruised from long hours of working in the fields, her dream of a happier existence did not leave her.

Sometimes Rita's sister, Aunt Teresa, and her daughter, cousin Lucy, would visit Maria and her family, making the trek from the nearby town of Salamanca. While Rita and Teresa talked, the girls would play in the dirt yard, chasing chickens or playing hide and seek in the bleak surroundings of the tiny hut that was their home. After these visits from her sister, Rita would become distant. Maria was not sure if her mother was sad or angry, but she knew she was unhappy.

"What's wrong, *madre* (mother)?" Maria asked. "Don't you like *Tía* (Aunt) Teresa?"

Rita gave Maria a long look, then shook her lovely head. Her large eyes took on a faraway look as she answered.

"She's my sister, *mija*. You can't dislike your sister no matter what. She's family and family comes first."

Maria received no further explanation.

❖

"Ma," Francisco approached Rita one day.

"I have decided it's time for me to leave. There is no way we will ever be anything other than poor peasants if we continue as we are. My friend, Jorge, writes there are jobs in Texas. I want to go."

"Mijo, Texas is so far away! What will Maria and I do when you are gone?"

Rita's concern was genuine. She loved her son dearly and had come to rely on him to help support the family. If he left, she would have neither emotional nor financial assistance.

"Don't worry, Ma. I will send money home and, when I see the work in Texas is steady, I will send for you and my sister. You know I won't desert you."

"Let me think, my son," said Rita sighing deeply. "We will talk of this again tomorrow."

Rita knew that her son was right. She had heard from friends that Texas offered jobs and many had left Mexico for the money, much of which was sent home to relatives suffering from the poverty afflicting the country. With a heavy heart she gave her son permission to leave. Francisco quickly readied for his sojourn. He knelt before his mother as she invoked a blessing in which she beseeched her special saints to watch over her firstborn. They embraced. Then Francisco held Maria close.

"Don't be sad, little sister. Soon we will be together again. Take care of our mother while I'm gone."

Francisco left the farm as mother and daughter stood together watching until he faded from sight.

<hr />

During this period, crossing the border was relatively easy, with official papers rarely asked for. It was as easy as saying one was crossing "to shop" and simply not returning.

It was several months later that Frank, as he came to be called, sent for Rita and Maria. The twentieth century had progressed to its second decade, and the years had not brought with them better days. Rita had spent years trying to think of ways to improve her family's life. Perhaps this would be the answer she sought, so she and eleven-year-old Maria made the trip to Texas, where Frank had found work with the railroad.

Living conditions were primitive. Housing consisted of old boxcars located virtually in the middle of nowhere. It was to this bleak environment that Maria and her mother journeyed to join Frank as they sought the American dream.

Their lives were isolated and hard. Never leaving the encampment, Maria and Rita spent their days keeping the house, making food, and washing clothes for the workers to earn a few additional dollars. Texas weather seemed to fluctuate from miserably cold and windy to unbearably hot and dry. The boxcars offered no amenities other than shelter and were cold or hot as the weather dictated. Cooking and washing were primarily outdoor chores accomplished over campfires. Days were bleak and lonely, especially for the work-weary women. Ironically, discrimination was one hardship they did not suffer. Other than the Anglo foreman who barked out orders and handed out paychecks, there were no Americans with whom to interact.

With each day, the hopelessness of the situation seemed more apparent. Despite Frank's work on the railroad and the women's work at home, little money was left after paying for food and the miserable lodgings. Each night they fell into an exhausted sleep with nothing to look forward to except repetition of the day before. After nine months Rita had had enough.

"Francisco, *mijo*, if this is what America has to offer, it is not for your mother. This land, it goes on forever! And never a house, never a village, not even a church to kneel and pray! Only this wind, which never lets go.

"I'm sorry, *mijo*, your sister and I must return home. There I at least know people I can talk with and a priest who can bless me with the Body of Christ. Maria and I will be fine. You stay. Do not worry about us. God tells me we will all be together again. But, for now, I must leave. I will pray. God will show us the way."

Frank did not try to persuade his mother to remain. He had known the endless stretches of land and the relentless loneliness only saddened her more.

"Go, Mother. I will miss you and Maria, but I understand."

Again they embraced. This time it was Frank who watched until his mother's train was lost in the distance.

Rita and Maria returned to their homeland to find that the uncertain conditions had not improved. Many families had fled from farms to towns where a relatively larger population offered some safety from the troops. Rita settled into this reality but continued to dream of an escape from such hardships for herself and her children. Determinedly, she schemed to find the path to the fulfillment of her dream.

2

The Bargain

Arranged marriages were not uncommon in Mexico during the early years of the twentieth century, as parental pressures often took precedence over notions of romantic love and adolescent freedom.

When Maria reached the age of fourteen, Rita hit upon a plan, the crux of which lay with a woman called Camila Arredondo. Camila owned property in town and had two sons, Miguel and José. She was a strong personality, and her arrival in the town of Salamanca was somewhat of a mystery. No one seemed sure of where she came from, though her light gray eyes hinted at European heritage.

In those days of upheaval and continual relocation it was accepted as more or less the norm for individuals to appear from nowhere to settle into a new life. Camila had a reputation for loving a good time; she was an excellent dancer and was said to have worn out a pair of shoes in a single evening. More important to Rita, she was also known as a shrewd businesswoman who ran a bar and soon had invested in a good deal of property. Camila had also met a man named José Peña, and the two had begun to build a life together. Rita made it her mission to discover more about this woman whose achievements, both financial and personal, impressed her.

"Tell me about this Camila woman," Rita demanded of Manuel, a tradesman she knew well. She had come to the nearby town of Salamanca to buy the little cornmeal her meager farm wages would allow and deliberately approached the tradesman at a quiet time.

"Who? Camila? The one who dances 'til she wears out her shoes? What do you care about the likes of her?"

"I was just wondering," continued Rita. "I hear she has done well. Did she bring money with her when she settled in Salamanca?"

"Ha!" exclaimed Rita's acquaintance. "Who knows? She comes into town one day with her little sons, flashing those gray eyes. Nobody seems to know anything about her. Before you know it, she is buying a bar and José has fallen for her, taking in her and her sons."

"Oh. She has sons?" Rita asked innocently, knowing the answer full well.

"Sure, like I said, two. But not for long. The older one, Miguel, is in love with a girl who works at the bakery."

Rita's expression remained placid but her mind was racing.

"So this son is to marry?"

"Not if Camila has anything to say about it!" laughed Manuel. "I hear she's not in favor of the match."

"Why?"

"Why? How should I know! What do you care anyway? The woman's hard as nails. I'd stay out of her way if I were you."

"Oh, of course you're right. I was just curious," smiled Rita, placing a few pesos on the counter as she gathered her bundles and left.

Rita had learned all she needed. She set about finding a way to link her fortune with the tough entrepreneur who had managed to gain land and property under the most difficult of conditions. To Rita the situation was supremely simple: Camila had a son of marrying age, and she, Rita, had a beautiful young daughter. A marriage between the two could improve both her and her daughter's future prospects.

After further initial queries into Camila's affairs, Rita discovered that the older son, Miguel, who was a handsome young man and a weaver by trade, had fallen in love with a young girl his mother disapproved of, not for the girl herself, but because of her father. Camila was adamantly against the match because the girl's father was a high-ranking military officer; his status would severely outrank Camila's own standing. Far from seeing this as a step up the social ladder, Camila foresaw that Miguel would soon be lost to her when the prospective father-in-law used his power to dominate and dictate to the couple.

Camila, accustomed to controlling both people and events, viewed such a union as detrimental to her own aims. If anyone were to wield influence over her son, it would be Camila herself. The situation was ripe for Rita to seize the moment. With Maria as her bargaining chip she concocted a straightforward

Miguel Vargas Arredondo (left) and his brother José

proposition: their children should marry. Such a forging of families would give Rita connections to a more prosperous way of life. For Camila it would squelch the possibility of a coupling that could diminish her influence over her son, Miguel.

Juan Vargas, Camila's first husband and Miguel's father, had been Austrian—a tall, blue-eyed blond who claimed his own father had been close to Emperor Maximilian and his wife, Carlota, when they ruled Mexico. Miguel had vague memories of fishing with nets accompanied by his father and grandfathers in the town of Pátzcuaro, Michoacán, Mexico, where Miguel listened to stories of glory in the "old days" when Napoléon's cousin Maximilian ruled Mexico. Camila had reinforced the idea that "royal blood" flowed through the family's veins, and Miguel always considered himself to be of "kingly" ancestry. The last name of Vargas had been changed from Varga in order to blend better into Mexican culture. True or not, the perpetuation of the story served to enhance the mystery of Camila Arredondo and her sons.

Rita's maiden name of Batalla had Spanish-Italian origins with the family's genealogy presumed to be rooted somewhere either in the southern part of Spain or Italy, although there was no proof other than the original spelling having been changed from Bataglia to Batalla through time (in truth, the vast majority of Mexicans were a mixture of indigenous native Indians and one or more of the numerous European groups).

Rita was not naïve. She realized her standing would be less than nothing in Camila's eyes. She had no money, no land, and no family connections. She was a poor peasant, a woman without a husband. But she had two things in her favor: her will was as strong as Camila's, and her daughter was a beautiful, unsullied girl. Carefully, she arranged a meeting between herself and Camila. An invitation of sorts was sent to Rita by Camila whose curiosity was peaked as to why this woman, a stranger to her, wished to meet.

Entering Camila's home, Rita found the woman sitting in a straight-backed chair, clearly awaiting her arrival. She made no move to welcome Rita, merely nodded and asked, "What is it you want?"

Rita did not flinch, but stood all the straighter as she put forth her proposition.

"*Señora*, I know that you have a son of marriageable age and that you do not bless the union he wishes," Rita spoke boldly without hesitation.

"And what is that to you?" snapped Camila, her face tightening. A beam of sunlight streaked in from the window causing her gray eyes to gleam menacingly.

Rita stood her ground.

"I, too, have a child of marriageable age. A beautiful, innocent girl who would treat your son and you with great respect. I believe that a union between them would give us both what we want," she hesitated before adding, "their happiness."

The matriarchs met each other's eyes as the moments slipped by. Camila weighed the proposal and saw it was a match that would offer her no worries. A lovely, malleable young woman with no standing in society who could be manipulated easily was all Camila had hoped for. Slowly she nodded.

"You are right, Señora Perez. Let us discuss this matter further."

———◆◆◆———

"Marry?" cried Maria when Rita explained the bargain she had made with Camila Arredondo.

"But, Mother, I don't know this Miguel Arredondo. What if he is horrible? What if he doesn't like me? What will I do? I know nothing about being a wife. What if *I* don't like *him*?"

Rita stood patiently as her daughter poured out her fears. When at last Maria ran out of questions and sat trying to absorb the news her mother had brought to her, Rita spoke.

Rita (Batalla) Perez and fourteen-year-old Maria
Perez on Maria's wedding day, May 30, 1922

"Maria, I know this seems sudden, but you must understand. This man is the son of a wealthy woman. As her daughter-in-law, you will be part of a family who has property and money. You will have the life you deserve and I, as your mother, will have a daughter who can help care for me.

"Don't you see, my child, we will all be better off. You worry for nothing. Miguel cannot help but love a girl as good and beautiful as you. And his mother wants this marriage. He is an obedient son. He will follow her wishes. Besides, *mija*, a woman should be married. She should have a man to care for her. To protect her."

Maria, hardly understanding the words her mother had spoken, struggled to comprehend what had taken place. Awakening that morning, her life had been one of a daughter living with the mother she adored—the only person who had cared for her and never, ever left her side for the fourteen years of her existence.

Now she was to become a wife to a stranger, expected to leave her mother. Expected to start a new life without the slightest idea as to what the future might hold in store.

By the next day, Maria had pushed her doubts deep within herself. She had prayed to her saints and reminded herself that her mother loved her. Of course, she would do as her mother asked. There was never any doubt of that, not really. Family was everything. If her marrying would give her mother a better life, all would be worth it. And who knew? Maybe she would love this Miguel. Maybe he would love her. Maybe theirs would be a happy marriage. Maybe, maybe, maybe.

Maria's beauty and purity is evident in the picture taken on her wedding day. She stands solemnly by her mother—herself a handsome woman—and peers out at the world with resignation and trepidation as she prepared to enter into an arranged marriage in which she had virtually no say. Only fourteen, she exhibited the kind of strength and stoicism that would serve her well during the twists and turns life had in store. While she might have had many misgivings, she knew her mother had struck a bargain, and she could not disobey her wishes.

Miguel, too, never thought to challenge his mother's plan, although the forced marriage was obviously not his choice. Having been an altar boy and deeply religious, he may have been a reluctant groom, but he accepted his fate. Both he and Maria adhered to the custom of the time, and the two were married on May 30, 1922. Miguel was seventeen years of age. After the wedding ceremony, each returned to their own home with their mothers. The couple met and talked daily until, eventually, the marriage was consummated.

3

From Texas Boxcars to Illinois Rails

Many Mexican immigrants to the Calumet Region first found work in Texas and, like Miguel Arredondo, were employed by railroad companies before becoming steelworkers. Most believed that their sojourn in America would be temporary and that they would return home. Miguel's son, Jesse, recalled that his father "worked one of those machines that you pedal with your feet to make a blanket. He figured he'd earn a thousand dollars in America and go back and buy that machine and be in business for himself."

Camila Arredondo may have been a woman of means, but she had no intention of sharing her money with anyone, including her son. After all, she reasoned, she had had no help in accumulating what she owned. Every peso she had, she had worked for. Why would her son or anyone else be entitled to what was hers? She would provide a home, but her son would work for everything else. Giving things only led to more being expected. Far better to let her boy make his way for himself. He would value it more. He would be a proud man.

It took little time for Miguel to understand that any idea of an easier life was not to be gained through help from a generous mother. Though he worked hard, there was never any money remaining from his pay. The dependency on Camila for housing only exacerbated the situation. Far from getting "free rent," Miguel was expected to earn his keep by helping maintain the property, while Maria was thrown into a role hardly more than a servant. She cleaned, prepared meals, and did Camila's bidding in whatever was asked.

Miguel realized that to support his wife he would have to leave Mexico. He made his way to the United States, but not before their first child, Juanita, was born on June 24, 1923. At the border Miguel was told he must choose only one last name to note his crossing. Traditionally, Mexicans used two last names, the father's and the mother's. Miguel chose his mother's, Arredondo.

The trek to the North was a circuitous one that saw Miguel spending years alone as he prepared a life for his wife and child. As with many Mexicans, he retained a strong sense of nationalism and planned to remain in the States only long enough to earn money to buy his own loom. This would allow him to set up his own business in his homeland and support his family as a weaver. Miguel was intelligent and ambitious. He was unafraid to set out on a new venture in a new land. His wide range of interests, avid reading habits, and a grasp of the "bigger picture," especially in the area of world politics, would eventually single him out as a leader in this new country, but at the time the young man's sole purpose was to garner the cash for the coveted loom.

"We can't stay here," Miguel announced to his young bride. "Mexico has nothing for us until I earn enough money for my own shop. Then we can have a home. My mother will help us after I prove I can earn a living. You will see."

Maria could only nod. A young girl who had seen America from the worst vantage point could hardly have been overjoyed at the prospect of returning. Yet Miguel was now her husband. Though not affectionate, he was handsome and persuasive. She visualized herself in a home of her own and was content to follow him to reach that goal. Even had she not been compliant, there would have been little choice. In Mexico the man was head of the house. His decisions were followed; his word was law.

Miguel left Mexico in the summer of 1923, forty days after the birth of his daughter, and eventually settled in Indiana Harbor, where he worked at the huge industrial giant, Inland Steel. But this final destination was years away. Prior to reaching Indiana, he worked numerous stops along the way, including a short stint in a Pennsylvania coal mine, where his brother José had found work. He discovered this to be the worst of all worlds. The dark, closed life of the coal miner was far too confining for Miguel. It was not until October 1926 that he at last felt he could send for Maria and Juanita and face the challenges of living in the United States as a family. He was living in Texas where he had found work on the railroad.

Having waited with rare stoicism and patience for three long years, Maria would journey, once again, to Texas. And, once again, she would leave Rita, to whom she had returned to raise her child when Miguel had traveled north.

Maria and three-year-old Juanita, along with a cousin, Josephina Gonzalez, and her one-year-old daughter, Adela, embarked on the first leg of the trip north by train. It was a journey fraught with fears and misgivings for the timid Maria, but the company of her cousin was a comfort. Maria was leaving her mother to meet a husband she had not seen in years. Salamanca, her hometown, remained a region of poverty and struggle. A new future in a new land with her husband was both scary and exciting; a past life that she would later describe as being "very sad and very poor" was about to be exchanged for one that—at the very least—was bound to be different. And, like Miguel, Maria viewed the departure as a temporary one. When they had enough money saved, they would return to Mexico and a home of their own.

"I wonder what it will be like?" Josephina asked Maria.

Maria did not answer. She looked down at Juanita sleeping on her lap, a child unaware that her life was about to change radically. Her Grandmother Rita remained in Salamanca and would not be there to comfort her first grandchild; her father, who had left when she was just over a month old, was waiting at the other end of their journey. None of this worried the sleeping child. Maria, however, knew all too well how harsh life could be. Her mind flashed back to days before she was to deliver her baby. She had gone to her mother-in-law, Camila, to ask for help. She'd been welcomed with a stony gaze.

"Go. Deliver your child beneath the trees out there. You're a girl of the fields. It shouldn't be hard for you. Go. Bring me my grandson when he is born, and then we'll see what you need."

Tears of humiliation and anger burned in Maria's eyes as she trudged back to the spare lodgings she shared with Rita. She told her mother the story and watched as Rita's mouth tightened.

"You'll have the child here," said Rita. "Then we shall see." Rita's voice was cold and hard, but she said nothing more. There were no words of scorn for Camila or her son, Miguel. Rita would wait. Wait and see.

When Maria delivered Juanita she knew Camila would be displeased. It was a grandson Camila wanted, a boy who would grow up strong and help support her in her old age. What good was a girl who would grow up, marry, and produce more babies? Just another burden.

"What do you think, Maria?" Josephina asked again, interrupting Maria's reverie.

Maria pulled herself from her unhappy memories and looked her cousin directly in her eyes.

"I think it will be better here. We will work hard and raise our daughters. We will have our own family and be independent. Yes," she nodded, her expression both hopeful and determined, "yes, I think it will be better."

Josephina smiled, reassured by her cousin. They were young and strong and healthy. Everyone said the United States was a place to live better and earn a decent living. Yes, they would be happy, she was sure of it.

Husbands Miguel and Domingo met the women and children in the Texas border town of Laredo. Here both men labored and saved money until they were able to work their way farther north to Dallas. Again, Maria lived in box-cars furnished by the railroad as she had as a child of eleven. Though still only eighteen and barely more than a child herself, she was now a married woman with a child, responsible for the care of her family.

The task was one she accepted as she accepted all things throughout her lifetime, with courage, dignity, and determination. As she had on her wedding day, she kept her misgivings to herself, though it was becoming more and more apparent that life gave her little in the way of options. She did as she was directed with one exception: the realm of motherhood. Here, she reigned supreme, for Miguel showed little time or interest for his daughter. His domain was the outside world of work and community; Maria's was home, hearth, and child. This division of power was established early on and would continue as a well-ingrained dynamic within the couple's relationship and within the family as a whole.

———◆•✳•◆———

Upon arrival in the States, Maria and Josephina set up housekeeping. A woodstove was used for cooking, and Josephina and little "Jenny," as Juanita was called, would go to fetch wood while shy Maria remained home with Adela. Again, the boxcar was isolated from most civilization save for the railroad workers. It was not as lonely with her cousin and their daughters, and the railroad company did provide coal for heat. Maria began to like the quiet solitude of her life. She became comfortable with her situation and looked forward to getting the yearly travel pass the railroad provided its employees. She missed her mother and the dream of a trip home helped sustain her through the work-filled days. She and Josephina cooked, cleaned, and did laundry for their husbands and other workers just as she'd done with her mother, but this time she had a purpose, a child to raise and a happier future to secure.

While the men worked on the railroad, Maria and Josephina established their own routine. They arose early to make breakfast and pack their husbands' lunches. In winter the women cooked over their outdoor fire, shivering as they stirred pots of beans and fashioned cornmeal dough into flat, round tortillas.

Laundry was done twice weekly or three times if the clothes taken in from other workers required additional time. A clothesline strung between the boxcar and a straggly tree weighed heavily with drying garments. During cold months the wash froze into icy scarecrows swaying stiffly in the wind until temperatures moderated. The women's hands grew red and cracked from plunging laundry into scalding water and rubbing each piece up and down on galvanized washboards.

In warmer weather both laundry and cooking grew less arduous. Shade from the boxcar gave some relief from the sweltering winds and blazing hot sun. In summer's heat the clothes first hung in the dry dusty wind were dry and ready to bring in before the last of the load was pinned at the end of the clothesline.

In the evenings, when temperatures cooled and the wind diminished to a steady breeze, Maria and Josephina would place their daughters on blankets to play and nap as they prepared supper. The wind harmonized with the songs of birds and insects as Maria watched the fire's hypnotic flame and considered her future.

She had gained what she had sought, at least in part. Camila, her nemesis, was left behind in Salamanca. She and little Juanita were reunited with Miguel. And, most important to a woman who had lived a life of constant fear and chronic insecurity, her family had reached the "promised land" where her husband earned a steady wage. To others, a life lived in boxcars in the flat, open plains of Texas might seem the stuff of nightmares, but for Maria it was a part of her dream fulfilled.

Oh, there was more she longed for, but such things could come later: a home of her own, sons, a life that did not require such a rigorous workload. Not that she coveted a life of ease. She accepted and, indeed, expected that hard work would be her lot. But, perhaps if she had sons, she would have someone who could care for her in her old age. Someone she could depend upon to love her and see to her needs.

And, she had not given up on Miguel's love. She knew he was a hard man with little ability to show affection. But then, how could he have learned to display love when raised by a woman who lacked compassion? A mother who had instilled a distrust of women and deliberately arranged his marriage to one she believed would be easily dominated could hardly qualify as a loving, caring role model.

Now that they were free of Camila's presence, now that she, Maria, had Miguel to herself, she would teach him that love between a man and a woman could be beautiful.

Oh, yes, she mused, she would prove to Miguel that his mother was not the person who had his interests at heart. She would convince him that it was she, Maria, who held his happiness, the one who cared for him. In time, she told herself as the Texas breeze brushed her face, in time, she would break Camila's stronghold. In time, Miguel would come to learn to love her as she had come to love him.

Maria imagined a time when she would return to Mexico on her railroad pass—return triumphant on the arm of her loving husband. Unfortunately for Maria, she and her little family did not stay long enough to earn the free travel pass. Miguel had heard that things were more prosperous in Illinois and Indiana, and his ambitions led him, his family, and the Gonzalez family to work their way across the country to Blue Island, Illinois. A friend, José Campos, was already established in Blue Island and took the families under his wing. In a pattern that would repeat itself throughout the years, these friends helped the Arredondos become established in the town.

The home of the Campos was crowded with the addition of their guests, but such was the culture of the times. Immigrants gave each other a hand up as they became accustomed to their new surroundings, for it was obvious that no one else was going to welcome them into the United States. Mexicans, like other nationalities before them, clustered together for mutual support. They were not wanted by other residents who had fought to garner their own place in America's vast melting pot and jealously guarded their hard-won position.

"Don't worry, Maria, you'll be fine here," Señora Campos reassured her houseguest. "If the storekeeper doesn't speak Spanish, just point out what you want. I'll help you to learn the money. The important thing is to remember most everyone here came from the old country. They understand. We're in the same boat. We help each other. Soon you'll have your own place and you, Miguel, and little Juanita will settle in."

Maria was grateful for such advice. She didn't mind sharing the living quarters and was thankful to have the Camposes to rely on. Sometimes at night she would shed a tear as she prayed for her small family and for her

Map of the Mexican colonies in the Chicago area in the late 1920s from Forging a Community: The Latino Experience in Northwest Indiana, 1919–1975, *edited by James B. Lane and Edward J. Escobar (1987).*

mother in Mexico, but she clung to her young daughter and remembered why she had come.

As Señora Campos helped Maria navigate the grocery stores, José Campos assisted Miguel in searching out lodging for his family and securing a job with the railroad. Miguel recognized that this country could offer steady work. He had traveled to California in his early teens to work as a fruit picker and, while the area was beautiful and the climate ideal, seasonal work held no promise of security. He thought the harsh climate and unlovely surroundings of Illinois were a reasonable trade-off for relatively good wages and long-term employment.

In these early years, Maria held the family close while Miguel worked for the railroad. A home was found, and the Gonzalezes shared living space with the Arredondos as each family adapted to life in yet another environment. As they had in Texas, Josephina and Maria worked out a routine of caring for home and family. Later in the 1920s, other relatives from Salamanca came and they, too, lived with the Arredondos until they settled into a place of their own.

This practice of multiple families residing together was common for housing was scarce. Families or acquaintances lived together in dreary, crowded quarters, making do as best they could. Single men, called *solos*, made up the bulk of the Mexican population, immigrating without families to earn money that they could send back to their loved ones in Mexico or, as had been Miguel's case, until they had funds enough to bring their families to join them. It was in this environment that Miguel and Maria entered a new phase of their lives.

On September 5, 1927, Maria gave birth to their second child, Jesus, who came to be called "Jesse." Maria consulted her calendar for the saint representing the date. It was Saint Lorenzo's day. Maria disliked the name and arbitrarily chose "Jesus" for her first son. After all, what better name was there than the name of God's own Son.

A midwife was called when Maria delivered in Blue Island, and the birth was relatively routine. If Miguel were delighted at the birth of his son, he gave little indication. "Women's business" is what he considered everything linked to home and child rearing. Miguel was a prototype of Mexican men of the time. His focus was on his work; his demeanor was stern and lacked affectionate displays; and he preferred talking with other men to spending time with his wife and family. Maria accepted this from her handsome husband; as long as he provided for her and her children, she sought little else.

"He's beautiful, Maria," her friends exclaimed when they saw the boy. Jenny was fascinated by her new brother. She had another happy arrival to delight her as well. Her Grandmother Rita and her Uncle Francisco had arrived in Blue Island. Both Maria and Jenny were happy to have real family near. For Maria, her mother was again close enough to provide advice, act as a confidante, and help with Jesse and Jenny. For Jenny, Grandma Rita brought her the love and attention she craved.

Francisco, who Jenny called Uncle Frank, found work with the railroad at the "Round House," the circular building in which train engines were cleaned. For Maria having her older brother and her mother gave her a sense of security that only a family could provide. Still very young and inexperienced, she turned to Rita for support and guidance. She felt that life was now complete and gratefully settled into a routine that included not only her husband and children, but also her dear mother and brother.

4

Tragedy Has Two Faces

During the 1920s the Chicago, Rock Island, and Pacific Railroad, known as Rock Island Railroad, operated a freight yard, repair shops, and a roundhouse in Blue Island, a city of approximately fifteen thousand residents located just south of Chicago in Cook County, Illinois. Although the workplace could be a dangerous one, the facilities provided employment opportunities for Slovaks, Italians, and Poles, as well as Mexican immigrants. Enterprising immigrants established groceries, eateries, barbershops, and billiard halls in the area that were frequented by fellow immigrants.

Maria's joy was cut short in 1928 when tragedy befell the family. Jenny entered the kitchen one morning and found her mother at the table nursing one-year-old Jesse as she cleaned beans for the evening meal. The scene appeared a normal one until Jenny noticed tears streaming down her mother's face.

"Ma, why are you crying?" asked the five-year-old, alarmed to see her lovely mother in such distress.

Her mother adjusted her large shawl called a *rebozo*, clutching it closer to her as if seeking its protection.

"Your Uncle Frank is in the hospital," she replied, her voice choked with tears.

"Why, what's happened? Is he sick?" Jenny's eyes widened with fear.

"Yes, he's sick. He is very sick," her mother answered. Her voice trailed away, and she said no more.

It was obvious that some monumental event had caused her mother great distress, but Maria remained silent and continued with meal preparations. Jenny was greatly disturbed but sensed that pressing the matter would only

Maria's brother Francisco (Frank) Perez

make her mother sadder. Later that day, Jenny learned that her uncle was not sick but had been in a terrible accident. Leaving work on his lunch break, Frank walked the short distance home to eat. Always reluctant to leave the comfort of home, he dawdled and realized he was running late. Impatient to reach work on time, he called "goodbye" over his shoulder and hastily made his way back to the railroad. It was then that he made the fateful decision to duck under a train that was blocking his way rather than taking the time to climb over it.

Just as he was crawling to the other side, Frank heard a loud noise and realized two trains were coupling. Though he frantically scrambled out from under the menacing wheels, he was not quite quick enough. His left arm was mangled. His forearm and left hand dangled uselessly. Frank's scream pierced the air, rising above the screech of the train's wheels as they braked. As he sat next to the track, he fainted at the shock; the pain and blood were overwhelming. People ran to his aid, calling for him to hang on. One man tied his belt above the elbow, slowing the bleeding. Others ran for a doctor. As Frank drifted in and out of consciousness, a priest was called to administer the last rites for he was in grave danger of dying.

Frank was transported to a hospital, where it was determined the arm had to be amputated just below the elbow. Seeing the result of his haste, Frank fell into a deep depression. How would he work? What would he do now that he had lost an arm? Cleaning engines required a strong, able-bodied man. What could he possibly do now that he was handicapped? For him the future seemed to hold only pain. Why hadn't he left home earlier instead of eating one more taco? Why hadn't he gone around the train instead of stupidly trying to duck underneath? He tortured himself as he relived that afternoon over and over.

As soon as possible, Rita visited him. As he lay bemoaning his fate, she looked at him sternly. She was having none of his self-pity.

"Stop, *mijo!*" she said loudly, cutting Frank off in midsentence. "Enough of this! You should be grateful to be alive. Stop this whining and be a man! Pray to God for help. He will show you what to do!"

His mother's words broke through Frank's pain. He began to rally. He began to think of his future and plan a strategy for his recovery.

In a rather macabre turn, he directed his arm to be formally placed into a tiny casket and interred in a local cemetery. With that task behind him, he set about healing. He had experienced an unfortunate mishap, to be sure, but he had survived hardships in the past; this was but another hurdle to overcome.

As with other events the family would experience throughout the years, this tragedy had a positive side. Whether it was Rita's admonishment to put things in God's hands or simply the excellent disability policy of the Rock Island Railroad, a settlement was awarded as compensation for Frank's injury, and he was guaranteed a lifetime job with the railroad. He used the settlement money to purchase a billiard parlor in Blue Island. With steady work as a railroad crossing guard and his own billiard parlor, the future brightened.

Such parlors served as primary gathering places for Mexican men. Here, the music and familiar language brought some comforts of home. These establishments became the nearest thing immigrants had to a community house. Over drinks and a game of billiards, the men discussed the news of the day, available jobs, family comings and goings, events in Mexico, and political topics. For these strangers in a strange land, the parlors were a haven from their harsh environment. Other than work, there was little opportunity for coming together with friends; young Mexicans were barred from most forms of socialization and entertainment. They turned to the billiard parlors for companionship and for a sense of belonging that was sorely lacking elsewhere. Frank had found a niche that served him well; the bawdy atmosphere of his establishment, coupled with the extra money it brought him, were a healing balm to the pain the accident had caused.

Frank and his mother lived in rooms behind the billiard parlor. Here Rita prepared meals for other Mexican immigrants and occasionally rented rooms to boarders.

——◆◈◆——

Frank's billiard parlor became a popular establishment for *solos* and family men alike. Frank purchased secondhand pool tables and with dining tables and chairs gathered from alleyways and repaired and painted, he completed the furnishings. Rita covered the mismatched tables with bright, checkered oilcloth and set about preparing batches of extra tortillas for the tacos his customers craved. Frank located a source of cheap peanuts, which he salted liberally, to provide a further incentive for drinking.

An old Victrola, an early type of record player, played Mexican songs whose lyrics plucked the heartstrings, especially of those without families and loved ones near. Strong men literally "cried in their beer" at the sad, sentimental ballads telling tales of lost loves, betrayals, and broken hearts. Spanish lent itself so much more easily than English to this often-maudlin "drinking music." When the atmosphere became so heavy with pathos as to become unbearable, the records were changed abruptly to lively polkas or songs celebrating life's happy moments. This music lifted spirits and encouraged cheerful conversations that inevitably led to boisterous toasts. In this way Frank controlled his establishment's atmosphere, and the sale of drinks soared.

<hr />

It was during this time that Frank met and married a lovely Lithuanian girl called Apolonia. With her blonde hair and blue eyes she had a striking resemblance to Ginger Rogers, a famous movie star of that era.

The marriage was a surprise to Rita. One afternoon Frank came home with his shy young bride in tow. She had just graduated high school and was very young and beautiful. The couple had been married at the county seat of Crown Point, Indiana, which had gained a national reputation for the "quickie" marriage. Even celebrities married there. Famous actor Rudolph Valentino exchanged vows in the big red-brick courthouse that dominated the town square.

"I hope you know what you're doing, *mijo*," Rita cautioned him. "She's young, and you're like an old man to her. She'll get bored."

"Don't be foolish," Frank answered, a frown in his voice. "I'm not old, just a few years more than she is. We'll live here; she'll help me in the billiard parlor. She can sing and play the accordion. It'll add some entertainment and pull more customers in."

Rita was quiet. She said no more to her son, but set about arranging a room for him and his new bride. She worried about Frank. He had taken to gambling even more than he had in earlier years. It was as if the loss of his arm had not taught him caution, but had made him even more reckless and hardheaded than before. But however many worries her son brought to her, she loved him fiercely and cooked special treats prepared for him alone. If a young wife were what he thought he wanted, she would welcome her. Rita, Frank, and Apolonia settled in.

While Frank and Rita operated their establishment, Prohibition made alcohol illegal, spurring the demand for contraband booze. Americans casually thumbed their collective noses at any constitutional amendment that had the audacity to tell them what they could and could not drink. The Chicago region became a hub of illegal speakeasies and liquor. Huge amounts of "bathtub gin" and other forms of homemade alcohol flowed nightly in the after-hour joints and homes of the area; Al Capone and other mobsters made millions from the sales.

Rita knew a good thing when she saw it. She expanded her financial base by brewing hard liquor and beer in large ceramic jars and bottling it with a machine that automatically capped the bottles, ensuring that the beer fizz remained sealed within. This improved beer became the drink of choice with Rita's boarders and with the customers in Frank's billiard hall.

Hard liquor had its own customer base in the city, and, with bottles filled and ready for sale, Rita and Frank would go into Chicago to sell their "product." Rita carried the liquor in shopping bags with clothes piled on top, effectively concealing the illegal booty. The sales on corners were brisk, and the police paid little attention.

Although Rita reveled in the extra funds from her hooch, Maria was frightened for her. When she first learned of Rita's enterprise, she confronted her mother.

"Ma, what if they catch you and throw you in jail?" she asked.

"Catch me? Who's going to bother a poor old lady? The cops don't care as long as they get a pint for themselves. Besides, if they really want to stop people drinking, they should go after those big guys who sell it by the barrel.

"Don't worry, Maria," she continued to reassure her daughter. "I don't sell enough to bother nobody, cops or the mob. And why shouldn't we get a little extra money? Everybody else does!"

This explanation did not fully set Maria's mind to rest, but she knew better than to try to change her mother's mind once she had made it up. And even Maria could not quarrel with the need for extra cash; no matter how hard they worked, there never seemed to be enough of that.

◆·✕·◆

The illegal liquor, which so worried Maria, concerned neither her mother nor brother. As Rita had predicted, the police and the mob had no interest in small-fry entrepreneurs; the profits of such businesses were a mere pittance when compared to the monies pulled in by large criminal organizations. What did it matter if a few Mexicans sold a little hooch to their *compadres*? Nobody begrudged them that.

What *did* matter was greed; for those who sought to horn in on the mob's territory, whether "civilians" or rogue mob operations, the mob moved quickly to shut them down. Eliminating the competition translated into bloody actions, and the Chicago region gained a reputation for vice and violence.

However, for Frank and Rita, their small share of the market held few risks; selling their special recipe was for them a profitable adventure. A couple of bags of whiskey hawked on Chicago's streets caused Rita to chuckle to herself; she felt as if she were participating in one of God's little jokes. Perhaps the odds were stacked against her in society, but He was seeing to it that her family was fed and cared for all the same. As she always insisted, "God knows what He's doing."

<hr/>

Frank was satisfied, too. The click, click, click as the balls touched, shifted course, and dropped neatly into the pockets pleased him. The smoke forming striated clouds above green felt infused a titillating touch of mystery. And, the talk and laughter of men exchanging stories offered a comfortable sense of camaraderie and well-being. Added to this scene was the delicious odor of Rita's cooking carrying just a whiff of beer and chalk dust. This atmosphere afforded Frank the satisfying belief that he was living his dream.

But a familiar voice that was never far from his ear whispered softly. Frank tried to ignore it as he would a worrisome mosquito's buzz, but the voice persisted like a temptress reminding him of the rush he had felt with each "Big Win." This gambling muse triggered glorious memories of races, games, and fights he had placed bets on and the euphoria of winning that nothing had ever rivaled. Try as he might to convince himself not to gamble, the voice returned with a vengeance.

"Come on, Frank, you know you miss the good times. Do you really want to sit in this hall listening to the same old music and stories you've heard over and over? Wouldn't you rather bet the whole bundle and let the die fall where they may—win or lose?—Wasn't *that* really the good life?"

Frank struggled against his seductive siren, reminding himself he had given much to gain a better life for himself, Rita, and his wife.

"Isn't this wonderful, *hijo* (son)?" Rita would say to him as she bustled around the kitchen filling orders for their customers.

"I told you God was good. He sent you tragedy and gave you this in return."

Her eyes danced with happiness as she surveyed their own small world of success.

Frank dearly loved his mother and delighted in her happiness. The life they had endured flashed back with vividness as strong as a body blow. Of course life was good and he would do nothing to disrupt it. Let Rita enjoy her sanctuary, even though it was nothing more than a hot kitchen and a smoky billiard parlor.

5

Secrets of the Past

As with other immigrants, when newcomers arrived from Mexico, they often moved in with relatives, a situation that complicated family dynamics but did not upset the primary bond between mothers and their children.

Miguel, Maria, Jenny, and baby Jesse lived in a frame house on Ashland Avenue in Blue Island, Illinois, not far from Maria's mother and brother. Worries over bootlegging or not, this was a far better situation than were the old railroad cars where the family had lived earlier. Here, Maria had a real house for her family, and her mother and brother were near. She faced each day with greater confidence. Perhaps the world was a kinder place after all.

In their new surroundings, the duty of caring for one-year-old Jesse fell to Jenny, a role she would continue with other siblings as more children were born. During Jesse's infancy, Rita's sister, Teresa, came up from Mexico with her family, living with the Arredondos during their first few months in the States. Cousin Lucy, Teresa's daughter, and Jenny loved little Jesse and would vie for time with the baby. Lucy and Jenny often quarreled over which girl would get to hold him. Once, as they wrangled for the baby, they tripped over the shawl in which he was wrapped, causing the little boy to fall and start crying. Jenny was terrified lest she be punished for not caring for her brother carefully enough.

"Your family is the most important thing. It's all you really have. Take care of your little brother," were words that rang continually in her head. Even as a preschooler, Jenny knew that the primary focus of everything in the Arredondo philosophy was family. Jenny was greatly relieved when she quieted Jesse and found he was none the worse for his tumble.

Although the cousins were unaware at the time, problems far greater than a tussle for baby Jesse were buried in their family's history. The reuniting of the sisters Rita and Teresa was fraught with complications. Years before, Rita Batalla had married a man named Inez Perez, becoming Rita Batalla Perez. Rita then gave birth to Maria's older brother, Frank. In time Inez became afflicted with a mental illness so severe and violent that he was chained in the yard of their pitifully inadequate home. So dangerous was Inez that his food was literally thrown to him in an effort to avoid any close encounters in which he could injure his caregivers. His madness lasted a full five years until he died, raving and hallucinating, believing himself cursed by a former suitor of Rita's who had vowed that Rita would never be happy if she chose Inez over him.

Whatever the cause of his madness, Rita struggled to survive in the most trying of situations as she cared for a mentally deranged husband and a young son. Benigno Perez, Inez's brother, left the city of Salamanca with his mother, Juliana Aguayo, to help provide for his brother's wife and son. Benigno, or "Ben," was a tall, handsome man with dark hair and green eyes. He sported a mustache and a slim build.

"Rita, you must let Ben help care for you and Francisco," Juliana told Rita when she arrived. "My son Inez is lost to us. He is mad. We must care for him as best we can, but his brain is sick. He cannot be your husband or little Francisco's father anymore."

Rita could not dispute her mother-in-law's words. Inez was mad and dangerous. Try as she might, she could not continue on as she had been much longer. She had a son to think of. She accepted Juliana and her brother-in-law's offer with relief, for she knew there were no doctors who would treat Inez and no money to pay them even if they would. Mental illness was misunderstood in those days, whether in Mexico or elsewhere. Those suffering from it were locked up or hidden away. Having Inez's family to assist seemed a godsend.

For some time the group lived amicably, working and coping with life on the ranch called Palo Blanco or "White Stick." They succeeded in their mutual purpose: to keep a family together. After a period of time, Juliana became weary with the grueling sameness of the ranch. She wished to return to the town where she and Ben had lived before the madness of her older son had forced a move.

"I must go back to town," she announced. "I have things there that must be done, and I am too old and weary for this farm life. Ben will stay and continue to help."

Maxima (Cervantes) Batalla, Rita's mother, and Teresa Batalla, Rita's sister

With that she bid farewell to her son, daughter-in-law, and grandson and went to live with her sister in Salamanca. Ben was left to care for his brother's widow and her child.

It was shortly after her departure that Inez sickened and died. Rita was still young, vibrant, and beautiful and had had no intimate relations with her severely disturbed husband for years. In hindsight, it may have seemed inevitable that two vital, young people, thrown together by such circumstances, would become lovers. With the absence of a chaperone and a growing attraction between Ben and his brother's widow, they soon entered into an affair that would produce a second child for Rita, her daughter Maria. The relationship continued after Maria's birth and brought happiness to the couple though the two never formally married. Ben was kind and loving, and his presence eased the burden Rita had carried alone during her husband's illness. He cared so well for his daughter Maria, as well as Francisco, that little Frank never knew he was not his biological father.

In the eleventh year of Rita and Ben's relationship, Rita's sister, Teresa, fell ill and came to visit the ranch to recuperate. Rita welcomed her sister and assisted her during the illness. Rita was aware that at one time Ben had been infatuated with Teresa, but Teresa had not reciprocated his interest. She had no cause to suspect that her sister felt any differently now. She could not have been more wrong. Before she left the ranch, Teresa succeeded in rekindling Ben's interest and proving Rita's trust in her had been tragically misplaced. Years later, Rita recounted the story to her daughter, her anger spent, the telling matter-of-fact.

Teresa was thirty years old and well aware that any union between herself and Ben would be leaving both Maria and Frank to be raised single-handedly by Rita. Yet this did not deter her plan. Teresa relentlessly pursued Ben and persuaded him to leave his family and marry her. A date was set with the parish priest. Before the ceremony took place, a friend of Rita's warned the town priest that Teresa was entering into a damned marriage.

"No! No!" Teresa protested to the priest when he confronted her. "Those are lies. My sister has no hold on Ben. He has been a kind and generous brother-in-law, trying to help her and her children, but he loves me. I am the one."

With no one to dispute her testimony, Teresa insisted that she and Benigno be married immediately. She was determined that no one would interfere with her plans. She knew she was far older than most brides of that time and, as the years passed, realized she should have taken Ben up on his initial attempts to court her. She was tired of her life alone and dreaded the thought of living it out as a spinster. She would have her way, and her sister could fend for herself.

The nuptials proceeded. Teresa became Señora Teresa Aguallo Perez. Rita, Frank, and Maria were left alone. It is doubtful that the children truly understood what had occurred. They merely knew that life after their father was "gone" became far more difficult and that their mother became weary and unhappy as she struggled to provide for the family. Bitterly, Rita cursed Teresa, promising her she "would never have one happy day" with Ben. She could do little else. Her sister had stolen Benigno away, and the Church had blessed the union.

<hr />

As for Teresa, she resented baby Maria and felt jealousy toward Rita. She would continually question her husband's love to which he would reply abruptly, "I married you, didn't I?"

Ben and Teresa had three children: the eight-year-old Lucy who would come to stay at her "Aunt" Maria's in Blue Island, a second sister, Emeteria (Emi), and a son, Antonio (Tony).

Lucy's life in Mexico was far different from what Maria's had been. She lived in town in a brick home that Ben built for his new family and went to school through the third grade in the town school. During this period, her father made frequent trips to the United States for work while Lucy lived in Mexico with her mother. Teresa dressed Lucy like a little doll in ruffled blouses and skirts, which covered bloomers tied at the knee. Sandals or lace-up shoes were her footwear, and her long hair was braided in pigtails that hung down her back or were elaborately twisted on top of her head.

Life was far easier for Lucy than her "cousins" on the ranch, though she did help her mother with small chores like sweeping the tile floors or accompanying Teresa to the market for shopping. For her, life seemed happy as she played children's games. Her favorite was "Ring Around a Rosy" and something called *"Vivora de la Mar"* (Snake of the Ocean), which was a version of the American game called "Red Rover" in which sides were chosen. Children on each side faced the other side, clinging tightly to each other's hands. Then one child would run to the other side singing, *"Vivora de la mar, por aquí pueden pasar"* (Snake of the ocean, here's where you pass) trying to break through the

Teresa (Batalla) Perez and Benigno Perez, 1920s

chain of children's hands. Lucy lived in blissful ignorance of the intrigue surrounding her parents' marriage and the rift it had caused between her Aunt Rita and her mother.

Lucy occasionally visited the ranch where Maria, Frank, and Rita lived. Chickens and turkeys ran in the yard, and vegetables were plentiful in the summer. Tomatoes and pumpkins were baked outside in large ovens. Though Lucy did know Rita was her aunt, the relationship to her half-sister, Maria, continued to remain deliberately vague. They were presented as cousins and, even though Maria was much older than Lucy, "cousins" they remained.

After her marriage, Lucy's mother, Teresa, had no desire to migrate north to the States, refusing to leave her father, called Bono, saying she "knew him before Ben and would never leave Mexico as long as he was alive." Having "caught" Ben, she now proclaimed to prefer her father's company and justified her decision to remain in Mexico by stating she must take care of him. Her life was comfortable, her fear of being an old maid allayed. The arrangement of Ben in the United States and herself in Mexico with her father and child suited her perfectly.

Ben continued to travel back and forth until 1927 when he immigrated permanently to work at the Rock Island Railroad, living in what was called "Gypsy Town" in Blue Island. Teresa's father died in 1926, and Teresa had run out of excuses for remaining in Mexico. Ben journeyed back to Mexico. He was blunt: "Either you come with me, or I go back alone and won't return."

Teresa now had no choice. It was then, when Lucy was eight years old, that mother and daughter crossed legally into the United States and came to live with Maria's family. Lucy became great friends with Jenny and loved Maria like a second mother.

Never mind the Byzantine twists and turns of the family relationships. As far as Lucy and Jenny were concerned they were kin and close friends. The troubled past of earlier generations impacted, if at all, only slightly.

But what of Rita? What were her feelings when her sister came to live with her daughter, Maria, flanked by Rita's former lover? What did she feel toward the sister who had stolen the companion who had nurtured her and her children for more than a decade? How did she view the woman who now came to take up residence near her, bringing her own children fathered by Benigno? Perhaps a modicum of bitterness and resentment remained toward her treacherous sister who had stolen what little happiness she had enjoyed in her homeland, but Rita was nothing if not a realist. She had survived a revolution, bargained away her daughter into a loveless marriage, made her way in an unfriendly land, and through it all, retained her dignity.

Long ago Rita had realized that, be they lovers or husbands, men were not destined to be the anchors in her life. Some might be blessed with the ideal soul mate, but not for her was this fairy-tale ending. Blood, on the other hand, ran thicker than water; a sibling, be it a betraying sister or not, was someone to whom one was bonded. This was a fact of life and not a choice to be made.

Children, likewise, were "forever." This axiom she believed wholeheartedly and demonstrated through her dealings with her own children. Rita knew the power of motherhood and wielded it with surety and skill. She bound her offspring to her as she wove a tight web in and out of their lives. Her children were her joy and her security; they were the object of her love, hopes, and dreams, and they were hers to manipulate and direct as she thought best. While men came and went in a woman's life, children remained a constant. Rita never wavered in her welcome when her sister arrived at her daughter's home. She continued with her life, reconciling with Teresa. If there were any feelings left for Ben, she never revealed them. She had her life, her work, and her children—they were enough.

Young Maria observed her mother's methods for holding fast to her children as she forged them into her strongest allies. She may have resisted at times her mother's hold on her, but she intuitively understood the power it gave to Rita. Maria watched and learned these lessons well.

Jenny was six years old when she began school in Blue Island. The school was called West Pullman, named for the railroad (Chicago, West Pullman and Southern Railroad) that established it. It was a half-day kindergarten. Enrolled by a friend of her Uncle Frank, Sam Dominguez from Las Cruces, New Mexico, Jenny was the first of the Arredondos to enter the American educational system. As her school years began, she left her parents' home and moved in with her grandmother, who wanted her company. She remained with her through her early years.

After the formality of enrollment was accomplished, Frank announced that he and his friend Sam were taking Jenny into Chicago to buy clothes. Through the years, Frank had become very conscious of his attire and bought beautiful suits and hats. He was quite a handsome man despite the loss of his arm. He wanted Jenny to have a fashionable wardrobe for school. Catching the streetcar, the threesome made their way into the city.

The shopping trip was a dream for Jenny as she reveled in the excitement of the city and its wonderful array of stores. She tried on dress after dress, modeling for her uncle and his friend as she darted in and out of the fitting rooms. Finally, two frocks were decided upon. One dress was blue silk with puffed sleeves, the other green velvet that Jenny wore on Saint Patrick's Day while she recited an Irish poem before the class. Jenny was proud of her lovely clothes, but Rita and Maria were doubtful.

"Why such fancy dresses for a little girl to wear to school? You could have bought five plain ones for what these cost!" Maria fussed at her brother.

"Never mind plain! She's a princess and should dress like one. What's money for if not to live a good life?" asked Frank who was feeling quite generous after having won a large bet on a horse race.

Maria shook her head while Jenny basked in the new clothes, thinking perhaps she was a princess, at least when wearing her new dresses.

Jenny attended a one-room schoolhouse a mile from home. She walked each way, and her waist-length braids were tempting to naughty little boys to pull. Later, she would have fond memories of this small country school with flowers growing in its yard. Each morning her Grandmother Rita would awaken her and pack her metal lunch box with a bologna sandwich and an orange soda. After Rita had combed and braided her hair, she would set out for

class. She proved herself to be a bright student and soon developed a love
for learning.

When Jenny's school ended for the summer, a field trip was arranged to
take the children on buses to the Chicago Arboretum. The night before the
big anticipated event, Frank's wife, Apolonia, wrapped Jenny's hair in rags. In
the morning when the rags were removed, lovely banana curls were revealed.
Jenny wore her blue dress and felt pretty. At the arboretum the peaceful
beauty of the trees and water awed her. She had never seen anything so lovely
as this vast expanse of nature uninterrupted by the constant noise and dirt of
the industrial Blue Island to which Jenny had become accustomed.

However, when another school event was offered in the third grade,
Jenny was not so fortunate. Mr. Blackwell, a famous magician, was to perform during the last class of the day. Her grandmother steadfastly refused her
permission to attend, fearing he would throw "something" into the children's
eyes and hypnotize them. Rita's odd mix of superstition and religion was an
integral part of the family's tradition. Prayers were an ongoing part of each
day, and their home always included a small "altar" on which candles burned
in front of favorite saints. The prayers that Rita had used to keep the family
safe in Mexico were repeated by her daughter, Maria, and passed on to Maria's
brood. Prayers for intervention in problems that arose or for health and safety
in daily life occurrences were recited with fervor. Special requests to Our Lady
of Guadalupe, Mexico's patron saint, were frequent, and Our Lady and other
Catholic saints were considered as members of the family. Mingled with
these traditional Catholic rituals were customs borrowed from ancient
Mexican times.

One obvious blending of beliefs had to do with Palm Sunday, celebrated
the week before Easter and symbolizing Christ's triumphant ride through
town just prior to His crucifixion. The Church passed out palm fronds to its
parishioners as a tangible reminder of that fateful Sunday. Rita would take
these and weave them into crosses, then place them in the home's windows
to "scare away" threatening weather. In addition to these "church" items,
Rita used knives to turn away the weather's threat. Standing in the doorway,
she would raise two crossed knives to the heavens to "cut" the storm clouds'
power. The addition of such old superstitions and wives' tales to church ritual
was a matter of course. Life was hard, and faith was a strong foundation on
which to survive its struggles. If the old beliefs seemed plausible, so be it.
Surely, the saints would not mind.

6

Safe Harbor

Nearly 55,000 people resided in East Chicago, Indiana, in 1929, incorporated as a city just thirty-six years before and nicknamed the "Twin City" because of divisions between the exclusive "South Side" and the "North Side" Harbor area. The Harbor area was home to Inland Steel's four blast furnaces and thirty-one open hearths, most of its workforce, and to a Mexican colonia *that included businesses, mutual-aid societies, and even a weekly Spanish-language newspaper.*

Early on in Jenny's educational journey, her father, Miguel, heard rumors that Mexicans were being hired at Inland Steel in East Chicago, Indiana. The history of Mexican labor in the steel mills was a checkered one. A large colony of Mexicans had been established during the steel strike of 1919. This was a period when workers had few rights, and many workers at major steel companies went on strike for better conditions. Determined to break any strike action, many companies resolved to import workers. Since tight new immigration laws had brought the influx of Europeans to a virtual halt, the companies turned to Mexico for labor, enticing Mexican men with good jobs and wages if they were willing to come to the United States. Anxious for jobs, many Mexicans had gone to the mills in 1919 often unaware that they were to be used as strikebreakers. Some returned home when comprehending the situation, but most of the *solos*, whose families in Mexico counted on the wages they sent home, remained in the States.

The Mexicans proved to be hard workers; some had past work experience in the United States with railroads, meat markets, and mining, but many were young *solos*, lacking education and speaking little or no English. The workers who staged the strike were European immigrants. They resented the newcomers who stood out from the Europeans; thus, the Mexicans became targets for discrimination. Because of this, the Mexican employees formed groups among themselves. Their work ethic soon made them valued workers, though sorely hampered by both nationality and language. Their ranks were composed of unskilled laborers assigned to the hardest and lowest-paying tasks. Both work and housing conditions were deplorable, and it was not unusual for single men, crowded into substandard housing, to sleep in "shifts." As one worker left for his job, another returning from a different work shift would claim the empty bed.

With such a large number of single men who had little outlet for their loneliness, it was inevitable that brothels sprang up. Women from surrounding towns, as well as East Chicago, would ply their trade to the lonely young men of "the Harbor," so called because of its proximity to Lake Michigan. Since men far out numbered women, they did not want for customers.

An important factor that worked against assimilation into American life was the desire of most Mexicans to return to their native country once they had saved sufficient money. This made them a less stable and settled community than their European counterparts who were more likely to establish themselves as American citizens.

In spite of the dark history of Mexican labor in steel mills, Miguel pursued the leads for employment always in hopes of securing a better life for his family. Once again it was a friend, Frank Ramirez, who helped. Ramirez walked nearly twelve miles to East Chicago from Blue Island, Illinois, to inquire about available work. When Ramirez brought back favorable reports, Miguel followed suit, and in January 1929, Miguel was hired. After locating houses on Pennsylvania Avenue, the Arredondo and Ramirez families moved to Indiana.

The Harbor, the area of Block and Pennsylvania avenues in East Chicago, became the primary settling place for Mexicans because it was one of the few areas that accepted Mexicans. The steel industry had built some housing around its huge industrial plants, but the cost and restrictions placed on residents resulted in a quick end to this arrangement. Any attempts to settle, quite literally, "on the other side of the tracks" were thwarted by landlords who charged Mexicans exorbitant rent or simply refused to rent to them at all. The Polish immigrants were especially anxious to isolate the Mexicans. Relatively new to America themselves, they viewed the Mexicans both as competition for their jobs (the attempted strike of 1919 was still fresh in their minds) and as people of "lesser value" than Europeans. Like all new waves of immigrants, Mexicans encountered discrimination from "older" immigrants who had

COURTESY OF THE ARREDONDO FAMILY

Miguel, 1920s

fought their own struggles for a place in America's pecking order.

Faced with limited options, Mexicans took what was available and often endured deplorable housing conditions. Quite simply, they paid more, but got less. And yet, they persevered. Often the first settlers assisted their countrymen who came later. This led to establishing churches, ethnic clubs, and mutual-aid societies, which led to combined efforts for equality. However, the path of being accepted as "American" was a long and sometimes tortuous one for Mexicans as for other immigrant groups, winding through generations before the acculturation process was complete.

———◆•❋•◆———

The move to Indiana proved a difficult one for Maria. She had grown accustomed to the relatively quiet life in Blue Island. East Chicago in the late 1920s seemed too noisy, too busy. The soft-spoken woman seldom left her home, both because she had small children to care for and because her lack of language skills made navigating the English-speaking world of stores and streetcars difficult. Her oldest daughter, Jenny, remained in Blue Island with her grandmother. With the birth of a third child, Socorro (Sue), born May 24, 1929, Maria found herself busy with settling into city life as she struggled with two small children. Her friend and neighbor, Maria Ramirez, whom the children came to know as "Mama Quita," pitched in to assist with cooking and caring for the new arrival. She and her husband, Francisco (Papa Poncho), who had scouted out the Inland jobs, hailed from Guanajuato, the same state in central Mexico as the Arredondos. The families had past, present, and future to bond their relationship.

Maria Ramirez took note of Maria's exhaustion and harried demeanor with empathy. She understood the difficulties inherent in the new environment and tried to comfort her new friend. "Maria, don't worry. This is like anywhere else. Once you become accustomed to it, you will see. Life will get better."

Part of the Inland Steel transport area where Miguel worked

Maria appreciated her friend's help though she had heard such reassurances before. She smiled her shy smile and nodded. She was not at all sure that she would ever get used to this new city filled with noise, factory whistles, and black soot. She picked up her new daughter and held her close.

"We'll be fine," she whispered to the infant. "We'll be fine."

———◆•※•◆———

While the family worked through the trials and tribulations of relocation, Jenny remained in Illinois with her Grandmother Rita and Uncle Frank, continuing her schooling and helping her grandmother with boarders throughout the school year. (In summer she spent two weeks in the Harbor to help her mother with the two little ones.) At her grandmother's, whom she referred to as "Rita" because everyone else at the boardinghouse did, she played with the neighboring Romanian grocer's daughter, building igloos during the snowy winters and playing outdoor games in warmer weather. One day her girlfriend brought over Christmas presents that Santa Claus had given her.

After she left Jenny asked Rita, "Who is Santa Claus, and why did that girl get all that stuff from him?"

Rita wasted no time in trying to make excuses for the missing-in-action Santa.

"Don't believe that girl next door. She's lying! There's no such thing as Santa Claus!"

Any illusions seven-year-old Jenny may have held regarding a jolly old elf who supplied little girls with presents were quickly squelched by her grandmother's no-nonsense approach. Rita was not being cruel. She was merely expressing the facts of life as she knew them: life was not sugarcoated. You worked for what you got, and no fat little man in a red suit swooped down the chimney to dump off free toys. For that matter, no one was giving anybody anything for nothing: there was no free lunch.

———◆•※•◆———

In December 1930 Jenny's father brought Sue and Jesse to stay with their grandmother. This was an unusual turn of events, but Jenny did not question; she was glad to have her brother and sister as playmates. On New Year's Eve, December 31, 1930, Miguel called to tell Frank that Maria had given birth to her fourth child, Sylvester, and that he would be coming soon to pick up the younger children. When Jenny learned of this, she cried bitterly, knowing she would miss having her brother and sister with her. But she now understood why the children had been brought to visit: the Arredondos had a new brother.

Sylvester, called Chive, did not enter the world with ease. New Year's Eve was not a fortuitous time to locate medical help, and he was born with the umbilical cord wrapped around his neck. Help, in the form of a Polish midwife named Christina, arrived in time for the delivery, but his birth was touch-and-go. Miguel was not on hand to comfort his wife during her travail. As with the previous births, he left the house and distanced himself from his child's arrival. If this upset Maria, she did not show it. A fourth child had entered her world. She had another being who would be dependent upon her for love and care. Maria welcomed the new boy into her growing family.

7

"Mill Rats"

There was a union at Inland, the Amalgamated Association of Iron and Steel Workers, that had been active since before the 1919 steel strike, but it was not recognized by management. It did not keep membership lists, and it operated underground out of concern over reprisals by company foremen. Because Mexicans generally were forced to work the dirtiest, most dangerous jobs for about three dollars a day, unionization had an appeal. When Lodge 1010 became invigorated by the formation of the Committee for Industrial Organization (now Congress of Industrial Organizations), known as the CIO (as in AFL-CIO), Miguel was one of its mainstays.

The atmosphere where Miguel labored in the mill was a far cry from that of Mexico. In Salamanca many families, including Maria's, had worked the same land for generations. Miguel was used to a life that revolved around the seasons, sunrise and sunset, holidays and religious observances that followed a set pattern. Now he was becoming accustomed to the steel industry whose goal was productivity. For most workers, who chose to work varying shifts in order to receive the added pay differentials, there was no standard routine. Life was one of continuously changing shifts and irregular days off. All the workers abided by strict rules and accepted onerous assignments. Any harmony with nature was out of the question. The only rhythms the steel bosses honored were those that resulted in more dollars finding the way into their coffers.

Every morning Miguel rose at 5:00 a.m. to ready himself for the early shift at the mill. Maria prepared his breakfast of eggs, beans, and tortillas as he shaved and dressed. As he listened to the early news, he interjected his personal editorial comments for Maria's benefit before leaving with his sack lunch of tacos or head cheese sandwiches.

Joining colleagues along the way, they talked and exchanged friendly jibes until they neared the shadow of the bulky mill buildings. Then a physical pall seemed to cast itself on the laborers: their chatter drifted off, their heads dropped, and the spring in their steps dwindled into a shuffle-like walk as they passed through the "clock house," punching their time cards before entering the plant's looming gates. Here they boarded buses that transported each worker to his respective work area: coal strip, tin mill, plate mill, sheet mill, rolling mill, annealing and pickling facilities, open hearth, blast furnace, and so forth. It was here that the metamorphosis from man to worker was complete. Now, they truly belonged to the mill.

The odor of each area was distinct. Chemical odors mingled with the scent of coal dust and waltzed with acrid steel shavings throughout the polluted air. Miguel was overpowered by the mill's peculiar odors when he first started his job. His lungs longed for Mexico's clean air where the days' activities were dictated by the timetable of the sun rather than the time clock of the steel plant. The stamp of the clock sentenced him to an eight-hour stint within a huge building that encompassed several blocks. It was a place where massive girders and corrugated steel walls transformed the sunniest of days into a cocoon lit with harsh overhead lights and the fiery glow of a blast furnace. What daylight that could be glimpsed struggled through the very top of the structure where high windows were situated. Even these gave no indication of outside weather, obscured as they were with mill dust.

This metallic dust filled Miguel's nose, mouth, and lungs as he entered the plant. It insinuated itself into his clothes, which grew more filthy as each day passed. At week's end his clothing was so saturated with dust, oil, and sweat that it actually crackled as Miguel moved. Maria's wringer washer took three separate cycles to swish away the grime.

As Miguel's days in the mill grew into months and years, dirt and odors became all but unnoticeable. The long days of perpetual twilight blended with the never-ending assembly line, lulling his mind into a state bordering on suspended animation. He functioned, but did not think any more than did the conveyor belt, which carried its gifts onward to the final reward of profit making.

But there was one characteristic of the plant to which Miguel could never quite become accustomed: the noise. The cacophony of trains that crisscrossed the multibuilding complex thumped and screeched. Steel plates bumped along on assembly lines. Cranes, perched high above the floor

on overhead rails, protested each swing with the shrillness of chalk on
a blackboard.

Miguel's ears rang until the noon whistle blew and the workers hastened
to eat their lunches. Occasionally the smell of cooking floated up from the sala-
mander heaters or newly produced plates of hot steel utilized by entrepreneurs
as taco stands. From their makeshift stoves they sold food to fellow workers
during their twenty-minute lunch breaks. Gradually, a normalcy returned.
Husbands complained of their complaining wives, while *solos* lamented their
lack of any woman, complaining or not. Sports plays were minutely dissected,
and the usual gripes about working conditions surfaced.

Seldom did a day pass when one of the complaints did not focus on the
dangers inherent in mill work. The obvious health risks incurred from breathing polluted air were compounded exponentially by the machinery itself, as
well as the red-hot open hearths and ingots they produced. Men frequently
were injured, sometimes fatally, crushed by heavy equipment or burned by hot
molten steel. Limbs were often lost (years later, Jesse Arredondo lost a finger
while cleaning a malfunctioning motor). Workers knew the risks; as they saw
their *compadres* hurt and maimed, it was difficult not to wonder if their turn
was next.

After twenty minutes the whistle sounded, ending the lunch break, and
the mill creaked and groaned back to life like an old man rising from his bed.
The rat race resumed.

And rats there were. Not abstract, symbolic ones; not the workers who
came to be called "mill rats," but real live rodents the size of cats that scurried along walls, their eyes glowing in the eerie red glare of the furnaces. They
were bold, brave rats, so nonplussed by human presence that they sometimes
ran across the tops of work boots. The laborers became as accustomed to the
rats as the rats were to them; they cohabited their living quarters with mutual
tolerance and respect, sweltering together in summer, shivering when the cold
set in, each species struggling to survive.

After punching out at the end of the day, Miguel and his coworkers exited
the gates exhausted. As the mill smells receded, gaits quickened toward home
to baths and dinners and a few hours in which a man, not his foreman, was
in control.

———◆•※•◆———

Maria's day passed in a similar assembly line, though no paycheck
rewarded her labors. She rose before her husband to prepare breakfast and

make his lunch. She cared for her children who arrived every eighteen months, waking those of school age for breakfast, caring at home for the smaller ones. She washed clothes, linens, and floors; cleaned bathrooms and kitchens; made beds; mended clothes; and shopped daily for meals while worrying and praying over the needs of her family.

Before Miguel returned from the plant, she prepared supper, drew his bath, and saw to her children. For her, the "shift" didn't end until the kitchen was cleaned and her babies were in bed. She, too, was exhausted, but while Miguel cursed his fate and thought of a better life, she thanked God for living in a country where jobs, food, and shelter were bountiful enough to provide for her family.

❖

As Maria wrestled with matters at home, Miguel dealt with his own issues as he entered the hot, dirty world of steel laborers. Unlike his wife, he was gregarious, interested in the world around him and eager to forge friendships. Though his spoken English was limited, he was a voracious reader, devouring the English-language classics and all available reading material. In time, he learned enough of spoken European and even Asian languages to converse with the wide variety of peoples who populated the area.

The world of the steelworker was truly a melting pot filled with multiple cultures, each struggling to assimilate into the so-called Promised Land that was America. While working alongside the vast mix of immigrants, Miguel's gift for getting along with everyone served him well. He began to realize that his interest in creating a better world for workers was finding fertile ground in this industry. Ideas for workers' rights thrived in the hellish surroundings of the blast furnaces and in the brain-rattling clamor of the rolling mills. Philosophically, Miguel had found his niche.

"There's so much that must be done, Maria," he would tell his wife as he returned home each day from the mill. "The workers are mistreated. We must stand up for what is right. We've got to change these conditions. We have to get the unions organized!"

His fervor frightened Maria. She had heard the stories of strikes and the way that employers blacklisted troublemakers. She had heard about how the companies fired anyone they suspected of union organizing, leaving them and their families with nothing—no money for rent or food. What would they do if Miguel had no work? One day she confided her fear to him.

Coke ovens at Inland Steel, 1937

"Miguel, I know things are hard for the workers. I know things aren't fair, but let someone else push for this union thing. Why should it be you? You have a family. We can hardly make ends meet now. Why should *you* be the one who has to cause trouble?"

"For God's sake, woman. What do you know about any of this? You're just an ignorant peasant. People all over the world are uniting to help the workers. What do you think the revolution in Mexico was about? People trying to get rights for the poor—for us!" Miguel's anger grew.

"For us? For us! Oh, I know all about the revolution. I saw what it did to the poor—it made them poorer. We came here to get away from all that. We came for a better life. What kind of life will we have if you lose your job?"

"*¡Cállate!* Maria. Shut your mouth! You don't know what you're talking about. Get back to the kitchen where you belong and make me something to eat!"

Maria did as she was told, but the fear remained within her. Her heart sank each time Miguel said he was going to a meeting. Try as she might to put

Miguel's union organizing out of her mind, it remained a continual worry in a life full of uncertainty and change.

As Maria's dislike for union organization grew, so, too, did Miguel's determination to move the workers' cause forward. As the years passed, he became well known for his generosity and caring toward newcomers and for his mesmerizing oratorical skills, which he employed as he expressed his views on changes necessary for the advancement of the Mexicans and other workers. His reputation grew along with the respect others had for his leadership.

While the wide breadth of humanity within the mills posed no problems for Miguel, becoming accustomed to the actual work routine took some doing. Miguel despised shift work, believing that the days were for labor and evenings for family, recreation, socializing, and sleeping. He refused higher wages in order to remain on "days" and used his nights to further educate himself and organize groups to advance the workers' cause. Fellow workers applauded his obsession with workers' rights, but to Maria, who was left to contend with limited funds and an expanding family, his activities only fueled her resentment. While Miguel basked in the admiration of others, she was left to raise a family on the smallest of allowances. She watched as other men worked the shifts and gained extra money. She trembled when she heard rumors of strikes. Being a woman, she knew her "place," but no amount of socialization could quench her fear and anger.

By the 1930s Miguel knew virtually everyone through his community activities. He and others had succeeded in founding the Benito Juarez Mutual Aid Society, which was later renamed *Unión Benéfica Mexicana* and became known as the UBM. This organization, as others of the same ilk, worked toward its mission of helping Mexicans in need and serving as a gathering place for social and political debate. The UBM sponsored dances and celebrations for holidays such as September 16, Mexican Independence Day, which marked the date of Mexico's victory over Spanish rule.

Over time Miguel's involvement in the steelworkers' unionizing movement became more intense. At one point he was preparing to join striking workers at Plant Number Two of Republic Steel, located in South Chicago. It was not unusual for men from one mill to support their brother workers, but it was rumored that things might become violent. "Don't go, Miguel," friends advised. "This could get nasty, and you're a married man with a bunch of kids. Let the *solos* take this one."

At first Miguel balked at not being in the forefront of the demonstration, but eventually less passionate heads persuaded him that in this case, caution was the greater part of valor. Miguel remained home. As events proved, his decision was a wise one. Violence did, indeed, break out at what came to be known as the Memorial Day Massacre. Ten men were killed including three members of Local 1010. Several workers were injured as was the Arredondos' friend and Local 1010 officer, Max Luna. He received a shot to the head and eventually took the steel company to court and won a settlement.

———◆◦◆◦◦◆◦◆———

Often union discussions took place in the UBM hall, billiard rooms, or bars. Miguel, who in his youth had never been much of a drinker, began to join in with the other men as they talked and drank beer. In time, as the meetings grew longer and the issues more intense, Miguel's drinking also increased until it became problematic. While the children were proud of their father's community standing, they learned to dread the effects that too much drink could have on him and the friends whom he often brought home after long hours of debating and drinking.

Sue was particularly leery of encounters with her father's drinking buddies and tried to avoid them as much as possible. On a cold December day in 1935, she was playing outside their apartment on Block Avenue when she saw her father and a friend coming toward their home. She feared they had been drinking and ducked around back, hoping to enter unnoticed through the kitchen. Meanwhile, Maria had been busy preparing tamales for their traditional Christmas feast and had set a large, deep pot filled with cooking lard on the back porch steps to cool. Sue, in her haste, knocked this over, severely burning her leg. She scurried across the porch and, crying to her mother, displayed the scalded leg.

"We have to get her to the doctor," Maria informed Miguel as he came through the front door, friend in tow and expecting a meal. Miguel dismissed Maria with a wave.

"Bring us something to eat," he demanded, "we're hungry."

Maria repeated again that Sue's leg required a physician's attention. The doctor must be called. Miguel rankled at the thought of a doctor bill. He brushed off Maria's plea a second time.

"Doctor? I've got no money for the doctor! It will heal itself," was his reply as he went back to discussing political issues after again telling Maria to prepare food for him and his friend.

Knowing Miguel as she did, Maria chose not to pursue the argument. Always stubborn, he became even more so when drinking. With no other recourse, Maria set about treating Sue's burns with the juice from aloe plants that she grew in pots on the kitchen windowsill. Home remedies were a large part of medicine in those days, and Maria knew them all, brewing concoctions from her herbs that often cured stomachaches, colds, and fevers. Many of these potions later proved their healing properties as modern-day medicine opened itself to less traditional medicine. But in this case, the burn was simply too severe to respond to her ministrations. After days of home doctoring, it became clear that Sue must have professional attention. Maria bundled her daughter in warm clothes and trudged to the doctor's office without asking Miguel's permission.

"Why did you wait so long to bring this child in?" demanded the doctor whose anger at the untreated, and now infected, burn was understandable.

Maria remained quiet as the doctor tended and dressed the leg.

"She must go to the hospital," lectured the doctor. "They'll be able to deal with the infection there. This is a serious burn. You must keep her in a sterile environment, and when she comes home, treat it with this ointment if it's to heal properly. We can stop the infection, but there will be scarring. Next time, don't wait!" the doctor reprimanded Maria.

Maria accepted his harsh words without comment and took Sue to the hospital where a tent was draped over her leg and nurses saw to her burns.

Her anger at Miguel grew, and once home, she berated him for his lack of compassion for his daughter. "Your drinking makes you crazy!" she shouted. "You can't even take care of your own daughter. All you think about is money. If money is so important, then stop your carousing and your damned politicking and work more hours at the mill. Your drinking and your no-account buddies from your precious organizations—I'm sick of them!" She raved, thinking of her daughter's pain as she lay alone at the hospital.

Sue's leg did get better, but a full year passed until it healed. The scar remained as a testament to a child's haste and a father's lack of it.

8

Change is Constant

According to the 1930 census, all but thirteen of the thousand or so Mexican families in Indiana Harbor rented their living places. They often shared their quarters with another family, paying inflated rates for inferior facilities with a leaky roof and scant heat from a lone potbellied stove. It was often left to their children to negotiate with landlords and other authority figures when one or both parents did not speak fluent English.

By the early 1930s Frank's gambling debts had grown to such an extent that he lost his billiard parlor. He had also lost his wife after a second tragedy struck his household. Apolonia had given birth to a boy whom they named Francisco Jr. The couple had moved to a cold and drafty wooden house where the infant soon caught a cold. The cold quickly worsened, and the child died. Frank was devastated and lashed out at his young wife in his anguish.

"You did it! You caused this! You gave the baby cold milk because you were too lazy to heat the bottle. It's your fault!"

Apolonia was crushed. In reality the death of the baby was probably due to poor living quarters with inadequate heating, but the words had been spoken and could not be recalled. A rift that would never fully heal had been caused by grief. For all practical purposes, Frank's marriage had ended, and the couple separated.

———◆◆◆———

Rita moved to Indiana, and Jenny returned to live with her parents. Jenny began to feel like a gypsy, always moving from place to place, never knowing where or when the next move might take her. This continued for many years as did dealing with landlords who were neither helpful nor friendly. Jenny and her family dealt with a succession of housing problems: leaky roofs that

*Frank and Apolonia's son Francisco
(Frank) Perez Jr., who died in infancy*

landlords refused to fix, landlords landing in prison for cheating on electricity by rigging the box into which pennies were dropped on a buy-as-you-need basis, lack of heat, and lack of space as the family continued to grow.

There was one particularly coldhearted landlord who delighted in wielding his power as he did when Maria discovered that the water heater in their apartment was leaking. The leak resulted not only in no hot water, but in a constant need to mop up the mess as well. At last Maria decided she must send Jenny to report the problem to the landlord. She had avoided approaching the evil-dispositioned man as long as she could, but the situation had reached such a crisis point that she feared the apartment would flood.

"Jenny," she directed her small daughter, "Go tell the landlord we have a leaky water heater."

"Ma, that man is mean. I don't want to go."

"Jenny," said Maria firmly, "Just do as I say. I can't leave the children, and I can't speak English. If we let this go, we'll have water all over the house."

Reluctantly, the little girl went to inform the landlord.

"Sir," she said hesitantly, "My Ma said to tell you the water heater is leaking."

"Oh, she did, did she?" the man leaned back in his chair and propped his hands across his fat belly. He glanced over at a man who was visiting him and winked.

"Well, let's see now," he chuckled, "How many kids does your Mama have over there?"

"Four," answered Jenny promptly.

"Well, tell you what, little gal. You just go home and tell your mother to let those young 'uns take turns sticking their fingers in that leak. There are plenty of kids. They can take turns!" With that he laughed uproariously.

"Now, run home, girl. Can't you see I'm busy?" finished the man, waving his hand in dismissal as he struggled to stifle his laughter.

Jenny returned home in tears. After relating the conversation to Maria, she yelled, "I hate that man!"

Maria hugged Jenny to her.

"Never mind, we'll get along. We'll just have to start looking for another place."

"But, Ma, I'm tired of moving all the time. Won't we ever settle down?"

Maria sighed and took her child by her shoulders. Looking into her tear-filled eyes, she instructed her, "Juanita, we live every day as God gives it to us. We can't do any better than that. Pray to the saints. You'll see. Things will work out. God knows what He's doing," ended Maria, repeating an assurance her mother had given her many times before.

Maria seldom complained. She accepted their lot because she knew she had no power to change it. As the seemingly never-ending moving cycles continued, she became expert at cleaning, organizing, and settling into each "new" home. For many of these moves, she was pregnant or had an infant on her hip.

So unhappy were the memories of her past life in Mexico that, to Maria, even the meanest of shelters seemed a haven when compared with the fear and deprivation that was the Mexico of her childhood. Her wish for her children was an easier life, and she was determined to do all in her power to achieve that wish. For now, it was enough to survive each day in the hope that tomorrow would be better.

Jenny followed her mother's example, and she, too, settled in, enrolling at Eugene Field School. It was here, as she entered the second grade, that Jenny made a lifelong friend, a friend who, along with her family, would come to play a major role in the life of the Arredondos.

As Jenny stood alone on the playground, she could not help but notice a vivacious young girl running along the grass, her coat unbuttoned as she flapped her arms like a bird. The energetic "bird-girl" made her way toward Jenny, suddenly coming to an abrupt stop directly in front of her.

"Hey little girl!" she greeted Jenny with enthusiasm. "What's your name?"

"My name is Jenny Arredondo." Too startled to say anything further, Jenny stood mutely and stared at this unlikely creature as if viewing an alien.

"Jenny," repeated the girl, undeterred by the dumbfounded expression on Jenny's face.

"Jenny. That's a pretty name. My name is Lupe Lopez. Do you want to play?"

Jenny shook her head vigorously. No, she most certainly did not want to play. In fact she wanted nothing whatsoever to do with this seemingly mad little girl who fancied herself a bird, "flew" across playgrounds, and accosted strangers in a most disconcerting manner. But Lupe persisted. Catching Jenny's hand, she pulled her along to a bench. Within minutes Lupe's friendly nature and happy chatter had won over Jenny. The girls were soon talking like old friends and became inseparable. Jenny had made her first friend in the Harbor. It was a friendship destined to last a lifetime.

Soon after the girls' meeting, the Arredondos moved to yet another apartment. This one was located on the second floor of a large building. Within weeks of their move, a vacancy occurred on the first floor. Jenny mentioned the apartment to Lupe who, in turn, told her mother, Lola.

In record time, Lola Lopez had rented the space and relocated her family there. With amazing quickness she became fast friends with Maria. Several years older than Maria, Doña Lola, as the family knew her, soon regarded Maria as she would another daughter, a daughter she felt needed and deserved her love and support. As the families grew close, Doña Lola would tell wonderful stories about her life as a young woman during the Mexican Revolution. It was during this chaotic phase of Mexico's history that Doña Lola had actually known and fought in the army of the great revolutionary hero, Emiliano Zapata. Lola had worn men's clothing and carried a rifle with bullets strapped across her shoulder. The Zapatistas, as the soldiers were called, fought and spoke passionately for their cause. Her early life in Michoacán had been filled with excitement and action in the thick of battle, so different from Maria's as to seem in another universe. While Doña Lola fought in the midst of rebels who were intent on overthrowing a corrupt government, Maria had cowered within her mother's skirts, doing her best to avoid any vestiges of war.

Doña Lola, older and virtually fearless, had placed herself deliberately into the violent fight for freedom. Life had honed her into a bold and assertive woman, unafraid to speak her mind and intimidated by no one and nothing. Lola was the antithesis of the accepted Mexican woman who remained quietly in the background, accepting her role of total obedience to her husband and never challenging any man on matters outside the realm of home and children.

Maria admired her friend's strength, wishing she could shed her timid nature and be as confident and outspoken. Doña Lola proved a strong and loyal friend, who in the future would become godmother to two of Maria's children.

On the matter of godparents, Miguel's philosophy was to seek out individuals who hailed from Guanajuato, his and Maria's home state. Doña Lola, born in Michoacán, was well aware of Miguel's bias and deftly ignored it. To her, one Mexican state was as good as another; she planned ahead to achieve her goal to do what she felt was best for Maria. She was unfazed by any objections on Miguel's part.

In 1934, shortly after Maria had given birth to her sixth child, José, Doña Lola announced to Miguel, "My husband and I will take this baby to the church to be baptized."

The petite, thin woman, whose appearance and manner portrayed no hint of her colorful youth, nevertheless managed to emanate so strong an aura of determination that Miguel never thought to question her pronouncement.

After the baptism of José, Doña Lola assumed the quasi-official position of godmother and baptized Maria's next daughter, Marie. Then she proclaimed that her daughter, Jenny's friend Lupe, would be responsible for additional siblings, should there be any.

"These will be Lupe's," she declared. She was, of course, unchallenged.

Another friend and neighbor, José Cardenas and his wife Lugarda, followed the baptism situation with amusement from their third floor apartment.

"Hey Mike," José Cardenas addressed Miguel one day, playfully hoping to needle him a bit. "You got a contract or something with Lola? Seems she's always taking your kids to church to be baptized!"

Miguel thought a moment, then shrugged, "What you gonna do? She comes to me. I don't ask her. She's good to the kids, Maria's happy, so what difference does it make?"

Exactly. What difference *did* it make? And more to the point, who had the guts to challenge a woman like Doña Lola?

The Harbor offered a wealth of activities, far more numerous and varied than Blue Island. The Arredondo children walked along streets filled with bustling crowds or played in city parks. Sometimes they would watch baseball games played in a large field behind their home. It was a busy community, and Jenny was stimulated by the constant activity.

The Harbor in the 1920s and 1930s was a town of wooden sidewalks and dirt streets. Boys hung out on corners or swam at "Bare Ass Beach" (BAB) during the summer, a strip of sand along Lake Michigan's cold waters that produced excellent swimmers who often went on to become champions in high school.

The girls' lives were much more controlled and sheltered than their male counterparts. Despite the raw and raucous surroundings of billiard halls, cockfights, and nearby brothels, the females of the Harbor remained innocent and protected, always chaperoned at any social outing they might attend. In a world so full of open vice, the Arredondo girls remained sheltered and beyond the fray. They were ignorant of much of life's realities and unquestionably accepted what they were told.

When Jenny was in the third grade at Abraham Lincoln Elementary School, a major snowstorm swooped unexpectedly into the Harbor. The harbinger of the storm was a few flakes that started to fall half an hour before school was to let out. Within a few minutes, dark clouds hung over the town, and white flakes tumbled down so rapidly that visibility plunged to a few yards. Most students had walked to school. Teachers had little choice but to bundle them up and send them on their way.

Jenny buttoned herself into her heavy wool coat and wrapped her knitted scarf across her head and face, leaving little more exposed than the tip of her nose and her eyes. She and the other students began trudging home, seeking landmarks such as trees, mailboxes, and lampposts to keep themselves on the sidewalk. The streets were now deserted of traffic. Jenny's eyelashes caught snowflakes that clung and crystallized, causing her vision to blur. As she walked carefully along, frightened and cold, she felt a large hand slip into her small one.

It was her father, Miguel, dressed in his winter coat and hat.

"Dad," she cried with relief, "what are you doing here?"

"Just wanted to make sure you got home okay," Miguel answered matter-of-factly.

Jenny was overcome that her father, who usually appeared oblivious to his children, would care enough to brave the howling wind and stinging snow to protect her welfare.

This was a memorable event for Jenny. Here was Miguel's inner soul that lay beneath the obligatory cultural *macho* veneer, a veneer that grew larger and thicker as time and experiences hardened him. But for one small girl on a snowy afternoon, the insight into the complex man who was her father would remain with her forever.

Jenny taking care of toddlers Jesse (left) and Sue (right), ca. 1931

One morning Jenny noticed a group of women sitting outside an apartment house next door. After a while, a doctor carrying a big black bag went into the apartment. When he left, all the ladies hurried in. Curious, Jenny and her playmates followed the women upstairs only to discover that a brand-new baby had mysteriously arrived on the scene.

Eight-year-old Jenny was shocked, demanding of her mother, "How did that lady get that baby?"

"Oh," replied her mother, "the man with the black case brought it. He had it in the case." This seemed a logical explanation, and it would be many years later before Jenny questioned it. Even the birth of her brother, Miguel, called Mikey, on May 24, 1932, did not shake the "black bag" theory of birth.

Shortly after Mike's birth, the family moved yet again to a second-floor apartment across from the Washington Hotel. During that period, Herbert Hoover ran for president. As Jenny and her mother were coming home from the hardware store where they had purchased kerosene for their three-burner cooking stove, they encountered a noisy crowd of people. Members of the group were standing on a flatbed truck, ringing a huge bell.

"¡Dios mío!" cried Maria, grabbing Jenny's hand and rushing her up the stairs to their apartment.

"What Ma?" yelled Jenny stumbling up the steps, trailing in her mother's wake. "What's wrong? What's the matter with all those people?"

By now Jenny had caught her mother's fear and began to cry.

"Hush, don't let them hear you. They have gone mad. Stay here and don't let them see you. Who knows what they might do? ¡Oh, *Dios mío!*" cried Maria wringing her hands in distress. There was no one in the apartment save for the mother and daughter.

Maria and Jenny stood stock-still and watched the melee from the safety of a second-story window. The noise and confusion seemed so great that Maria feared it was the end of the world. Later, when a neighbor came by, she explained to the shaken woman that the commotion had been supporters of Hoover holding a political rally for their presidential candidate.

Although a bright, intelligent woman, the social isolation that was common to most women at the time, coupled with her full-time occupation of raising a large family, conspired to keep Maria ignorant of most world events. Her knowledge of life outside the scope of the home was gained almost exclusively from Miguel as he regaled the family with facts and opinions during dinnertime.

For Maria, days consisted of cooking three full meals. Miguel insisted on home-cooked breakfast, lunch, and dinner, which was to be ready and waiting when he returned from work. With no "fast foods" available everything was made from scratch. Add to that washing clothes, bathing children, and continual cleaning to combat the dirty pollution of the steel mills, and Maria's days were consumed with household chores.

During this phase of her life there were hardly any occasions when she ventured from the house. She dressed in housedresses with an apron, shawl, and lace-up shoes with small stacked heels. Her beautiful hair was tightly wrapped in a chignon or knot at the back of her head. She saw that all of her children got to catechism classes to learn about the Catholic faith when they were old enough, but she, herself, was seldom able to attend church when the children were small. Gathering the brood, dressing them, and getting them and herself to Mass was simply too much, especially when she was expected to have lunch ready and waiting at noon.

Once, when a lady who lived in an apartment downstairs was married, she and Jenny did manage to attend the wedding at Our Lady of Guadalupe Church. Here Maria enjoyed the ceremonies and the music of cello, trumpet, violin, and organ. But this was a rare occasion. Most of Maria's outings consisted of trips for groceries or other necessities, always in the company of one of her children who acted as interpreter to English-speaking clerks.

During the 1930s women sat to the left of the aisle, men to the right. The Latin service was delivered with the priest's back to the congregation, facing the Crucifix. Hats and covered shoulders were obligatory for women, and slacks were simply unheard of. Communion was served with recipients kneeling at the railing near the altar.

When it was time to make her first Communion at age ten, cousin Lucy was Jenny's sponsor. Lucy was vigilant in her duties and prodded Jenny to attend all Sunday masses, to attend Holy Days of Obligation, and to get holy water when a situation warranted its powers.

In later years Lucy changed her religion to Jehovah's Witness and urged Jenny to follow her. To Jenny such a switch showed indecision and weakness.

"Don't be silly," Jenny answered testily. "You're the one who brought me to the Church. *I'll* never change!"

———— ◆•✦•◆ ————

Because Miguel insisted that the children speak only Spanish in his presence, Maria never learned to speak fluent English though she did learn to understand. Miguel's dream that he and his family would eventually return to his homeland persisted even as he worked to change conditions in the United States. In anticipation of that day, he demanded that his offspring embrace Mexico's language and customs.

"In my home you speak Spanish," he instructed his children. "Someday, when we are back in Mexico, you will be glad you know the mother tongue. You don't want to be like some of these Mexican kids who can't understand a word of Spanish! Ha! What good is English when they go home to Mexico?"

Teachers of the day held it as their duty to see that all foreign-language-speaking students learned English. They would instruct their charges to tell their parents that they should speak English at home. In that way, the kids would practice continually and not just in the classrooms where it was mandatory.

"Ma," one of the boys rushed in one day, "the teacher says we have to speak English at home. She says it will make us speak better, and we should practice *all* the time."

"Oh, your teacher says that, does she?" responded Maria, brushing a stray lock of hair away from her face and stirring up a pot of beans. She was tired and in no mood for edicts emanating from some teacher's bright idea.

Left to right: Jenny, Sue, and Jesse, ca. 1931, on porch of Frank and Maria Ramirez, early neighbors of the Arredondos in the Indiana Harbor area of East Chicago

"Well, I'll tell you what. You just tell that teacher to trade places with me and come here to feed you. Then you can speak English all you want. And tell her she can explain her great plan to your father, too. See what he says about it."

With that the discussion was dropped, never to be resumed.

Maria later came to regret that the children spoke only Spanish. One day as she was sweeping the steps, a young girl came in search of Chive. She spoke only English. After she related this to the children that evening, they asked, "Well, ma, what did you tell her?"

"I said," and here she switched from Spanish to English, "I said he was slipping."

This triggered laughter from the kids. One of them said, "No, ma, not 'slipping.' That means falling down. It's 'sleeping.'"

This embarrassed Maria, who seldom ventured into English because she feared such missteps. In later years she confessed to Sue, "Maybe I should have let you kids speak English at home. Maybe then I would have picked it up. After all, we live here. We should all be able to speak the language."

While Maria and Miguel moved forward in their lives, Rita opened another boardinghouse catering to single men working at the steel mill. The boarders provided her a source of income. Jenny returned to live with her, changing beds in the ten bedrooms and setting the table for dinner. Much of Rita's business was in preparing breakfast, lunches, and dinners for workers who would stop in to eat, take a bag lunch to the mill, and, perhaps, return for an evening meal as well. She charged thirty-five cents per meal, one dollar for three meals a day. Some men rented rooms, but many more came only for the delicious food. Her tacos, beans, soups, tortillas, chili, and other tasty dishes were much sought after. Rita also continued making her beer, which was a popular beverage for her diners.

"Ma, you keep selling that beer and you'll get caught one of these days. The police will arrest you and throw you in jail!" Maria cautioned her mother once more despite her mother's earlier reassurances that all would be well.

"Are you still worrying over a little beer? You're like a dog with a bone," Rita chided her. "Let it go. There is plenty to worry about without borrowing trouble. Besides, what do you think all these mobsters are doing? You think they aren't making money on illegal liquor? You see any police arresting them? Of course you don't! If they can do it, so can I. You think cops care about a little beer? Humph! They're getting rich, too. Why shouldn't we get a few extra dollars?"

Maria shrugged. Maybe she was making a mountain out of a molehill. Her mother had a point. No one worried about enforcing Prohibition in the Harbor.

Rita faithfully attended Mass while she did what she had to do. She saw nothing untoward about breaking the law and going to church. Surely God understood His people had to make ends meet. Desperate times called for desperate measures.

Boardinghouses such as Rita's remained as popular and necessary as ever. Mexican laborers still found many social aspects of the Harbor difficult. They were hardly welcome in the more affluent Anglo areas of the town. The "One-Hundred-Percent American" philosophy expounded by Nativists in the 1920s held that white Anglo-Saxon Protestants were the backbone and hope of America. Some went so far as to suggest shipping Mexicans back across the border where they belonged and building a wall so high they could never get back.

Of course, other minorities were discriminated against, but in the Harbor the police often singled out Mexicans for minor offenses, then jailed them or demanded bribes. The theaters were segregated, and, other than the Mexican pool halls, gathering places for young Mexican men were severely limited. Boardinghouses continued to provide them a safe haven in which to relax, speak their own language, and, perhaps most important, eat authentic Mexican food, which was such a staple of their home life in Mexico. The mere scent of Mexican dishes brought a comfort to those so far from home, and Rita's meals were the best around.

All food was bought and cooked fresh daily. Always a hard worker, Rita would begin preparing breakfast before dawn, fill lunch bags for workers to take to the mill, and start dinner in the early afternoon after shopping for ingredients.

Despite the travails of her life, Rita was optimistic, happy, and personable, making a fine hostess. But she had one habit that caused her problems: her love of cigarettes. She had a small machine that actually rolled the tobacco into the paper and, while she never smoked in public, she held a cigarette in her lips as she prepared meals in the kitchen. No doubt with the responsibilities and stresses of her life, smoking was a release for her. But when a boarder complained of the tortillas smelling of smoke, she quickly stopped. As satisfying as smoking may have been, it took second place to earning a living. Jenny was relieved when her grandmother let go of her cherished cigarettes. Rita's routine had included a last cigarette at bedtime, and Jenny could never close her eyes until she was sure her bedmate had squashed the final butt, and the bed was not in jeopardy of burning.

Kicking the nicotine habit may have been a positive change for Jenny, but for Rita it was a true loss. Smoking brought a moment of relaxation in her harried schedule, a brief respite in the midst of a demanding life that gave few options for personal indulgences. Even in her old age, Rita would watch others light a cigarette and exclaim, "God, that looks good!"

Often Rita's boarders became friends, some even entertaining amorous designs on the cheerful, vivacious woman. After all, her strong features retained a classic beauty, and her optimism in the face of adversity was a tonic for those lonely and homesick gentlemen who lived there.

One very old man with an eye problem that made him appear to be perpetually in tears would beg to massage Rita's back. Long hours over a hot stove resulted in a chronic backache, but Rita was not sure she wanted to become quite so intimate with her elderly boarder.

"Why not teach Jenny how to give a backrub?" Rita suggested after she had skillfully avoided several offers.

Eager to please, the man quickly agreed. Jenny was placed on a chair as the grandmother's admirer demonstrated his techniques and directed his young pupil. She was a quick study and soon mastered the art of massage. From that point on, the boarder sat contentedly as Jenny rubbed the aching muscles of her grandmother's back.

A second hopeful suitor took dinner at the boardinghouse each evening. Again, Jenny became the perceived instrument to Rita's heart. All were aware that she was her grandmother's pride and joy. Why not win over Jenny through a bit of bribery and in doing so gain the affection of Rita? The gentleman caller began to insinuate himself into little Jenny's consciousness through depositing small gifts of peanuts and candy on the table as he took his leave. After a week passed, he slipped a letter addressed to Rita under the basket of goodies. More letters followed. It fell to Jenny to read these to her grandmother. As they lay in bed, the two would giggle together at the flowery epistles.

Rita was not interested in suitors; she had more than enough to keep her busy. She continued to appear oblivious to the man's attention, and after a few weeks of fruitless courting attempts, he settled for Rita's delicious dinners. Rita had rejected him without losing a customer, but Jenny regretted the loss of nightly baskets of goodies.

9

Depression and Repatriation

Having come to Indiana Harbor recently, for the most part, and facing discriminatory hiring practices at the steel mills, the Mexican community was hard-hit by the economic breakdown known as the Great Depression. Families made do with hundred-pound sacks of flour, hundred-pound bags of beans, and what little else could be scrounged from grocers and charitable agencies. Many voluntarily sought to return to their homeland, but others were coerced by public officials and harassed by police into accepting repatriation. Coordinating this effort in East Chicago was Inland Steel's transportation agent, Paul E. Kelly. During a four-month period in 1932, approximately twelve hundred deportees were put on trains headed to Laredo, Texas, and from there, across the Rio Grande into Mexico.

Except for all the personal troubles and adjustments, life was improving. Miguel was becoming well known and respected within the Hispanic community, and home life ran to his specifications. His children were obedient, his wife attractive, and, though often at odds behind closed doors, publicly submissive and catering to his needs. His meals were always hot and waiting for his arrival, his bath was drawn when he returned from the mill, and his paychecks were regular. The family began to position itself for the future, which, if not exactly bright, at least seemed to hold hope.

It was during this time of relative calm that a world event changed the lives of not only the Arredondos, but also the country as a whole. The Great Depression with all its emotional and economic devastation descended on the country, jobs became scarce, and men took to riding the rails in search of work. Breadlines formed around city blocks, and families were torn apart as poverty and hunger moved into homes like uninvited guests. America's raw optimism gave way to despair. The nation's trouble struck the northern Indiana region with a fury. Steel had always been immune to economic fluctuations. Workers had come to view factories as invincible and their jobs, however onerous, equally secure. The Depression dispelled this myth with ruthless speed.

For Mexicans the consequences struck with the greatest rapidity. Their jobs were cut to minimum hours or eliminated altogether. Others in the area, who were virtually all naturalized citizens, the majority from eastern Europe, wished the Mexicans would "go home," leaving the jobs that remained for them. Since most Mexicans had not pursued citizenship, they were not considered true Americans and were viewed by most as temporary workers. Other immigrants who had migrated over vast oceans to reach American shores had put their homelands behind them. They tended to pursue citizenship and embrace the United States as their own. Mexicans had clung to a homeland that was easily accessible by foot, road, or rail. Moving them back across the border was seen as a relatively easy task.

The steel industry, so eager to import these workers when ruthlessly striving to crush the labor movement, now had no more use for them. The general community agreed. Why pay subsidies to these "non-Americans" when the rest of the population had their own problems? Why use the region's relief funds on people who were no longer necessary? Those who had once been an essential cog in the great machine of industry had become nothing more or less than an extraneous gear that slowed the machine's progress.

The Mexican population had not yet reached an economic plateau that allowed them to save money. When work grew scarce, there was no nest egg available. With many citizens needing help, noncitizens of all nationalities had difficulty acquiring aid from relief agencies and were not eligible for the public works projects that were eventually established by the federal government. Perhaps even more difficult for those of Mexican heritage was to ask for assistance in the first place. A proud people, used to coping with their problems alone, they considered it a blow to the manhood of Mexican males if they were humbled to seek help.

For the first months after Miguel's wages dropped, the Arredondos struggled to make ends meet. Miguel's huge network of friends came to his aid, including the grocer who extended credit to the family. But as months passed with no work, the family suffered from hunger. When given a single tortilla shell sprinkled with salt, Jesse begged for more. Maria explained there was no money for more, while Rita spread on hot sauce as if that could fill his stomach. Still hungry, little Jesse cried himself to sleep, praying his father would soon find work.

Miguel at last was forced to seek assistance. This stung the usually self-reliant man, but he, like so many of his fellow workers, had no choice. Our Lady of Guadalupe Church was the main source that helped provide food and clothes. With church assistance, the Arredondos soldiered on. Maria and her children walked to the church, pulling a little red wagon to carry items from the food pantry back to their home. The nuns also distributed clothing, shoes, and sneakers so children did not have to go barefoot. Once, Jenny was issued a cream-colored dress. After a time, Maria dyed it pink so another dress was created.

Maria never forgot this generosity. "In Mexico no one helped us. Never gave us anything, not so much as a tortilla. Here, we were given help. It's the biggest reason I love this country," she often stated to any who would listen.

Everyone in the family was expected to do his or her part, and even the smallest were not exempt. Little Jesse had sold a Mexican paper, *La Prensa*, since the tender age of four. He hawked his wares along the streets, his papers clutched under his arm. The parental injunction to work hard was manifested and put into practice as soon as the children could contribute.

Sometimes hardship was a catalyst for inspiration. As Jenny was in the kitchen watching her mother cut a cantaloupe, she came up with an ingenious idea. She scooped up all the melon's seeds, washed and dried them, and using Maria's needle and thread, patiently strung each seed into a necklace that she wore with pride.

The Arredondos accepted the consequences of the Depression without complaint, recognizing that the entire country was in the same boat. Like thousands of others across the country, the family sought any means available to sustain the most meager existence. The Office of the North Township Trustees for example, distributed staples such as eggs, beans, and potatoes on a weekly basis.

***

If the Arredondos hoped to wait out the ill feelings toward Mexicans, they were disappointed. Resentment toward Mexicans, the latest of the immigrants to arrive on American soil, did not subside. A national scheme to send them back to Mexico was devised and christened with the title "Repatriation." The concept was simple: transportation would be provided for Mexicans to return to their native land, where they could start anew. This was easy to justify since

Indiana Harbor repatriation train that took Harbor residents to Mexico, June 8, 1932

most Mexicans had retained close ties with family and friends in their home-land. No huge body of water separated the immigrants from their home of origin. A truck or train ride could easily transport Mexicans home. Less than twenty dollars would do the trick. They were promised transportation to the border with drop off in their home state. On arrival, local authorities would be waiting to help them settle and find jobs. For many, already homesick and unemployed in the United States, this seemed an attractive proposition. For those who were more reluctant to leave, threats often caused them to go, however unhappily. The repatriation plan was by no means a strictly voluntary one.

Miguel considered this route, but Maria held steadfastly against it. She wanted no part of the sad memories that life in Mexico evoked. No matter how difficult the conditions in the United States, she preferred them to her early life in Mexico.

"We should go. This is our chance to get home," Miguel argued. "My mother will give us a place to live—she has houses. I could work, and we'd have family around to help us."

Miguel may have wished to return to his mother, but Maria did not relish living under the thumb of a domineering mother-in-law. Maria had her mother and brother with her in the United States. Miguel's mother and brother in Mexico were certainly not Maria's idea of the ideal support group.

Miguel continued his argument.

"But, Maria, think. What good is it to stay here? The mills don't want the Mexicans anymore. They used us when they needed our hands and backs to do their dirty jobs, but now there are not enough jobs even for the Anglos. We are of no use to them now. They even talk of building a wall along the border to keep Mexicans out."

"A wall! Humph! There is not enough clay in the world to make the bricks! Are they crazy? Besides, who will pick their crops and clean their houses? Steel isn't the only dirty job for Mexicans!" countered Maria, her voice rising with anger.

"Then think of the children. They could go to their homeland. They promise us we will be taken back to our hometown. And the government will see we have jobs!

Maria responded with surprising bluntness.

"Huh, that country didn't give me anything! It's just coming out of a revolution, and you want to go back? How can they help us? What work will you do? No! There's nothing there! The mills are trying to fool you. This government is lying. The Mexican government is lying. This repatriation thing is nothing but a ball of lies, I tell you!"

Their friend, José Martinez, joined Maria in her protests.

"Look, Miguel, I don't trust the guys and their promises. I think they just want us to fall for their line and get rid of us.

"I'm your son Mikey's godfather. You know I want the best for you. I'm still working, and I'm a single guy. Let me help you and your family out. Take some time. See what this repatriation is really all about. *No se vaya.* Don't go."

Miguel was convinced to wait.

Many Mexicans did go, however, believing the promises and hoping for a new beginning to their lives. Others were virtually forced to pack up all their belongings and leave. Several friends of the Arredondos were among those boarding trains to head south. The family went to see them off, waving and wishing them luck as they loaded every possession they could manage, from brooms to beds, onto the railroad cars. The expression on the faces of those leaving and those staying reflected a mixture of hope and fear.

Soon stories came up from the border confirming that the repatriation promises were hollow. It seemed Maria's assessment of this situation was correct. There was no true organizational process to find jobs for those who went south, and the promise of being taken to their home states never materialized.

Those who chose to accept the offer to leave were dumped just over the border and left to their own devices.

Some were forced to sleep on the floor of the railroad station with their few belongings and the little money they had at grave risk of being stolen. The friends that the Arredondos had seen off in the summer of 1932 found themselves stranded and abandoned with no resources other than their own wit and faith. They went where rumors sent them in search of work, their homecoming worse than their lot in the Harbor. The only winners were those who had rid themselves of the now-unwanted Mexicans.

In the end, the Arredondos hunkered down and waited for life to improve.

10

"Take Me to the Fair"

Around forty million people of all ages, races, and social classes attended Chicago's Century of Progress International Exposition in 1933 and 1934, gawking at the wonders of the "Rainbow City," in contrast to the "White City" theme of the city's Columbian Exposition forty years before.

Ironically, one of the brightest times in Maria's early life came during the Great Depression when the city of Chicago was chosen to be the location of the World's Fair. Everyone was thrilled to think that visitors from everywhere would come to see the exhibitions and new ideas on display at this major event. The newspapers were filled with articles touting its wonders.

Maria, like everyone, heard the talk of the great fair and the marvels it held, but never expected to see it for herself. How would she get there and, if she did manage the trip, how would she ever have the money for the entrance fee? As far as Maria was concerned, the fair might as well be held at the North Pole. Chicago might be just across the state line, but the odds of her seeing the great event were on par with those of trekking to the Arctic.

Besides, her friend, Lupe's mother, had taken her once to a carnival set up in a vacant lot in the Harbor. It was a small show with a few games and rides, but what Maria remembered most was the resident "cannibal," a man who leered at the audience as he feasted on rats. This bit of theater had appealed to Maria not at all. If the World's Fair was anything like the Harbor Carnival, Maria was not interested!

As it turned out, Maria did have an opportunity to visit the fair and found it one of the highlights of her life. The Arredondos' good friend José Martinez

Front cover of sheet music for a waltz by Luther A. Clark and M. Curtis Pittman, commemorating the 1933–34 Chicago World's Fair

came to the house early one day and confronted Miguel and Maria with a grin and a command.

"Get ready! We're going to the World's Fair!"

The couple looked at him and laughed, thinking this was a great joke.

"Honestly! I'm not kidding. I've got passes and money. We're going! Bring Jenny, too. We can't miss a chance like this!"

After startled confusion and half-hearted protests, the group made ready. Rita would stay with the children, except for Jenny who was to accompany her parents. The happy band of merrymakers headed for the bus stop. It was a beautiful summer day as the sightseers came to see the Century of Progress exhibits that showcased American know-how at the fair of 1933.

President Franklin D. Roosevelt had welcomed the world to the event, which was the highlight of Chicago's centennial celebration. On the shores of Lake Michigan there had sprung up a model city focused on soaring architecture, color, and movement. Wondrous visions of a bright future swept away— if only for a moment—the darkness that the Great Depression had brought to the country.

Maria, Miguel, José, and Jenny marveled at the sights. Novelty items like the twenty-one-story Havoline Thermometer drew crowds of people who gaped at the bright neon tower. A sky ride carried passengers more than two hundred feet above a lagoon in glass-sided cable cars.

As they entered through the main gate on Twelfth Street, Maria viewed pavilions that represented life in a number of foreign countries including China, Egypt, Italy, Sweden, and Czechoslovakia. There was such a mixture of architecture, technology, art, culture, and carnival that visitors far more worldly than Maria were overwhelmed.

Chevrolet set up a full production line that was especially fascinating to the men. Not to be outdone, Hollywood had outdoor sets that filmed movies daily, appealing to star-struck girls. Coupled with this overload of science, culture, and plain old fun was music and food to keep the fair's patrons upbeat and well fed.

Everywhere she looked Maria was awed. Each step seemed to produce a wonder more spectacular than the one before. And the people! They seemed to Maria like a million ants streaming down the aisles of pavilions or along the open walkways. Never had she dreamed that she would be a part of such a magnificent event. As the sun streamed down, she felt giddy—she had to keep reminding herself that this was real. The hope and optimism that the great World's Fair generated rubbed off on Maria and millions of others who entered its gates. Hard times would pass. This was their America to come. And she, Maria Perez Arredondo, had seen it for herself. She had seen her future!

As the long day ended and the tired travelers sat on a bench near the Adler Planetarium, Maria felt she had visited a truly magical place. Often, when she felt discouraged, she would pull from her memories a snippet of her day at the fair and smile to herself remembering the wonders she had known there.

11

Betrayal

In their book Mexican-Americans in a Midwest Metropolis: A Study of East Chicago *(1967), sociologists Julian Samora and Richard A. Lamanna note that Mexican American families in Indiana Harbor held up quite well against all the challenges they faced and comment on the "extremely high fertility of the group." Still, during the early part of the twentieth century, many Mexican American men feared the traditional family structure was weakening and dreamed of returning to the Old Country, even though their wives and children might have felt differently.*

Maria remained grateful and relieved to have escaped repatriation. However hard things were, she had her family, they were fed and clothed, and she was not forced to make the long, arduous journey south to a life she had happily put behind her. But she could not foresee that a seemingly inconsequential remark would trigger the national plan for the repatriation of Mexicans and disrupt her life once again.

Rita had long purchased her groceries for the boardinghouse from a local store. One day the owner, whose name was Augustine, casually asked her how she had entered the United States. Rita had known the man for years. Little Jesse stopped by the shop daily to ask if there were any odd jobs he might do for a little change to give his mother. Augustine had even taken Jesse to his Baptist church, where Jesse learned gospel songs he had never heard in the more sedate and ritualistic Catholic ceremony.

Rita often exchanged small talk with Augustine. There was no reason for her to be wary of her old acquaintance.

"Oh, I just came across to Laredo with my son," she answered without hesitation.

She thought nothing of their conversation until days later when authorities knocked on her door and informed her that she was to be deported to Mexico as she was an "illegal." There was a $25 reward for anyone turning in illegal aliens, and her "friend" the grocer had informed on her.

The news of Rita's impending deportation threw the entire family into panic. By this time Maria had three more children: José (Pepé), born March 2, 1934; Marie (Mary), born September 30, 1936; and Camila (Mila), on July 28, 1938. This pattern of a child approximately every two years would be repeated twice more for a total of ten children. In fact, Maria was pregnant with her ninth child, Ramón (Ray), when the news of her mother's misfortune was discovered.

Maria found herself in the throes of a true dilemma, torn between love and loyalty for her mother and her almost obsessive dread of returning to Mexico. Memories of her difficult childhood flooded back. The hunger, the fear, and the sense of abandonment resurfaced in her thinking. She remembered the early days of her marriage and the long years of anguish inflicted upon her by her mother-in-law.

"Oh, please, help me with this decision," she prayed to Our Lady of Guadalupe. She kneeled before the brightly painted statue of the saint and could not stop herself from adding, "Please, please, don't let me go back."

She also talked with her mother, who knew that her boardinghouse and the life she had made for herself through hard work and sweat was coming to an abrupt end. Rita was angry and afraid, but she told her daughter, "Maria, do what you must. Of course it will be hard alone, but I can make it. You must make your decision on your own, not because of my needs or Miguel's wishes. You must think of yourself and your children."

What to do? Could she let her mother return to their home city of Salamanca alone? Yet, how could she possibly pick up stakes yet again and leave the land she had come to love? How could she return to a place that held nothing but a past she had tried to forget?

The decision came from Miguel, and his mind was irrevocably made up.

"Go with your mother. Take the children, and I'll send you money from here. My mother will give you a house and everything will work out. I'll come later."

This was not the course that Maria had hoped for, but with a mother in dire circumstances and she, herself, pregnant, she had neither the strength nor the energy to argue further with her husband. With few exceptions she had been an "obedient wife." There was no way Rita could remain, and the move must be made immediately. The alternative, that Rita make the journey alone, was not one Maria wished her mother to endure. With great haste arrangements were made for the departure of Maria, her mother, and her eight children.

Ironically, on July 4, 1939, America's Independence Day, a pregnant Maria, along with her eight children and her mother, packed up all their belongings and took the train to Laredo. Their possessions consisted of two trunks, eight suitcases, a sewing machine, a washing machine, and a large radio. From Laredo they made their way to Salamanca.

Miguel's mother, Camila, had been writing to her son, assuring him that she had a house for him and his family. There was indeed a house with a large living area, tiny bedrooms, and a kitchen that surrounded a courtyard. There was no bathroom. The family was forced to go down the street to their Grandmother Camila's or use a primitive outhouse in the backyard. The outhouse was not a favorite because of ticks, which thrived in its dark, smelly confines. The boys improvised and used the courtyard when nature called, shooing away turkeys and chickens.

Maria's first act upon arriving was to bathe her children. She lined them up at a pump in the yard. One by one she washed their hair, leaving bathing to be done later in the privacy of the house. Soon the little group had gathered a bevy of gapers. No doubt she and her band of bedraggled children made for an unusual sight. Maria steadfastly ignored her unsolicited audience as she continued the task until her last child was clean.

Maria was unhappy from the start but attempted to settle in and wait for Miguel to send the promised money and, later, join them. Jesse and Sue were enrolled in school. Jenny, as in times past, stayed home to help out with the smaller kids. Baby Camila was a special problem because she had been born with a clubfoot. A caring social worker had contacted a doctor from Billings Hospital in Chicago who agreed to operate to correct the foot's defect. There had been no openings at the hospital at the time, and before an appointment could be scheduled, Maria and the children had begun their journey to Mexico. Jenny spent much of her time holding and caring for her handicapped sister. The familiar friends and surroundings were behind them. They were left to fend in an unfamiliar environment with only the support of a cold, unfriendly woman to aid them.

Maria and her mother were unwelcome guests. Camila was not a woman who showed affection, even to her grandchildren. She had supplied lodging

COURTESY OF THE ARREDONDO FAMILY

Miguel's mother, Camila Arredondo

and in doing so had fulfilled her promise to her son. Anything further was not to be forthcoming, at least not until the day her beloved son appeared. Unwanted, Maria was humiliated. She also doubted that Miguel would come soon, if ever. She felt isolated and abandoned. She was also exhausted and pregnant. Hardly an auspicious beginning to a new life "back home."

It took only a short time in this difficult situation for the children to become extremely ill. One by one, they each came down with a sickness. The sole exception was Sue. Chive was the last of the children to become sick. It was only then that Camila's second husband, José (her first husband had passed away earlier), took Maria and the children to a doctor in Irapuato, a city in the state of Guanajuato.

"In six months we'll see how many will live and how many will die," pronounced the doctor after examining the family.

Maria paled with fear.

"I didn't come down here to have half my children die!" she exclaimed.

"It's the change," explained the doctor, "they are not used to this country, its water, its food, its climate. If you stay here, you will almost surely lose some of them."

Maria resolved then and there that, whatever it took, she would return to the United States with her children. Miguel had yet to send money and certainly had not indicated any intention of joining them. Maria had a house, but her mother-in-law had not changed in her absence; the relationship between the two women was contentious at best. Camila was not a nurturing in-law—quite the contrary—her treatment of Maria was more that of master to servant than a loving mother-in-law to her son's wife. For Maria the whole situation was a regression to an earlier life of hardship and repression.

Maria wrote to Miguel telling him of her living conditions.

"What should I do?" she inquired.

Miguel lost no time replying, "I didn't send you there on a pleasure trip. I've got no money to bring you home. You'll have to stay."

This moment was a watershed in Maria's life. The years of suffering and sacrifice, her deep devotion to her children, and her innate strength, courage, and intelligence welled to the surface. Maria was going home with her children. She would not stay and risk losing them, nor would she continue to live under the intolerable treatment she received from Camila. No matter how hard, no matter what the cost, Maria was going home. She went to her mother-in-law's home to inform her of her decision.

"I am taking my children home," she told Camila.

Camila was seated in her high-backed chair, working on ledgers, which outlined her holdings, profits, and losses. She raised her gray eyes to meet those of her daughter-in-law.

"Don't be a fool, Maria. You have no money to go anywhere. Be grateful for what you have and stop behaving as if you've lost what little sense you had."

With that, Camila lowered her eyes and returned to calculating her worth. Maria stood for a moment regarding her husband's mother.

"I will never forget this moment," she thought, memorizing the image of her mother-in-law, the room and its furnishings.

"Whenever I am treated unjustly, I shall think of this moment and remember how small Camila tried to make me feel. Never again will I let anyone treat me like I am nothing more than dirt beneath their feet. Never again," she vowed to herself.

Maria straightened her shoulders, held her head up, and walked slowly and deliberately away.

José, who had overheard the exchange between his wife and Maria, entered the room just after Maria's departure.

"Why were you so hard on her, Camila?" he asked. "Her children are ill, and she's carrying another child. She's scared and worried. Couldn't you spare her just a little kindness?"

Camila searched her husband's face before responding. She seemed to be looking for something that wasn't there.

"Kindness?" she repeated slowly and softly. "Kindness? Don't speak to me of kindness. What has 'kindness' ever done for anyone? Was anybody ever kind to me? Did I get what I have because people were kind?" Her voice rose and bitterness crept in.

"No, José, I have what I have because I learned that it's not your 'kindness' that helps one through life. It's strength and hard work and making up your mind to get what you desire, whatever it takes. Do you think I saw 'kindness' when the soldiers marched through my town? Do you think I was welcomed here with 'kindness' when I first arrived? No, my husband, there is little of your 'kindness' in this world. What there is, is a great abundance of hate and greed and envy. If one is to succeed in anything, one must learn that no one will hand you an easy way. No," she shook her head and her eyes glistened. José was not certain if they did so because of anger or tears as Camila continued.

"People are very predictable, my dear. When you are poor and can be of no help to them, they spit on you and pass you by. It is only when you have something that they give you respect and even then they are filled with envy.

"I don't fool myself. I know what people think of me. I know there are those who wish me ill and think I am hardhearted. They wait for the day that I topple or they wish me to change my stripes—to be 'kind,' as you wish, my husband. Perhaps once long ago I was kind, but I can assure you such kindness brought me nothing but pain.

"No, what my daughter-in-law needs is not 'kindness' but, rather, hardening. Look at her, barely thirty and already with eight kids and one on the way. How will she and my *hijo* ever have anything if all they do is produce children like the hares in the fields?

"If Maria stays here, she and Miguel and their brood will someday have half of all I own. I am an old woman now, nearly twice her age. I want my son here with me. My daughter-in-law must make her choice. Whatever she does, she must do it because she believes it is best for her. She's still soft, José, and no woman can stay soft and succeed in getting what she wants. Let her make her choice and live with it. We can only wait and see."

José looked at his wife as she returned to her accounts, her words still ringing in his ears. He knew his wife had suffered and that suffering had made her what she was. Perhaps she was right. Maybe Maria had not learned the lessons necessary to reach her goals, despite the difficulties of her past. In any case, he knew better than to try to change his wife's mind.

12

"Don't Look Back"—The Homecoming

Though reared to be docile and subservient to their husbands, Mexican women also had primary responsibility for their offspring's well-being. When, as in Maria's circumstances, the two directives came into conflict, Mexican women often acted with an iron resolve to ensure the safety of their children. In Maria's case, this meant bringing her children back to the Harbor, even if it meant facing Miguel's wrath.

Determined to return home, Maria immediately acted upon her decision, selling everything she had brought with her. Her sewing and washing machines went to a rich family in town. A friend knew a man at the railroad station who bought their radio. She sold clothes, and the kids even parted with their marbles for a *centavo* (penny) apiece. Still, it was not enough for the trip back to Indiana.

It was at this crucial juncture that an old friend from Maria's childhood named Pilar stepped forward. She had reconnected with Maria upon her return to Mexico and was witness to the miserable conditions under which Maria and her family had been living. Pilar had watched as Camila lorded over Maria and ignored her requests for help.

"Here's some money," she said, holding Maria's hand. "You don't have to pay me back. I don't like how your mother-in-law has been treating you. Take this. Take your children home."

Maria was speechless for a moment, then whispered, "I will never forget this, my friend. You will be in my prayers till the day God takes me."

Her despair had turned to gratefulness. Maria, Rita, and the children began their long trek toward the border. When they reached Nuevo Laredo, they stayed with people who knew Rita. Their hosts were poor and could offer little more than jalapeños wrapped in tortillas. No matter how meager, the family was grateful for their hospitality. It was with them that Rita remained, fearful of crossing the border without papers. The pregnant Maria continued on with eight children and two suitcases, all she had left in the world.

Early in the day she reached customs.

"My children and I are going home to Indiana to join my husband," she explained to the guard at the border.

"I think not, Señora," replied the guard gruffly. "Nobody goes across without passports."

It was true. She had no documents. She had left the documents at home. When she hurriedly left the States, her discouragement was such that she believed Mexico would be her home until she died; why bother with documents if one never planned to return to the States? She saw now she had acted without thought, but it was too late.

She explained again that she was returning to her husband in the States. With no proof of her story, no papers supporting her claim, she was turned away once more. At that point Maria was ready to take all of the children and leap into the river. To the desperate and exhausted woman, drowning seemed a better solution than remaining in Mexico. She was discouraged, pregnant, tired, and hungry. She would not go back to Salamanca, and she could not go forward to her life in Indiana Harbor. There was nothing left but to let the Rio Grande bring eternal sleep to her and her children. Just when she was ready to abandon all hope, another border guard, noticing her distress, walked over to her. He took in the desperation on her face and the eight wide-eyed children who clustered around her.

"Go sit over there," he pointed to some shade, "and wait until evening. The guards are not as hard then. They may let you cross, but be careful. Do not make them angry."

With that small modicum of encouragement, Maria resolved to make one more attempt. She prayed hard to her saints, pleading for a miracle, "St. Jude, saint of all things despaired, please help me," she murmured over and over.

That night the bedraggled little band tried to cross once more. At first demands for documents were repeated. As the night wore on, the guards relented somewhat and asked for proof that Maria had only been in Mexico a short time. Did she have receipts or other evidence that their stay had been less than six months?

Fence at border between El Paso, Texas, and Juarez, Mexico

Jenny began to explain in English. She repeated the story as her mother had instructed her: they had come to visit their grandmother and were now returning to their father who worked at the steel mill in East Chicago, Indiana. Tangible proof, however, by way of receipts or other paper trails, was simply not to be had, no matter how carefully they searched the two pathetic suitcases with their meager cache of clothes and sundries.

It seemed as if the river was fast becoming the only option as the contents of the suitcases stubbornly failed to produce evidence to validate their story. Another guard, who had turned his chair backwards as Jenny and Maria rummaged through their belongings, gazed at the mother and her children. Seeing the hopelessness in Maria's lovely face, he cleared his throat and spoke for the first time since the border drama had begun.

"I've been talking to this boy here, and he's answered every question in English. He knows his name, his age, and where he lives. He says his Dad is waiting for them in the States," he said to his colleague.

"So what?" replied the other customs man, disgusted with the delay caused by the family. "They have no proof!"

"Let them go," answered the other. "There's no way this little boy could speak such good English if they'd been in Mexico any length of time."

The little boy was Pepé, who had been discussing his life with the second guard with great detail and enthusiasm. Pepé's talkativeness proved the family's salvation.

"Oh, very well, go! You'll only keep worrying us all night if we make you stay. Take those snotty-nosed kids of yours and get out of my sight before I change my mind," said the customs officer, tired of the aggravation the woman and her children were causing him. It was late, and he wanted to relax and drink his coffee, not hassle with a nearly hysterical woman and her brood of sad-eyed kids.

The guard motioned the mother and children to cross. Maria bustled her children into one of the many taxis stationed at the border before the guard could change his mind. She and her eight offspring were squished tightly into the hot car before Maria allowed herself to believe that they were truly going home.

As they crossed the long bridge to stateside, Jenny looked back. "Wow! Ma, look how long this bridge is!"

"Don't turn around!" Maria admonished her. "What if they call us back?" Wiser than Lot's wife, Maria stared fixedly forward until they were safely delivered onto American soil.

From the border they caught a Greyhound bus to Dallas. Maria steered her children to the back so they could all sit together. When the bus stopped, Jesse was sent to purchase hamburgers, which were shared among the nine travelers. Hours later a mother and her daughter who were on their way from Guadalajara to New York shared some of their bread with them. The bread was so stale and hard that little Mikey chipped a tooth as he bit into it, but it helped stem the growling of the little stomachs, at least temporarily.

When they reached Saint Louis, there was a six-hour layover between buses. Sue began to hate the city as they passed dreary hours waiting for their next bus. The longer they lingered, the higher the brick buildings seemed to grow. By that time there was no money left, and the children were hungry once again. The wait began to seem an eternity.

Maria pulled her wedding ring from her finger and directed Jesse and Sue to go find a pawnshop.

"Take this ring and sell it. We'll use the money to buy food." Then Maria instructed the children on a dollar amount they were to bargain for.

The two young children set out in search of a pawnshop. Years later, Sue recalled the ugly buildings and how famished she had been. That Maria would have sent her children out into a strange city on such an errand was indicative of the desperation she felt. She was a woman on a mission, driven to see to it that her children lived in America. She almost felt she would sell her soul if that was what it would take to reach her goal.

Jenny remained with Maria to help with the rest of the children: Chive, Mikey, Pepé, Mary, and Camila. When Jesse and Sue returned empty handed, explaining that the pawnbroker would not pay the amount Maria had requested, little Pepé, who had been peering hungrily through a restaurant window, his hair sticking up and clothes rumpled from the long journey, was called back by Jenny.

"Come sit down," she demanded.

"No," he responded stamping his feet, "I want to eat!"

Jenny, who had learned early on that her responsibility was to control the young children and teach them manners, got up and made him sit. However, even her authoritarian manner could not stem his loud crying.

After a few more minutes of Pepé's noisy, snuffling tears, a gentleman came up to Jenny and inquired, "What's wrong with him?"

"Oh, we've been traveling for a long time. I guess he's hungry."

"Here," said the man pulling out thirty cents. "Take this to that store across the street and get some milk and bread."

Whether this generosity was because of compassion or because Pepé's incessant screaming was too unsettling, the result was the same. The children had a slice of bread and some milk to squelch their hunger, though Pepé grabbed the milk first and drank far more than his share.

Maria marked the incident well and, in later years, used it as a lesson to her children.

"Remember, you should help people when you are able. Think of that man—he didn't even know us, and he took pity and gave us money for food. You never know in this life who will be there for you, who will rescue you in times of trouble. Be sure you treat everyone as well as that man in Saint Louis treated us."

After many more harrowing miles the ragtag band reached Chicago. The last leg of the long sojourn required a taxi ride from the Windy City to Indiana Harbor. There was no money.

Jesse, again, was pressed into action.

"Go and find a taxi driver who will take us. Tell him your father will pay when we get there," his mother directed him, her voice so filled with fatigue as to be nearly inaudible.

Though very young, Jesse had learned much as he had worked to help his mother. He was wise beyond his years and succeeded in finding a driver trusting enough to take the family to the Harbor. They piled into the taxi, some sitting on each other's laps and others sharing the front seat. Late in the afternoon of Labor Day, 1939, they arrived on the doorstep of their dear friend, Doña Lola, the only address where Maria felt certain she would find a friend awaiting. Jenny knocked on the front door. Peering through the window, she spied her father sitting in a chair as he visited with Lola. She called to him.

"Dad, we're here. Please pay the taxi driver."

Miguel was furious when he saw his family. Maria had gone against his wishes and returned. Far from a loving greeting for his pregnant wife and children, he strode out of the back door muttering that he "wanted no part of it." No doubt he, himself, was overwhelmed at what the future held. Work at the mill was still "iffy" at best. Each morning men lined up at the gate while a foreman picked those who would work and those who wouldn't. They favored lighter complexioned men and, as Miguel was very fair, he was chosen more often than most. Yet money remained scarce, and now he would have to search for a landlord willing to rent to a man, his wife, and eight kids. Sure, Mexico may not have been pleasant for Maria, but at least Miguel could be assured his family had a roof over their heads. So what if Maria and his mother did not get along. Women seldom did. Now she and the kids had turned up, and he was supposed to take over with a shaky job and a couple of dollars to his name.

Though Maria did not know it at the time, Miguel had another reason for wanting his family to stay in Mexico: he had been having an affair. A woman with a bright red convertible had been seen driving him around town. Miguel clearly enjoyed playing the part of a single man with nothing more on his mind than where he and his attractive companion would go for a drink. He felt young and carefree, relieved of the burdens and responsibilities he had shouldered for so long—the burdens, which often grew so heavy he was at a loss as to how to cope.

Luckily, Doña Lola's reaction was exactly the reverse of Miguel's. She embraced Maria and welcomed her old friend and her family, happy to have them all back. Reaching into the pocket of her apron, she produced a small change purse.

"How much is the fare?" she questioned the driver.

"The meter reads $3.90, but I said I'd bring them for $3.50, so $3.50 it is."

Doña Lola paid the honest cabbie and welcomed the family into her home.

"Don't worry about Miguel," she reassured Maria. "He'll get over his anger. In the meantime you'll stay here with me," and she set about preparing food while the weary travelers washed away the dust of their long ordeal. Later she arranged cots on the floor, and the family slept, clean and well fed. Once Maria and the children were settled in at her house, Doña Lola set about finding Miguel. Having once been a soldier in Emiliano Zapata's guerilla army, Lola did not hesitate to give Miguel orders when she located him.

"Find a home. Take care of your family and forget your no-account lady friend! Be a man!" Lola shouted at him.

———————

In a few days Miguel had located a house next door to the Alex Hotel. The lodgings were so filthy that Jenny and Maria quite literally swept bushels of dirt from the floor. A bed was found for Miguel, Maria, and baby Camila; the other children slept on the floor until additional beds could be had.

During this time Miguel sensed a change in his wife. Usually a man who took things in a literal, intellectual manner, this time he intuitively sensed that Maria would no longer suffer in silence. Something had occurred during the time she had been away. She held herself taller, and the ordeal seemed to have forged a harder, tougher persona. She reminded him of someone he knew, but he could not quite think of who it was. He resented the change, but at the same time recognized it for what it was—a shift, however subtle, in the balance of family power.

Already Maria had sent Jenny to retrieve him on one of his Saturdays away from home.

"Jenny," she directed. "Go find your father and bring him home at once. There's work to be done to get this place halfway livable, and I need his help. You'll probably find him in the bars with that floozy he hangs around with. Go on, now. Do as I say."

Reluctantly, Jenny bundled up in the hand-me-down coat Doña Lola had given her and began her search of the many bars that lined the streets of the Harbor. She was cold and angry as she went from one tavern to the next.

She was old enough to realize how badly her father was behaving and wise enough to understand how it reflected on her and the family.

It did not take long for Jenny to locate Miguel. Sure enough, there he was, sitting in a tavern, lounging back in his chair, drinking with "that woman"!

"Papa, Mother says to come home. Now!" she announced to her father who was seated at a back table. Miguel reluctantly followed her, muttering something about another damned emergency. He could see from the determination on his daughter's face that she would cause a scene if he did not leave.

"I'll be back later," he called with a bravado he did not feel.

Jenny confronted him as they went along the sidewalk toward their home.

"How can you be with that terrible woman? She is nothing compared to Ma. How can you do this to all of us?" Jenny's voice quivered with hurt and anger, but Miguel said nothing in reply. He was the man of the house—why would he feel obliged to answer such a question from his daughter? Then he rethought his position and replied with a timeworn excuse, "What do you expect? Your mother was in Mexico, and that woman came chasing me. She'd pull up to the mill in that fancy car and wait for me until my shift was over."

Striding into the house, he shouted at Maria, "What's the matter with you?"

She did not deign to look at him as she continued placing bowls of food on the table.

"You belong here, Miguel," her voice soft and hard. "You have a wife and a family. Whether you like it or not, you belong here now."

Miguel remained shocked at his wife's new demeanor. She was not crying or screaming at him. Instead she was giving ultimatums and in no uncertain terms. It was obvious to anyone who could see her at that moment that she was not a woman to be trifled with.

Miguel made up his mind that he could not accept that kind of behavior from any wife of his. He vowed to himself he would show her who was boss. It took only a few days before his showdown occurred. A neighbor lady, as they are wont to do, came to report to Maria, "Did you know your husband's sitting in that woman's house right now?"

This time Maria accompanied Jenny to retrieve Miguel. Grabbing up her youngest child, Camila, she and her daughter marched down the street to the little house where "that woman" stayed. As they came up the walkway, they could see through the screen door that Miguel was sitting at the table.

Hanging in the background with her baby, Maria sent Jenny to call her father home. Opening with the same words she had used before, Jenny said, "Pa, Ma says for you to come home."

"Tell her I'll be there shortly," Miguel answered. After all, having vowed to prove who was in charge, he could not acquiesce immediately.

That was enough for Maria. She strode to the door clutching her baby and with a strong, determined voice told Miguel, "You come right now, or I'll call the police and tell them that hussy is selling beer!"

"Go, go," the woman inside waved Miguel away. Jenny could see her grabbing bottles of beer and pouring the contents down the sink. Miguel, Maria, Jenny, and the baby returned home together.

Realizing that he had lost this particular skirmish, Miguel turned his attention from his wife and lashed out at his firstborn instead. While she, too, had been acting out of character by daring to question him, at least she was still a child and one who knew better than to defy him. He would show Maria who was boss even if it had to be done indirectly through his oldest daughter.

"You're going to have to stay home and take care of the kids. You can't go to school anymore," he spat out the words to Jenny.

Jenny, who always loved school, burst into tears. "All these years I've had to babysit and stay home each time a baby was born. And now you want me to quit school and take care of these kids who aren't my responsibility!" She sobbed angrily at her father, resenting his decision but afraid to disobey.

Just the act of talking back to Miguel was a major breach of family mores, occurring only because her outrage outweighed her years of rigid obedience. At age fifteen she had spent much of the time caring for her siblings and, along with her mother and brothers and sisters, had just returned from a nightmarish journey to Mexico and back. And, on top of all this, had found herself in a barely livable environment with a father who had made no secret of preferring that his family had stayed in Mexico, a father who sat in a tavern with a trashy woman not his wife. Little wonder the years of being the oldest daughter with all that such a role encompassed had finally caused a dam of resentment to burst.

As for Maria, she held her tongue and waited. The horrid little house now teemed with tension. Maria had learned of Miguel's philandering and had challenged him. Miguel felt smothered by the responsibilities of his family.

Jenny grudgingly cared for her younger siblings while wishing she were in class. It was as if the very walls held their breath in anticipation of a break in the silent standoff. That break came soon enough in the guise of a stranger at the door.

Early one morning a tall, husky female wearing a uniform knocked heavily on the Arredondos' front door. Jenny answered the door, peeking out curiously at the odd visitor who stood before her. The stranger stared down at Jenny, rocking slowly to and fro.

"Are you Jenny? Why aren't you in school?" the woman demanded with no preliminary small talk. She did not pause to let Jenny answer, but continued unabated. "I'm the truant officer from Washington High School. I was sent to find out why you haven't attended school. Your brothers and sisters are there. Why aren't you?"

Jenny regarded the feisty female who towered over her. She decided quickly to drop back and call in reinforcements.

"Ma," she called out, "this lady wants to know why I'm not in school!"

"Tell her," commanded Maria in Spanish. "Tell her it's because your father wants you home to help with the little kids."

Upon hearing this explanation, the woman exploded.

"No, no, no!" she shouted vehemently. "You're only fifteen years old. You tell your father that you *have* to go to school, and you'd better be there tomorrow morning!"

With that, the woman left, her unfinished threat reverberating through the humble house. She walked quickly away, not lingering to hear any protests that Jenny might have made. Had she stayed, she would have been surprised to learn that, far from being upset, the teenager was overjoyed by the turn of events.

Jenny listened with barely concealed glee as her mother reported the conversation to her father. The next day she was back in class, grateful to the gruff lady who had won for her the battle to remain in school. She had missed a few weeks but quickly made up the work. Despite Miguel's anger at the turn of events, he was wise enough to recognize a challenge to this woman's authority could only bring trouble. He felt suddenly besieged by females! First Doña Lola, then Maria, then Jenny, and now this stranger. He quickly weighed his options and determined that his best recourse was a trip to the tavern and a beer!

13

On Watling Street

Indiana Harbor was a culturally diverse community in which daily life consisted of a mix of experiences that brought both fun and frustration. While children in the area held on to their own ethnicities at home and in churches, they also were exposed to the cultures of other national groups and were learning those American customs necessary for survival and ultimate success.

From September to December the Arredondos lived in the little house across from the Alex Hotel. Maria's days were spent as before: cooking, cleaning, and caring for her family. No matter how much she cleaned, the house remained dark and gloomy. The wall toward the hotel had no windows; some daylight penetrated the entrance but did not extend to the rooms within. Only the south side of the house had light from windows looking onto a small yard with a clothesline and sweet potato plants growing in clay containers that sat in wooden crates.

This yard was shared with a neighbor, Maria (China) Perez, who was a cousin and one of the few people the Arredondos saw regularly. The mother of small twins, Señora China had devised an ingenious way to keep her toddlers from straying while she and Maria were hanging clothes and chatting. Fashioning a makeshift "baby chair" by cutting four small holes in the bottom of the crates that held the plant pots a few inches above the ground, she inserted the twins' legs. This prevented their crawling away. The twins, comfortable on their blanket, kept one another occupied while their mother tended to their laundry without worrying about having to chase them.

In January 1940, a large hall-like dwelling became available on Watling Street. The family moved again. Though huge, the hall was bleak and unwelcoming. On one side stood a bed shared by Jesse, Mikey, and Pepé. The other side of the room held a bed for Jenny, Sue, and Mary. In a corner was Miguel and Maria's bed and baby Camila's bed. Only Chive was not with the family. It was his turn to stay at the boardinghouse, keeping his Grandma Rita company. Frank had secured the appropriate papers for Rita's return to the United States, and she now ran her boardinghouse with the security only official documents could bring.

Initially, the only other furniture on Watling was a table with orange crates for chairs. The only privacy in the big hall was the bathroom. Jenny stayed up until 11:00 each night studying her lessons, trying to grasp the little quiet time available in a home with eight people sharing one room.

Jenny continued the rest of her high school years while the family lived in the big room on Watling Street. However, school still presented a problem for Jenny because there was no money for books. Jenny's best friend, Lupe, spoke to her mother, Doña Lola, about the problem. At Thanksgiving Lola asked Maria if she could take Jenny along with her for a few hours.

"Yes, okay." Maria gave permission knowing Doña Lola was a trustworthy friend and had Jenny's welfare at heart. She and Doña Lola had spoken of the book dilemma and Maria knew this outing was somehow related.

Doña Lola took Jenny to a home in which a woman dressed in the traditional mourning clothes known as "widow's weeds," replete with black head covering, sat waiting in a huge wing chair. The woman was Doña Lola's good friend, Señora Segovia, mother of one of the Mexican men who had become a player in the region's political scene.

"Señora, this is my *compadre's* daughter, Juanita," explained Doña Lola. "She wants to finish high school and is a very good student, but her father has no money for her books because there are too many children. Could the school loan her books so that she may finish her work in school?"

"Don't worry, I'll take care of that," replied the widow. "It will be no problem."

For the last two years of school, Jenny was loaned textbooks. She gloated in the fact that her father had no excuse to keep her home and tried even harder to excel in her studies.

During the family's stay in Mexico, the social worker from Billings Hospital in Chicago had come looking for Maria regarding Camila's clubfoot. She had left a message that there was now an opening for the surgery, and the

COURTESY OF THE ARREDONDO FAMILY

Left to right: Mikey, Chive, Sue, Jesse, and Jenny, late 1930s

Arredondos should contact the hospital immediately. Arrangements were made by Doctor Arthur Brody just prior to Thanksgiving 1939; he drove Miguel and the pregnant Maria with their sixteen-month-old daughter to the hospital. The procedure was explained by Doctor Brody to the Arredondos, and the infant was left in the hands of the Billings staff until her bones could be broken and reset in the proper manner. Doctor Brody kept tabs on the child's progress, and when the foot was sufficiently healed and placed in a cast, Camila was brought home.

Subsequent treatments were required. Miguel had never driven or owned a car, so public transportation was their only option. Miguel and Jenny would bundle up the baby and catch the bus into Chicago where Jenny was given instructions on follow-up care for her sister. When the series of hospital visits ended, Camila wore a built-up shoe to assist in correcting her walk until she was five years old. Camila's foot eventually healed completely, though weather changes brought on aches throughout her life.

One month later, on February 9, 1940, Ramón was born. He was the first child born in a hospital, Saint Catherine, where he was delivered by Doctor Brody.

The doctor had come into the Arredondo's life before Camila was born. He had visited the family's home, knocking on the door and introducing himself as Doctor Arthur Brody, a new doctor in town. He had heard of Miguel Arredondo from others who spoke highly of his knowledge and influence within the community.

"I'm setting up practice here in the Harbor," he explained to Miguel. "I was hoping you'd consider using my services and perhaps recommending me to your friends and neighbors." Miguel took an immediate liking to the young man and soon became a major promoter of the new doctor, helping him to establish himself among the families of the Harbor. Doctor Brody was grateful and treated the family for no fee as a way of thanking him. In fact, he home-delivered Camila as his first "repayment" for Miguel's assistance with starting his practice. Maria was grateful, too, since now she was relieved of the concern of wondering if a sick or injured child's cries would result in a medical bill for which there was no money.

Once, while they sat in the waiting room as other patients were called in, Jenny questioned, "How come we have to wait while others who came in later are already done?"

"Because," explained Maria in hushed tones, "those people pay. This doctor treats us because your father was good to him. We wait because it's free. The doctor has to earn a living, so he has to see the people who pay him first."

Jenny nodded. She understood this logic.

Doctor Brody continued to help the Arredondos. He delivered both Ramón and Lorenzo (who were to be the last of Maria's children) pro bono at Saint Catherine Hospital. This kindness was sorely needed. The cavern-like hall in which the family lived during the boys' births afforded no privacy for the usual home delivery, except for curtains hung to divide the "rooms."

The doctor continued to play a part in the family's life after the boys' births. Jenny would later work for the doctor, and he would encourage her in her studies, advising her to take classes that would help with her future direction.

—◆»◆«◆—

Maria had been under such stress during her pregnancy with Ramón that she fully expected to lose her ninth child, but Ramón, though an underweight baby, survived and prospered. Maria always considered this son, whom she had carried and borne under such difficult circumstances, to be her "miracle baby." Maria chose the name Ramón because she had heard tales of wondrous miracles performed by Saint Ramón. Throughout her pregnancy, she prayed fervently to this saint and to Saint Jude and credited them with the birth of her healthy boy.

The addition of a fifth boy had little effect on the family's life. Home, church, mill, and school defined their days. They worked hard and depended on one another for everything. The fare remained hundred-pound sacks of flour, beans, and potatoes, supplemented when possible with vegetables, fruit, and, occasionally, meat.

Miguel's standing in the community, as well as the children's industriousness, enabled the family to begin faring better during their many tough times. The pharmacy on Main Street extended Miguel credit, as did "Red," the storeowner on Watling. Work gloves and other necessary sundries were available for a pittance at the store by the railroad tracks that catered exclusively to steelworkers' needs. In addition, Jesse supplied bread from his job at the bakery, and Jenny, who was working for a local grocer, often brought home fresh fruit and produce.

Within the Harbor, life had its own rhythm and hummed along to the noisy, smoky beat of industry. Working conditions at the mill were as difficult as ever, but the neighborhood was lively with activity everywhere. The billiard parlors' popularity continued, and music from their establishments was heard daily on the streets. "The Beer Barrel Polka" was the favorite song of the day, its strong rhythm adding a happy lilt to the pulse of the streets.

In winter, days were often dreary, gray, and cold with the ever-present wind howling off Lake Michigan, down alleyways, and around street corners. Snow and ice became blackened with the soot spewing from the factories' many chimneys. Dirty coal dust settled on rooftops and frozen streets; leafless trees stood like sentinels guarding the Harbor's frozen visage. The very air had a harsh, metallic taste as the chemicals belching from smokestacks permeated the area. A sharp acrid smell hung over the town as low gray clouds pressed down like an icy, smothering blanket. People bundled up against the bone-chilling cold, hurrying along mean streets to seek a warm refuge.

But in summer, when the weather was mild and breezes teased the leaves of trees that lined the streets of the Harbor, the air smelled sweet with the scent of flowers overflowing window boxes and gardens. The unmistakable odor of fresh roasted corn wafted from stands on street corners, alongside peddlers selling sweetly flavored *paletas*, a frozen fruit treat, as they pushed carts down sidewalks drenched in sunshine.

After winter's grip had given way to the glories of warm weather, the Harbor bloomed as brightly as the flowers themselves. People crowded the streets as they shopped; deliverymen made their rounds in the neighborhoods, and children reveled in a summer free from school and studies.

The "Egg Man" delivered dairy products. Peddlers came to the door with fresh vegetables or various items such as thread, needles, and other household necessities. The "Knife Man" pushed his cart as he announced his presence with a bell, seeking items to sharpen; women gathered knives and scissors that needed attention from his sharpening wheel. Sparks flew as the spinning wheel did its work, and the implements gleamed with newly honed edges that seemed to proclaim their readiness to participate in the new energy of the season.

One of the best-known delivery men was a muscular black man in a leather apron who carried large blocks of ice from the icehouse and delivered them to households that displayed signs in their windows, the color of which indicated the poundage of ice required to keep their iceboxes cool. Neighborhood kids would follow along the iceman's route, catching slivers that fell from the truck and eating them as a summer treat. The "Ice Man" deftly cut the requested amount for customers, hoisted the cold block to his shoulder with one mighty heave, and strode up to his customer's home. While the iceman delivered his ice, kids would scamper onto the back of the truck and gather still more chips.

Another familiar face, to those up early enough to see him, was the milkman. Once home from Rita's, Chive and his brother Mikey worked for the milkman on his early morning runs. (In later years Ray and Lorenzo took their places as the milkman's helpers.) Glass bottles, nestled in wire-mesh baskets, were delivered daily to households before dawn. When the milk froze in winter, cream popped up from the bottles. Jenny would hurry to bring the milk in, scooping the cream from the top and eating the rich treat before her siblings arose.

Jesse and his friend "Gopher" hauled melons for the "watermelon" man who paid each fifty cents a day. He drove through the neighborhood selling his wares crying, "Yo, wa-de-o melons." On hot, sweltering days juicy melons were a perfect way to cool off. Children ate large slices, spitting out seeds and letting the sticky juice drip down their chins. Housewives came to the sidewalk to buy melons, using this time to gather and share a bit of neighborhood gossip with friends as they shook and thumped the fruits, searching for the ripest and juiciest.

Fresh produce was also sold from the back of trucks, which traversed the neighborhood streets. Young boys were hired to help sort and lift the fruits and vegetables to customers gathered on the sidewalk. Often the boys' buddies would gather around the back of the truck. As the driver returned to the cab of his vehicle, his "helpers" would throw fruit to them, knowing that they and their friends were safely hidden by the trucker's blind spot.

Chive and Sue helped to fill the family coffers by carrying buckets of tortillas to taverns, selling them to men drinking at the bars. Those somewhat unsavory destinations were considered less than desirable for the children to enter, but times were hard. Money was made where it could be. Maria did not worry for her children's safety because they could roam the streets without fear of being accosted by strangers. Everyone knew their neighbors and looked out for their own and each others' children. If Chive and Sue were exposed to foul language or loose women, well, that was how life was. They took it in stride as they did all that happened in the Harbor.

The whole atmosphere of the town was one of good-natured encounters spiced with friendly talk and camaraderie in the same happy manner that chili peppers of different sizes and colors joined together to enhance the flavor of traditional Mexican dishes. Main Street was a hub of commerce. Here, house-wives shopped for fresh produce, fish, and live chickens, who squawked in their cages as if they realized the fate that awaited them. Customers such as Rita and Maria would inspect the birds, choose their fowl, take it home, wring its neck without so much as a shudder; then they would pluck, cut, and cook it for the next meal.

In grocery stores, food was sold in bags or boxes, measured out as the buyer requested. Canned goods were rare or nonexistent. Meals were made from fresh ingredients, and preparation time was often hours. The Arredondo girls learned to cook by watching Maria. Recipes were stored in the mind, rather than a cookbook; measuring ingredients simply was not done. A pinch of this or that and a quick taste to determine proper flavor was the rule of the day. The results were delicious. Just the smell of something simmering on the stove was a treat.

The one exception to these glorious odors was the cooking of *menudo*, a soup made from tripe (pig's stomach). It was simmered on the stove for hours emitting a distinct odor, which could never be characterized as pleas-ant. Deemed a delicacy by many, *menudo* was served with chopped onions, hot peppers, and oregano, then topped off by squeezing lemons over the whole concoction. Sometimes garbanzo beans were added for additional texture. The flavorful dish was a favorite of many and often considered the perfect meal after a night of drinking.

It was while living in the huge one-room house on Watling that Maria's last child, Lorenzo, was born on September 5, 1941, eighteen months after Ray's entry into the world. Maria now had a total of ten children, six boys and four girls. Her family was complete, they were all together, and despite the Great Depression, deportation, and the variety of problems experienced by all families, they were surviving. The hall was by no means the ideal living space, and Maria found herself forced to bed her infant boys upon the table of the home, staying up through the night to ensure that no rats crept out from the flimsy walls to harm the babies. But this was a precaution Maria accepted as she accepted all difficulties thrown her way. Her prayers had been answered, and she was grateful. She thanked her saints for her family and her life.

14

Graduation, Illness, Accidents, and a Vision

The first Latina to graduate from Jenny's high school, East Chicago Washington, was Rosa de Lima Buitron in 1925. Starting in the late 1930s there was an increase in the number of high school graduates of Mexican ancestry, rising from ten in 1939 to nineteen in Jenny's class of 1941.

Jenny's graduation in 1941 was the first for the family. Her perseverance with her studies paid off. She had mastered business skills: typing, shorthand, bookkeeping, and calibration, which involved working with a machine similar to a cash register. It was Doctor Brody who was responsible for the bookkeeping addition. One summer she had worked for the doctor answering the phone and performing general office duties. The doctor recognized Jenny's ability and encouraged her to add the course.

"Bookkeeping will give you a broader range of skills," he told her. "And it will open doors for a larger variety of jobs. You're a smart, attractive girl, and you'll do well. The more you know, the farther you can go in this world."

This was the first time Jenny had been told by a man that there were opportunities for women in the workforce. Her father had not encouraged her in the least; in fact, quite the opposite. Her mother had never even entertained working outside of the home; the sheer number of children she had to raise would have prevented it, even if she had wanted to. The only women Jenny knew who worked were schoolteachers, secretaries, or clerks in stores. Other than teachers, who, for the most part were single women, girls graduating had no role models and thought little about college, at least those in northwest Indiana's Calumet Region. The issue was not only lack of money, but also a mindset that men were breadwinners, while women were homemakers. Why waste time and funds on a woman who would only marry and stay home?

Society's rigid view of male/female roles precluded any belief that to educate a woman resulted in a benefit for the family. Jenny was grateful for the doctor's advice and found that the advanced courses served her well.

———————————

A few weeks before Jenny was ready to graduate, she was rewarded with a beautiful prom dress provided by Doña Lola. Doña Lola had insisted on being godmother to two of Maria's children, Pepé and Mary, and had been good to them. Watching Jenny struggle to obtain her education, she decided to take the girl to Chicago for a special dress. They decided on a gorgeous gown of blue from Lerner's Department Store. The cost was six dollars; Doña Lola added a white cape for another three dollars.

Of course, there was no discussion of a date. It was understood that Jenny would be chaperoned by Doña Lola's daughter, Lupe, and her brother Salvador, as well as Jenny's cousin, Tony. Under no circumstances could she have attended in the company of "a stranger." The prom group borrowed a navy blue Buick from one of Grandma Rita's boarders and left for the gala evening. Arriving home, Jenny found her mother and siblings sitting up on the porch awaiting an account of the night's events, though her mother was more interested in seeing that Jenny returned home by the designated curfew than she was in hearing a recount of the night's events.

———————————

By the time Jenny graduated, all but the younger children were enrolled in the public school system. Jesse, Sue, Chive, Mike, and Pepé were winding their way through grades ranging from elementary to high school. They were still living on Watling Street, and like all kids of the times, there were the usual rounds of chicken pox and measles. When an outbreak of a contagious disease occurred, the city nurse would come to the house and place quarantine signs in the window in hopes of stemming the spread of easily transmitted diseases. Children who had been exposed remained inside so that exposure to others was minimized. In the case of the Arredondos, if one child fell ill, the other nine were grounded. The edict to remain indoors rather than go out and play was probably as much a trial for Maria as it was for the restless children who became more and more "antsy" as their conditions improved. They begged to be let outside and, when they were "released," it was hard to say who was more relieved, the mother or the children.

Bumps, scrapes, and cuts were routine, though other more serious injuries and illnesses also occurred. Little Ray came down with scarlet fever. About four

Indiana Harbor kids make their own form of play, floating "boats" in a puddle at the corner of Washington and Pennsylvania streets, ca. 1941.

years of age, his thin body was wracked by high fever. His mother wrapped him so tightly in blankets that he could not move. She then employed another famous home remedy at the behest of Doña Lola. Cabbage leaves filled with raw hamburger meat were placed on his body in the belief that they would somehow draw out the fever. Doctor Brody had also prescribed more traditional treatments, but when these did not work quickly enough, the cabbage leaf was added. Whether the illness responded to medical treatments, home remedies, or simply ran its course, the frail boy rallied and regained his health.

Earlier Ray had another mishap when in the care of his sister Sue. He was a sweet and obedient child, and both Sue and Jenny enjoyed taking care of him. On this occasion, Sue had him out for a walk in the stroller when she stopped to chat with a friend. The toddler spied a playmate across the street and the usually "good" baby quickly escaped the stroller and was toddling toward his friend. Before Sue realized what had happened, a car bumped him as he attempted to dart to the other side of the street. Luckily, he suffered only a few scratches, but Sue was mortified. Once she knew he was okay, she began to fear the punishment she would incur for not watching her baby brother more carefully. She was somewhat let off the hook when the gentleman who had been driving the car came to the house to offer to pay for any medical costs that the accident may have caused. He offered Miguel seventy dollars, a great deal of money at the time. Since Ray was basically fine, the money went a long way in lessening the dressing down Sue would have otherwise gotten. Still, she was harshly reminded of one of the family's cardinal rules: take care of each other. No excuses were sufficient when it came to that mandate.

Lorenzo followed Ray's example a few years later and had his own run-in with an automobile. This time, however, he was old enough not to be under the care of older siblings. Playing ball with his buddies, the ball got away and bounced from the sidewalk to the street. Lorenzo ran to get it and was struck by a car. The driver was the wife of the landlord who owned the building in which the Arredondos lived. She scooped up the child and rushed him to the hospital. He was given basic care, paid for by the landlord, though his jaw remained somewhat out of line.

To Maria, this was just another sign that Providence was watching over her family. Given that there were ten siblings, having each remain healthy and relatively unscathed proved "the Lord was with them."

<hr>

One day Ray and Lorenzo were playing tag with some of the children in the neighborhood. Little Ray was "it." Standing with his back to the house, while the others ran to hide, he began to count with his eyes squeezed shut.

"99, 100," the five-year-old called out, turned around, and opened his eyes. He was startled by what he saw. There, directly in front of him, was an elderly bearded man sitting on a bench. Neither man nor bench had been there when Ray closed his eyes. He was dressed in white robes and held a staff in his right hand. His body seemed to glow as if illuminated by a thousand candles.

Ray stood stunned as the old man gazed steadily into the little boy's eyes with great intensity. He seemed to be searching for something in Ramón's small face. The old man continued to hold Ray's gaze until, after what seemed an eternity, Ray fainted dead away, crumbling into a heap.

A neighbor passing by saw the child as he fell to the ground. She ran to call Maria who hurried out, reaching her son just as he was regaining consciousness.

As the little boy saw his mother kneeling beside him, relief flooded his mind and body.

"What happened, *mijo*?" asked a worried Maria.

"It was a man," he managed to say, still shaken by the experience.

"A man? What man? Did you know him?" His mother continued to question. She was shaken by her son's unusual behavior.

"No, Ma. I never saw him before. He was old and had a beard. His clothes were funny."

"'Funny'?" What do you mean 'funny'? Were they dirty or torn? What did they look like?" Maria now began to worry in earnest. Had some stranger tried to accost her son? Nothing like that had ever happened, but there were bars and pool halls close to their home. Who knew if some of the patrons were perverted or drunk or even on drugs? Maria's imagination galloped with the speed of a wild gazelle. Sensing her fear, little Ramón began to cry. He tried once more to explain.

"No, Ma. He wasn't dirty or raggedy at all. He was real clean. His clothes looked like the ones the priests wear only they were all white. They glowed."

"Like the priests wear?" Maria's face frowned with puzzlement. "You mean like robes?"

"Yeah, Ma, that's it. White robes that glowed. He was sitting on a bench, and he was holding a big stick. But he didn't look mean or anything. He looked real nice." The boy rattled on. "Not like he was going to hit me or do anything bad. He just looked at me. Real serious and peaceful. It was nice. He seemed like he was a real nice old man. And then . . . then, I just went to sleep. I guess. . . ." Ray's voice trailed off.

Now it was Maria's turn to be stunned. She folded Ray into her arms and looked around. There was no old man now. In fact there was no bench and never had been. The only people present were the small children who had been playing with Ray. Their eyes were round with wonder. What had happened to their playmate?

"Did any of you see an old man?" asked Maria of the little cluster of children.

"No, Señora," one spoke up as the others shook their heads in agreement. "We were running to hide; we didn't see no man."

"What about you, Lorenzo?"

"No, Ma, we were hiding," the toddler answered, wondering why his brother had been lying on the ground.

Maria nodded. She picked up Ray and took him inside.

"You lie down, *mijo*," she told Ray as she put him on the bed, tucking the bedclothes around him. She felt his forehead. He had no fever. He did not appear sick at all. What in the world could have happened?

"I want you to rest awhile. I will bring you some *atolé* to drink. Sleep awhile and you'll feel better."

Ray nodded. He felt fine and was beginning to enjoy the unusual attention the odd incident was giving him. It was always special when his mother was alone with him. As the next to youngest in a house with nine other children, the quiet boy sometimes felt lost in the crowd. As he sipped his *atolé*, a warm, thick drink made from milk, oatmeal, and chocolate, Ray thought again of the nice old man. He was glad he had seen him and wished he knew who he was.

After some more discussion about Ray's strange experience, the episode faded into the many memories that composed the family's history. Not until many years later, did Ramón learn the identity of the old man he had seen that morning in the Harbor.

——————◆•✦•◆——————

Illness, accidents, and visions notwithstanding, Jenny had graduated, and it was necessary that she find work. Girls moved directly from high school into the workplace. Miguel had worked hard to get two men elected to union offices; when Jenny graduated, he went to them seeking a position in the union for his oldest daughter.

Shortly after Miguel's inquiries, two men came to the Arredondos' Watling Street home to interview Jenny. Her embarrassment at having them see the family's living conditions almost kept her from successfully completing the interview. The home was furnished primarily with beds and little else.

After they left, she ran to her mother in tears. "Oh, Ma, I knew they were looking around trying to figure out how and where all these people in the family slept! I was so embarrassed, I wanted to die. I could tell they were more interested in our awful surroundings than they were in me. I'll never get the job now!"

If Jenny had expected sympathy from her mother she was sadly mistaken.

"Stop it, Juanita," Maria scolded. "Stop your crying. Never be ashamed for things you cannot help. Those men don't care about how bad this house is. They were here to decide if you would be right for a job, not because they wanted to rent a room! And don't forget that your father worked hard to see they were elected. They owe him something for that. You're a smart girl. Act like one! Where you live won't matter if you have what they want."

Despite feeling mortified, Jenny got the job. She also learned a valuable lesson about the system, much ingrained in the Harbor, of doing favors for neighbors and coworkers and calling in those favors when one's family was in need. Jenny got the job because she was very qualified and because her father had helped to start the union and was one of its mainstays.

15

The War

War in Europe revived the American economy but brought anxiety to those with loved ones overseas. A dozen Mexican Americans from the Harbor were killed in action. Meanwhile, hundreds of young Mexican American women became war workers.

On Sunday, December 7, 1941, World War II started in earnest for the United States when Japan bombed American warships in Pearl Harbor, Hawaii. By early 1942, the Depression's hardships were giving way to the war effort. When food and other items became scarce, families were issued ration books, their amounts based on the number of members residing in the household. Because of their large family, the Arredondos actually fared better during the war. Maria saw it as a time when food became a surety thanks to a little book filled with stamps and coupons. Life's struggle had eased somewhat. In the early stages of the war, her sons were not old enough to join or be drafted; the fear of losing a loved one, which haunted many mothers, had not yet come to Maria.

As the steel mills geared up for war and men began leaving for the service, jobs became plentiful once again. Though working conditions for the laborers were still poor, and there was discontent among steel men, at least the paychecks were regular. Miguel was soon working double shifts, and the children saw him only at evening meals. Jesse recalled years later that sometimes when there was a heavy snow and Miguel was working a double shift, Maria would give him warm food to take to his father at the steel plant's gate.

Jesse continued to work numerous jobs after school and on weekends. He added shoeshine boy to his resumé. Muño, a good friend, made him a box for polish, brushes, and supplies, and he was in business. In the little spare time he had left, Jesse and his friends searched alleys to get cardboard boxes and bottles to sell for movie tickets. The theaters presented matinees with serial films. *Flash Gordon*, starring Buster Crabbe as an early space hero, cowboy and Indian films, as well as feature films were shown. For Sue, *Heidi* became an early favorite. All-day tickets for weekend matinees were twenty-five cents. The theaters were segregated, but even though the ushers directed the Arredondo kids to the right-hand side of the aisle, they were blissfully unaware of any discrimination. In their excitement to see their movie idols, they sat happily wherever they were ushered and enjoyed the entertainment before them.

What the children *were* aware of was the war in Europe. They could not help hearing of war on the streets and at school as more and more of their friends saw older brothers, uncles, and fathers leave for the service. Dinner discussions at home had long centered on Miguel's views of the war in Europe; but now the fighting became far more than talk. It became real. The mills needed extra men to meet their goals.

During the attack on Pearl Harbor, Chive was in the alley playing with a group of kids when someone ran out shouting about the attack on America by the Japanese. He sensed the excitement and concern of the adults, but as a youngster, it had little direct impact on him at the time. Sue, at eleven, was inside listening to the radio when the broadcast was interrupted to announce the bombing. While not realizing all the implications of the strike, she knew a grave event had occurred. Later, as newsreels at the movies began showing fighting in the Pacific Islands and, later still, when they showed the horrors of the German concentration camps, she would shiver as she watched the films, realizing their seriousness.

Miguel kept himself closely informed through the papers and radio, and his interest in world affairs escalated to a fever pitch. Over meals with their father, the children sat enraptured as Miguel related war news to Maria.

Once returning from his early shift, Miguel bathed and settled in to listen to the radio for news of the war. The reception became poor in the middle of the broadcast from Schenectady, New York, and a frustrated Miguel leapt from his chair and raced to the roof, bent on adjusting the antenna. In his haste he took a misstep on the ladder, fell, and broke his arm.

A trip to the hospital for X-rays showed the arm required setting and a cast, which remained on for several weeks. When the cast was removed, the injured arm was stiff, the muscles having atrophied.

Miguel quickly hit on a way to increase his arm's strength. He walked to the store and traded ration stamps for needed groceries, drafting Jenny to accompany him. After completing the purchases, he would carry the heaviest items, such as the five-pound bags of sugar, to build up his arm. On one such jaunt, a friend of Maria's saw Miguel toting his burden back to their apartment.

"Oh, Maria," she exclaimed. "I saw Miguel bringing home groceries the other day. How nice for you that he does the shopping."

Maria chose not to reply, but later she made it clear to her daughters that the day Miguel went shopping to lighten her work would be the same day hell froze over.

On another occasion Miguel came home between evening shifts. He had missed the Civil Defense sirens that signaled a blackout to the citizens of East Chicago. This was a drill used to ensure preparedness in the event of enemy air attacks. If city and factory lights were dark, enemy pilots would have difficulty finding their targets. Volunteer Civil Defense wardens took their duty to protect the homeland very seriously and monitored citizens' responses diligently.

Miguel, however, was focused on a hot bath and meal. He burst into the house flipping light switches and demanding, "Why are the lights off? Why are you people sitting in the dark?"

It took a few minutes to remind Miguel of blackout drills and why they needed to participate. After all, for a hungry man, food was first and foremost.

———————

While the children may have been seated at the dinner table, Maria herself seldom was. She continued serving and heating tortillas throughout mealtime, making innumerable trips back and forth from kitchen to the dining room table. Early on a system was established whereby the girls helped out in the kitchen as soon as they were old enough, and the boys got "first seating," eating while the females waited on them. This traditional role of women was not questioned anymore than Miguel's insistence that the family speak only Spanish while in the home.

"What you do outside is your business," he would say, "but here in my house you remember your heritage, and you speak Spanish." This remained a familiar refrain in the household.

———————

The war discussions were not lost on the children's imaginations. One day Pepé and his group of friends decided to play "Army" on the sidewalk.

He directed the boys to systematically remove the metal rods used to turn the awnings on the storefronts. Shouldering them as rifles, Pepé led his band of brothers in a march down the street. The police were called by irate storeowners, and older brother, Mikey, arrived at the same time as the law. Mikey, always responsible and worried about his younger siblings, almost throttled Pepé when he saw what was happening.

"Don't worry. I'll see they put the poles back," he reassured the officers. After this was accomplished and the police had moved on to more pressing matters, he lectured Pepé and threatened him with bodily harm should he ever pull a stunt like that again.

"What do you think Pa would do if he found out about this? Do you want to go to jail? Are you crazy? Don't ever let me see you do something this dumb again!"

Pepé nodded obediently as Mikey continued his tirade. His buddies faded away as quickly as they could to escape Mikey's wrath.

Ray and Lorenzo, the youngest of the family, devised other ways of playing war games. Having heard about the enemies "over the water" and gazing at Lake Michigan's vast expanse, the boys assumed the "Japs" were lurking somewhere just beyond the horizon. The concept was a logical one for boys raised in the Midwest. Having been given an old World War I helmet with "real blood" on it from a man sweet on their sister Jenny, Ray and Lorenzo dressed with play guns and canteens and dutifully defended their coast from invasion.

<hr />

For Jenny, the war's impact was felt in a couple of ways. She detested the powdered milk that was a standard issue of rationing inventory. "It always tasted chalky, nothing like real milk," she complained.

More important to Jenny was the lack of silk stockings, which were nearly impossible to obtain at any price during wartime. She put a beige makeup on her legs in lieu of the stockings. This popular substitute for hosiery worked well until one day when she was caught in a rainstorm. The makeup ran down into her shoes, spoiling her carefully chosen ensemble. While such a shortage might sound laughable, wardrobe was no minor matter to a young, attractive girl.

By now Jenny was a secretary for Steelworkers Union Local 1010. With her salary added to the household finances, the Arredondos were soon able to move to a better home on Michigan Avenue, and Jenny was able to indulge her love of clothes. She made sure each outfit had matching shoes, hat, and gloves.

Steelworkers at the end of a shift during World War II, October 1942

The family's new dwelling was located on the top floor of a three-story brick building at 3410 Michigan. It was a large apartment with eight rooms and a porch. The largest bedroom held an iron double bed where the four youngest slept sideways to make room for all. The dwelling's original purpose was that of a medical clinic, purportedly the first in the Harbor. The ground floor housed a Rexall drugstore with second floor devoted to attorney offices and a dentist. The living quarters afforded both space and privacy. It had gaslights and a linoleum floor, which was mopped and then dried with newspapers that were placed over the linoleum to absorb the water. This home was a major improvement over any they had ever lived in—either in the United States or Mexico. To the Arredondos, it seemed a palace. It was spacious, clean, and its view offered an ever-changing vignette of Harbor life.

Located across the street was Nagdeman's, a large, exclusive men's store; from their vantage point in the third-story apartment the children watched customers stroll into the store and leave with fine new clothes. The times in that apartment were some of the happiest of their lives. Maria and her children sat near the window and watched the comings and goings of people to restaurants and movies, catching buses, and shopping. The panorama was as entertaining and exciting as attending a Broadway show. Mary was fascinated by the parades that marched by their windows on special occasions. Huge floats and columns of army and navy units trooped by to cheers and whistles of the bystanders as celebrations were held on Columbus Day, Veterans' Day, and the Fourth of July.

Camila liked Michigan Avenue because the drugstore owner would give the kids treats of candy, something her father vehemently discouraged because it could lead to diabetes, an illness he feared. She also enjoyed the Saturdays when she would accompany her mother shopping. Often they would stop for lunch at the Broadway Grill, whose specialty was delicious hot beef sandwiches. The only drawback she saw in their new abode was the elderly Polish woman who lived alone in an apartment at the back of the building. She would holler at the children if they ran up the back stairs or talked too loudly on the porch, which was just above her apartment. Also, if the kids happened to be home from school during work hours, they had to be quiet so as not to disturb those in the offices below.

The younger children played in the alley with neighborhood children of all races and nationalities. The alley was their park, their skating rink, their private kingdom. They seldom visited each other's homes. By some unspoken arrangement, all the kids scattered to their respective houses at 4:30 p.m. Since none had watches, they developed an internal clock, which signaled it was time to go. José and the older siblings played ball on a cinder field nearby. Skinned knees were de rigueur, though once, as he slid to make a base, he scraped his knee so badly that he was helped home by his buddies and required stitches.

The radio was a favorite form of entertainment. At night a station from Mexico City could be gotten on the shortwave link. Maria would often listen to Mexican music as she cleaned up after dinner, but big-band music and popular American tunes could also be heard in the Arredondo household. All the kids had their favorite radio shows. Movie theaters were another form of entertainment. Sue's favorite movie, *The Valley of Decision*, starred Greer Garson. It was set in the mill town of Pittsburgh, a region with which she could easily identify. All the children were movie buffs, and they became walking encyclopedias of film trivia.

———◆•※•◆———

Maria encountered her personal war crisis in the area of food preparation. Though their rationing stamps had raised the family's eating standards, pinto beans, which were such a mainstay of their diet, became scarce. At one point they were nowhere to be found in the Harbor. Sue was commandeered to get Maria and her friend Doña Lola to South Chicago where rumor had it the precious beans were available.

"I want you to take me and Doña Lola to South Chicago," Maria told Sue one day in the most unconcerned of ways.

Sue, who was not yet in her teens, was astounded by the request. Her sheltered life never allowed her to venture far beyond her home and school, much less to strike out to the big city of Chicago! What had gotten into her mother to make such an outrageous request? Why, her mother hardly ever left the house except for groceries and an occasional movie. Surely she must be joking. She was not!

"Ma, I don't know how to get there!" the young girl protested when she realized her mother was serious.

"We'll take a bus," her mother answered confidently. "You ask the driver where the stop is, and we'll get off," said Maria, sounding as if a trip to the city was a routine, everyday occurrence.

"But why are we going to Chicago?"

"To buy pinto beans," her mother explained, citing the temporary shortage in the Harbor.

Sue remained dumbfounded but knew better than to question Maria's decision. Saturday morning the three set off on their mission with a timid Sue asking the driver for help in locating the area that was pinto plentiful. They descended from the bus, found the sought-after store and, purchasing an ample supply of beans, retraced their journey home. Maria might have been loath to leave her home under ordinary circumstances, but wartime was wartime, and courage was called for, be it in combat or on the home front.

Sue, when not in search of beans, would go with a girlfriend to the bus station to watch servicemen leaving. The two girls alternated between giggles and tears as they spied on the young soldiers kissing their wives and girl-friends good-bye. No soldier could be sure that he would return home, and the emotion of departure was very moving to the impressionable girls. A second favorite pastime was to go to the tracks where crowds of children would stand and wave good-bye to the soldiers leaving on the troop train. This small gesture meant much to children and troops alike.

The entire population of the Harbor embraced the wartime patriotic fervor. Recycling became an expected duty. Citizens brought scrap rubber and metal to recycling drops to be used for the manufacturing of war

During World War II, women went to work inside the steel plants as male workers joined the armed forces. Shown here is a "Rosita the Riveter" at Inland Steel in 1943.

materials. The local junkyards prospered, and steel mills regeared to make tanks and other equipment. Laborers worked around the clock, turning out whatever was required for the war effort. The Region's young men of military age enlisted en masse to fight for their country. Women also served in non-combat capacities, many in military hospitals. The shortage of nurses was filled by volunteer "gray ladies" who handled many duties ordinarily performed by nurses. Everyone came together in a concerted effort to defeat the Axis (mainly Germany, Japan, and Italy).

Initially, men away at the fronts caused a labor shortage. Women took jobs in the steel factories to fill in for men who had shipped overseas. Such jobs as "Rosey (or Rosita) the Riveter" were considered a temporary fluke; however, the newfound freedom and independence gained from the time in the work-place would carry over into postwar America. Women were getting a taste of working outside the home, and many discovered they liked it.

Other major sociological shifts were taking place during this period. Mexican Americans proved their valor in numbers disproportionate to their population. Such fierce devotion to America from a group that had long declared their undying loyalty to Mexico may seem incongruous, but the war was a catalyst that bonded Mexicans to their new country in a way never before seen. Additionally, a majority of those enlisting were of a generation born in America with little or no recollection of the "homeland." Mexican Americans displayed heroism and bravery on the battlefield; in fact, there were more Mexicans among Medal of Honor winners than any other nationality. This exceptional record helped to gain acceptance for Mexicans in the fabric of American life.

The war touched the Harbor with a patriotic fervor extending beyond factories and the military. Jukeboxes played songs that echoed sentiments of those caught up in what most felt would be the last great war for freedom. Sentimental ballads and big-band sounds could be heard blaring from radios and taverns around town. Pedestrians could walk for blocks listening to the same song playing on radios along their route. Families displayed small flags in their windows with stars indicating the number of children serving in the military: a blue star for a family member in service, a gold one for a loved one lost to war. Everyone joined in to do their part in the war effort, and those in the armed services were accorded special honor.

The military progress or lack thereof was the topic of virtually every conversation. Major battles were waged not only on the battlefields, but also in everyone's minds and hearts. People gathered on street corners, in bars, shops, billiard halls, and restaurants to exchange news, while newspaper headlines screamed the latest war maneuvers. "The March of Time" newsreels in theaters showed pictures of actual war events. The residents of the Harbor sat with eyes glued to the screen, eagerly hoping for a glimpse of friends or loved ones. Maps of Europe and the Pacific were posted on walls with tiny pushpins charting victories and defeats.

President Franklin D. Roosevelt held Fireside Chats, which were broadcast over the radio. The Arredondos, along with millions of Americans, sat around and "watched" the bulky radios as he reassured and inspired the country with his stirring orations. "The only thing to fear is fear itself" now took on a different meaning than when first uttered in 1933. Miguel, along with many of his generation, worshipped Roosevelt, holding him up as the champion of the workingman. Soldiers were shipped throughout the country and overseas. Many met and married women from areas other than their own hometown and brought a further mixing of ethnicity and culture to the Region. Throughout all this, the country rallied together as never before.

Of course, not all was rationing, victory gardens, and recycling. Daily life and its necessary routine continued: wives kept house, men worked jobs, and kids played a lot of games that did not have war as their theme. Alleyways, commandeered by kids, were playgrounds for the pastimes they invented.

"Real" toys, such as tricycles, scooters, and toy soldiers, were not part of the Arredondo household; they were simply too expensive. However, thanks to the generous sharing of friends across the alley, Danny Castillo and "Little Ray" Acevedo, Ray and Lorenzo did have access to such "luxuries." Even when cousins from Mexico, Luis and Frank Mosqueda, came for extended visits, the neighbors welcomed them to participate in elaborate "soldier" war games and to ride trikes and scooters. Visitors were quickly accepted into the play group.

Other forms of play called for more readily available props. "Bounce Back" was a game where a ball was thrown against a wall, and players tried to catch it. The last player to make a catch was designated as "loser." This was a favorite of the Arredondo children. Another version, played in fields, was called "Piggy Back" and consisted of throwing the ball to players with the person catching it becoming "batter." "Red light, Green light," "Simon Says," "Tag," and "Hide and Seek" were other perennial favorites. Perhaps the most complex of the invented games was one called "Cricket." A triangle was chalked on the concrete and cans stacked at its base. The object of the game was to knock down the cans with a tennis or rubber ball while the "batter" or goalie attempted to fend off a score using a broomstick for interference. Players ran back and forth from the apex of the triangle to its base during these plays with one point awarded per each successful run. This convoluted version of the British national pastime would hardly have been recognized on the cricket fields of Eton, the famous English preparatory school; nevertheless, it provided many happy hours to the children of East Chicago.

The ever-popular game of "Cowboys and Indians" was inspired by the matinee serial films. Sue, a tomboy in her early years, often played with her brothers and for this reason was nicknamed "Stone" after a cowboy character, Stony Brooke.

Mikey was the official nickname giver for all of the family. He simply shortened some of the original names, though others had more obscure origins. Juanita was, of course, Jenny; Jesse, "Rounds;" Socorro, "Stone;" Sylvester, "Chive" or "Seco" (thin); José, "Pepé"; Mary, "Mare"; Camila, "Mila"; Ramón, "Rawl" for a favorite baseball player; Lorenzo, "Lorry." Often the abbreviation of a name was used only within the family.

Neighbors, friends, and acquaintances were christened with their own unique monikers that often bordered on the bizarre; most were based on a habit or physical characteristic such as thick-lensed glasses or distinctive overbites. No cutesy names that might have cropped up in East Coast preppy circles found their way into the Harbor. The Buffies, Barbies, Bunnies, and Sugars had no place in the hardworking steel town. Instead, chums garnered such distinctive nicknames as Blind Boy, Mundo, Gopher, Half Pint, Bamba, Miho, Bomber, Choppers, Canoe, Pacos, White Mouse, Stubs, Porky, Fito, Baby Lou, Babe, Little Guy, Half Inch, Bright Eyes, Yoyo, Rubs, Cuco, Babaloo, and Dim Dom. While these names may sound somewhat disparaging, none took offense. Having a nickname was considered an affectionate token of belonging to an inner circle of friends, rather than a mean-spirited put-down, and Mikey was the undisputed champion at assigning these tags to friends, just as he did for family. He, however, remained "Mikey."

The Arredondos also formulated an internal language all their own. Family discussions were peppered with terms such as: "lube" (jealous), "Sev" (repetitive), "Soyv" (deaf), "Ledos" (hard of hearing), "Pauch" (fat), "Jake" (tightwad), "Flood" (pants too short), "Circumference" (huge head), "Mel" (lazy), "Strickly" (good looking woman), "Rick" (prostitute), and "Thump" (big feet). This language allowed the siblings to converse among themselves with bystanders not knowing what they were talking about. This odd exercise in semantics further forged the tight knit clan into its own exclusive world. No matter how close friends became, the family remained a unique and closed circle in many aspects.

16

Celebrations and Losses

Anxious to keep alive pride toward his mother country, Miguel was one of the organizers of the Mexican Independence Day celebrations and parades, often speaking publicly at them and putting up red, green, and white banners. Meanwhile, like most first-generation Mexican American women, preparing for church holidays such as Christmas and Easter was Maria's prime responsibility, but it did not differ greatly from her daily routine.

In the Arredondo household holidays improved though Santa remained as elusive as he had been for Jenny when she was a young girl in Blue Island. Tamales, made of cornmeal filled with either shredded pork cooked in lard and laden with a special sauce or with sugar for "sweet" tamales, were the main course of the Christmas feast. These cornmeal pockets were then wrapped in cornhusks and steamed. Making the dough was a huge job, particularly as the size of the family grew. Forty pounds of dough was not an overly large quantity, and when Pepé became old enough, he was recruited to the tedious and difficult job of mixing the dough. Though it was difficult, Pepé's love of food made his task an enjoyable one. He loved working in the kitchen with its delicious odors and access to quick bites of dishes as they were prepared. Like kids everywhere, he loved licking the bowl of its leftover dough. Rita and Maria made the meat and sauce, and the sisters manned a production line to assemble the finished tamales.

The Harbor decorated itself for Christmas, especially as the economy improved during the postwar 1940s. Inland Steel put up a huge light display on Watling Street, and people came from miles away to "Ooh" and Aah" over the fantastic offerings. Multicolored lights decorated the stores on Michigan

Avenue and Main Street, turning them into a winter wonderland with their twinkling reds and greens.

On the corner of Guthrie and Michigan, across from Larry's Busy Bee drugstore, rabbits, deer, and other meat hung in a kiosk ready for Christmas dinners. A diner that displayed a huge decorated tree and a pair of super-sized Great Dane mascots advertised prepared Christmas feasts for those who did not have a home-cooked meal available to them. Christmas music and carolers were on every street corner, along with Santas ringing bells for Salvation Army kettles. Shoppers were barraged with the sights and sounds of the season, and "Merry Christmas" was the greeting on everyone's lips. For the children, it was a wondrous transformation of a town usually lit by the flames emitting from the factory chimneys.

One Christmas, Mary decided it was time for her siblings to have their own visit from Santa. She was an imaginative child and longed for the happy Christmases she saw in books and movies. She gathered up old toys she found around the house and wrapped them in paper for her brothers and sisters. When they saw the "presents" under the tree, her siblings squealed delightedly, "Oh, Santa Claus has come!" only to be puzzled upon unwrapping them. When Ray opened one, Camila, recognizing it as a plaything that was hers, yelled, "That's mine," and grabbed it from her little brother's hand.

"I just wanted you all to have Christmas presents!" explained a tearful Mary, disconcerted that what she had meant to be a thoughtful gesture resulted in such discord.

In spite of such letdowns the children came to love the Christmas holidays and as the years went on and times improved they put up their own tree, purchased from one of the city lots converted into tree lots for the holiday season. Inland Steel's local steelworkers' union sponsored Christmas parties where each child received bags of candy and popcorn as well as gifts of tablets, pencils, and erasers for school. These parties became a favorite with all the children of the town and provided treats for many who would otherwise have gone without.

———◆·✦·◆———

Some years before, Rita's son, Frank, had briefly reconciled with his wife, Apolonia. As a result of this attempt to save their marriage, a second child, Robert Peter, was born in 1935. His arrival was not traditional; he was born in the elevator at Roseland Community Hospital when Apolonia's delivery was just minutes too soon to make it to the maternity ward. The birth of their second child did nothing to heal the bitterness still felt about the death of their first child, and Frank and Apolonia never lived as man and wife again. Little Bobby was sent to live with Apolonia's parents in Illinois, returning to the Harbor for two weeks each summer and at Christmas.

Bobby loved life with his grandparents, but the summer hiatus held new adventures. His mother scheduled his visits to coincide with her vacation breaks at Inland Steel. Bobby's grandparents would put him on a train in Roseland, Illinois. From here the little boy rode to Kensington, then transferred to the South Shore line to East Chicago. His beautiful mother always awaited him, greeting his arrival with hugs and kisses. Though estranged, Frank and Apolonia spent time together with their son, taking him to dinner at the restaurants of the Region and to local stores where, at the age of five, he was thrilled when his parents bought him an "army suit." Fascinated by the war raging in Europe, he also got an army tank that rolled backward and forward as soldiers popped up from its turret when Bobby turned its crank.

Store window displays, then as now, were magnets to a child, especially during the Christmas season. On a special holiday trip to the Harbor, Bobby spied a wonderful window replete with a carnival scene, which abounded with chalk figures and "fake" snow. The Lone Ranger and Tonto were among the figurines. His parents saw his interest in the cowboy and his Indian companion and bought a Lone Ranger costume, complete with two "six shooters" and the famous Lone Ranger mask. Other treats were "Tootsie Toys," forerunners of Matchbox Cars, though slightly larger.

Visits to Grandma Rita were a traditional portion of Bobby's visits. Rita adored the boy and contemplated kidnapping him and spiriting him away to Mexico each time she saw him. Children were viewed as God's blessings and all were welcomed and cherished. The child of her own beloved son, Frank, held a very special place in Rita's heart.

Perhaps having a child was one factor that caused Frank to not entertain the notion of returning to Mexico when his mother was deported. For whatever reason—the tug of a child, the painful memories of his early years in his home country, or something as mundane as employment—Frank never once considered a move south of the border.

Frank grew comfortable in his life as a single man. He took up residence with his mother, Rita, when she returned from Mexico. In addition to his railroad job, he indulged his love of an extravagant lifestyle by earning extra money at bookie joints, recording the numbers of an illegal lottery and acting

COURTESY OF THE ARREDONDO FAMILY

Apolonia (Pochinskas) Perez and son Robert (Bobby) Pochinskas, ca. 1940–43

as a bouncer. Despite having only one arm, he was inordinately strong, and customers realized they were no match for his strength. When Chive was around seven or eight, Frank would take him to the "joints," hold him up to the counter, and have him shoot dice for the American or National Baseball League Association for "luck."

The National and American Baseball leagues consisted of divisions. Each die represented one of these divisions. During the day, scores came in on a Teletype, a machine that looked similar to a typewriter and picked up telephone signals. Tickets were marked and scores were recorded on a chalkboard as they came in. The team that received the most runs, won. There were no odds on it. It was strictly a game of chance. In later years, Ray and Lorenzo became Frank's "lucky" dice tossers as they took over for Chive.

Frank Perez was a complex person. While he could be tough and hard, he also had a generous and kind nature toward those he loved. He was egotistical, feeling himself as good or better than most men. He despised being looked down upon and insisted on dressing the part of what he considered the "upper crust." He had little regard for "working types," calling them "low riders" because they wore their pants low on the waist. Frank made a point of wearing his trousers high.

"Look, this is how the rich men wear their pants," he would instruct Ray and Lorenzo. "Don't wear them low with your belly hanging out. People judge you by your clothes. See? I wear only the best."

Frank purchased his suits and other sundries at Nagdeman's, the high-end men's shop across the street from the Arredondo's Michigan Avenue apartment. He always had the finest shoes and accessorized his clothing with matching silk ties and handkerchiefs. If clothing made the man, Frank was a success.

Apolonia did not fare as well as did her long-estranged husband. As years passed, her health deteriorated, causing her to lose hours and wages. She had, for a time, lived in an apartment in the same building as the Arredondos, which allowed Bobby to play in the halls with the middle boys, Pepé and Mikey, during his visits. Later, his mother moved to smaller quarters.

One Christmas season, as she awaited Bobby's visit, Apolonia fell ill with a serious dental infection. She visited a dentist who pulled some teeth, gave her a prescription for pain and warned her to stay in bed. He instructed her that, under no circumstances, was she to venture out into the bone-chilling cold that gripped the area.

Determined to buy gifts for her son's impending visit, Apolonia ignored the dentist's orders and set about Christmas preparations as usual. The cold that year was even more frigid than were the usual piercing temperatures of December. When she returned to her room she was wracked with ague. Her body trembled first with a hectic flush, then with a chill that made her very bones ache.

Thinking her illness would run its course in a few days time, Apolonia at last admitted to herself that she was desperately ill. Only then did she call her parents for help. They arrived with her son and transported her immediately to the hospital. They prayed for her recovery, but in vain. The infection had spread, pneumonia had set in, and the antibiotics of the time were helpless against the sickness that attacked her frail body.

Apolonia died in 1944. Bobby lost his beautiful mother. Frank was a widower. His child was all but lost to him. Gambling became an even more integral part of his life.

———◆◈◆———

It was during this period that Rita's longing for her grandson began to weigh heavily on her mind. After all, he was her firstborn's son and, with his mother gone, it was proper and right that he should be with his father, not Apolonia's parents. The more she thought, the more she convinced herself that her idea was one she must pursue.

She dreamed of teaching Bobby Spanish, feeding him his fill of home cooking, watching him grow and become a man as part of the family. The presence of the child would bring Frank a new sense of purpose—a new lease on life that could lessen the grip of gambling. And shouldn't a son be with his father?

"*Mijo*, you could bring Bobby here. He would have a good life, and you could raise him as a father should," she coaxed.

His mother's words struck a deep chord in Frank's heart. The lack of a father in his life had left a gaping vacuum in his own childhood. Should he not try to ensure that his son, his blood, would not endure the same emptiness he had suffered? After much thought and a great deal more of Rita's persuasion, Frank decided that his mother was right. He petitioned to gain custody of his son.

The little boy had lived happily with his grandparents and, by the time Frank determined to reenter his life on a permanent basis, Bobby was well established in their home. His friends, his school, his sense of belonging revolved around his mother's parents. His father and Grandmother Rita were people he deeply cared for, but knew only through occasional visits.

The court date was set. Rita accompanied Frank to the hearing, as eager as he to bring "her" grandson home. Testimony was heard from both sides and, when completed, the judge turned to young Bobby.

"Who do you want to live with, son?" He asked.

Bobby, not wishing to hurt Frank and Rita, but also not wishing to be uprooted from his home, answered, "With Grandma and Grandpa Pochinskas."

Given the stability of the boy's present circumstances and his obvious desire to continue as he was, the judge ruled in favor of the Pochinskas. Frank was disappointed, Rita devastated.

Children had always been the center of the universe for the Arredondo family. Quarrels, misunderstandings, even betrayals were set aside for the sake of the next generation. The women held their offspring to be their most precious of gifts, the product quite literally of their labors and their hope for the future.

These lives were strong symbols not only for them, but also for the Mexican culture and race. No sacrifice was too great, no burden too heavy.

Following the court proceeding, a heart-wrenching scene played out in the halls of the courthouse. Weeping, Rita held Bobby close as she promised they would continue to miss and never, ever forget him.

To fight the ruling never occurred to Rita. She accepted the law's decision; perhaps, deep within her, she understood that her grandson was better off where he was. Love Frank, she did, but she was well aware of his weaknesses.

◆◆◆◆◆

With Frank it remained feast or famine. At times he would carry as much as four thousand dollars in his pocket; when times were lean, he would scramble to borrow ten. He would take one of the watches or cuff link sets he had purchased at upscale Reaven's Jewelers and hock it to keep afloat. But through the ups and downs of Frank's fortunes, he and his mother's combined incomes allowed for a fairly stable financial situation. They were as secure as could be expected.

Frank was by no means unique in his love of gambling. Gambling was an entertainment that virtually everyone took part in. East Chicago and the rest of the Region was always more closely connected with Chicago and its "wicked ways" than with the rest of Indiana. In fact, Indianapolis, despite its role as the capital, was called "Indian-nap-olis" and "Indiana-no-place" by Regionites because it was so dull and provincial compared to Chicago's big city glitz. The gambling aficionados of Chicago actually sought out the illegal casinos in East Chicago and surrounding Indiana towns. Not only did Frank work the joints and use his nephews as lucky charms, but so, too, did Doña Lola, who would sometimes take little Mary with her to write down "the numbers." Even Maria, who seldom ventured from home, was known to play the slot machines at the American Legion on the corner of Michigan and Guthrie. Long before river-boats became the Mecca for those hoping to strike it rich on the roll of the dice or turn of a card, East Chicago offered a Vegas-like ambience, albeit without the excess of neon.

———◆◆◆◆◆———

Rita began a new venture, opening her own Mexican restaurant, *La Paloma* (The Dove) near the steel mills. It was very popular because her cooking was among the best anywhere. Miguel had convinced Rita that the *solos* and other mill workers would flock to a restaurant that was convenient to the mill and served good food. He was right. Rita's restaurant was a great hit with the mill workers and others living in the Harbor. Sue would often go to her grand-mother's establishment, fascinated by the big jukebox that sat in the corner. Though she had no money to feed the neon-lighted tempter, she stood around hoping customers would drop in coins. Her favorite choices were ballads called *rancheras* sung by two sisters, *Las Hermanas Padilla*.

Cousin Lucy, who adored Rita, begged to be allowed to help out in her restaurant. She went to her father, Benigno, with her request.

"Only if you stay in the kitchen. I don't want you out serving the custom-ers and being bothered by men. Also, you must sleep in the same bed as Rita does and leave on the light to protect you," was her father Ben's reply.

Lucy was a pretty young girl and followed her father's injunction to the letter. She loved being in the restaurant and faithfully helped Rita make torti-llas. One day a very handsome man caught sight of her and deliberately chose a table near the kitchen where Lucy worked. He watched as the tortillas puffed up on the flame. Catching Lucy's eye, he motioned for her to bring him one.

"I'm not your maid," she quipped. "Come get your own."

She turned her back to the brazen man and was shocked when he came into the kitchen and meekly waited for his tortillas. That was the beginning of a romance between Lucy and Antonio Del Rio. The smitten young man pursued the young woman who played hard to get. This made Antonio all the more determined. When Lucy returned for a stay in Mexico, he wrote her love letters that she ignored. Eventually, Antonio's persistence paid off. Ten years after their first meeting, the two were married.

◆◆◆◆◆

All the kids who were old enough hung around Grandma Rita's place. Chive was a great help to her, running errands and buying supplies as needed. Maria's children looked to their grandmother for love and comfort; despite her grueling schedule, she always found time for them and for her son, Frank.

Despite, or perhaps because, Frank was a gambler and was involved in somewhat questionable activities, Rita treated him like a prince, saving for him the best pieces of meat and other delicacies. She made him a special black chili sauce using long chili peppers as the main ingredient. No one but Frank was allowed to eat this, though little Mary once sneaked a taste and found it had a different but good flavor.

Other "Frank-exclusive" treats included an expensive white cheese purchased at Andy Micu's corner store on Ivy Street. The cheese would be cut from a large hunk and placed in a cup for carrying home. Rita sprinkled ground black pepper on the cheese, which was considered a gourmet garnish by the kids. Another dish made especially for Frank was dried beef. First, Rita pounded the meat with a mallet, then hung it to dry on an indoor clothesline; there was never a doubt as to when it had reached readiness—Rita knew exactly when it peaked and was ready to serve to her beloved son.

17

Church and School

On September 2, 1939, a fire broke out in the Harbor's Catholic church, Our Lady of Guadalupe at 3855 Pennsylvania, when a votive candle tipped over and set fire to the carpeting. Within little more than a year, a new church was constructed on Deodor Street. The parish had a number of youth activities intended to keep children out of trouble and to hasten the process of Americanization. Although this was the Arredondos' parish, not all churchgoing Mexican families went there as some preferred the more emotional evangelical denominations.

In the summer Rita often took her youngest grandchildren, Ray and Lorenzo, to Our Lady of Guadalupe Church, where she attended early mass almost daily. The young boys were roused out of bed for the five o'clock morning Mass and groggily accompanied their grandmother. Often they would doze in the hard wooden pews until Rita noticed they were abnormally quiet and elbowed them awake. The church itself was cool and dim, lit by many candles, flickering around the altar and statues of saints, and smelled of incense, burning wax, and flowers. The boys would amuse themselves by watching specks of dust drift through the early morning sunlight, catching the reds, greens, and golds of the stained-glass windows. Other times, when days were short and no sun cheered the sanctuary, they would count the Stations of the Cross (a number that never varied) and try to name each event depicted in the fourteen scenes.

Rita insisted that they kneel and rise on cue, though they often let their attention wander during the service. When the collection plate was passed, Rita faithfully put in a dime. Should she not have the necessary coinage, she would drop in a dollar bill and retrieve the ninety cents that was her "change."

Rita fervently believed in giving God His due, but her contribution was limited by necessity—the family had to eat!

Too young for Holy Communion, the boys kneeled and watched the adults walk to the altar, the crucifix looming above as the priest intoned the Latin ritual. They loved to hear the bells tinkle and whispered to each other as the worshippers trooped by.

"How stupid is that hat," one would remark, as an elderly lady in elaborate headgear returned to her pew.

"Look at her hair. It's blue!" The other would point and giggle.

This banter ceased immediately as Rita came back from the altar. The boys sat quietly until the final hymn was sung and the small number of early morning churchgoers began to file down the aisle. A quick greeting to the priest— whose ever-changing robe colors fascinated the brothers—and they were on their way back to home and breakfast, each holding tightly to one of Rita's hands as she led them along the sidewalk.

Often, they would linger to pray as Rita knelt before her favorite saints. The Virgin of Guadalupe looked like a little doll, dressed in brightly colored full skirts, a smile on her sweet, round face. St. Jude's statue depicted him as a young man, dark hair and mustache adorning his face as he held a staff in one hand and a replica of Christ's face in the other.

Our Lady of Guadalupe Catholic Church, dedicated September 15, 1940

While weekday mornings saw Ramón and Lorenzo rising early and accompanying Rita to Mass, Sunday mornings brought with them another religious experience altogether. Caught up in the business of running a large household, Maria had no energy left to see her younger boys got to church on the traditional day of worship. While the older siblings usually got themselves to church, the Sabbath was a "free" day for her two youngest. Their mornings were spent with friends playing in the alleyways while Maria prepared lunch.

Around mid-June a group of Salvation Army members started offering "services" to the carefree alley urchins. Showing up with Bibles and candy, the dedicated "soldiers" would hold impromptu Bible readings using steps of any handy building as their "church." Initially leery of anything that would interfere with their games, the boys' curiosity gradually lured them to see what these people in the navy and red uniforms were all about.

Sitting in ragged rows on the improvised "pews," they and their buddies heard exciting biblical tales of near escapes from lion dens or the belly of a whale. These stories were told in a straightforward manner with no timeouts for kneeling and no unfamiliar Latin phrases to interrupt young imaginations. The boys pictured giants slain with slingshots or temples cleared of money changers by a boy Jesus hardly older than they.

Coupled with this was the enticement of hard candy and rousing songs just right for preschool voices. "Jesus Loves Me" was a particular favorite followed closely by "Fishers of Men," featuring energetic hand gestures as the children cast their nets into a sea teeming with unsaved souls.

When these entertaining religious lessons first began, the boys eagerly told their mother of their experience and proudly sang the newly learned catchy Bible songs.

Maria was not the appreciative audience they had hoped for.

"You boys shouldn't be doing this. The priests wouldn't like it. Who knows if these people are trying to turn you against the Church?" Maria scolded.

Well aware that Catholics were not universally liked and that the Church forbade attending services of other denominations lest their parishioners be "contaminated" by non-Catholic propaganda, Maria felt obligated to caution her boys.

Ramón and Lorenzo nodded solemnly as their mother continued to explain the dangers of straying from the "true church."

The next Sunday as they lustily sang the rousing tunes of Protestant salvation, the boys chose not to mention their new Sunday pastime.

Careful to eat their candy before reaching home and avoiding even the humming of "happy songs," the boys solved the dilemma of the Salvation Army's Sunday proselytizing through the tried and true sin of omission.

Some evenings after meals had been served and the kitchen cleaned, the family would sit on the porch and look over the evening activities of the town. Maria would darn clothes or crochet incredibly intricate patterns for curtains

COURTESY OF THE ARREDONDO FAMILY

Maria crocheted these curtains, including the image of Our Lady of Guadalupe, without using a pattern.

or bed coverings, using no pattern, but relying strictly on counting stitches. The Virgin of Guadalupe or the Eagle, the emblem of Mexico, would appear as if by magic. Her needle caught the crochet thread up and up again and again, transforming the mundane string into works of art. Though she had had minimal schooling, her ability to devise astounding pictures in stitches required exceptional mathematical skills.

During these lazy summer evenings, Rita would tell tales of her childhood; tales of the revolution, hunger, and roving wolves, and tales of superstition passed down through generations. At times these stories would have specific meanings for the listener. Sometimes they offered a grain of wisdom; sometimes they simply frightened the audience. The tale of a woman dying in childbirth during an eclipse of the sun would culminate in the message: "If labor begins during an eclipse, the pregnant woman must take shelter under a bed with a metal rod across her stomach." Not a particularly likely scenario, but handy information should it occur. A sudden death that followed the eating of peaches with cream sometime in the distant past resulted in an injunction against that particular food combination.

"Never wash your face after reading late at night," Rita warned, explaining that to do so would adversely affect one's eyesight. Jenny followed this instruction religiously after her late night homework sessions. Another remedy for the eyes was to place a drop of lemon juice into them, guaranteed to prevent cataracts.

Perhaps one of the strangest warnings was "never iron clothes following bathing or washing one's hair." The resulting effect was not possible electrocution but a very bad complexion. The truth was borne out by an acquaintance who routinely defied the caution and suffered terrible skin as a result. This "rule" obviously applied only to females, as no man would be caught with an iron in his hand unless he earned his living in a laundry.

Not all the special admonishments were directed toward the girls. For the boys there were special instructions and warnings regarding the very touchy arena of love. One evening Ray and Lorenzo were sitting on the rooftop perch when their Grandmother turned to them. "Watch out that no woman puts something in your food or drink. She can trick you into loving her, and you'll be caught like a spider in a web," Rita said, shaking her finger at her grandsons to emphasize the seriousness of such a situation.

The brothers were taken aback. They were hardly at an age to think of girls. While they snickered and rolled their eyes, they became aware that their grandmother was serious.

"Don't ignore your grandmother," Rita continued with a hard glance at her grandsons. "You don't know how many men have been given a love potion and never even knew it. There are many spells that can help or hurt, *mijos*, and you had better know of them. You laugh at the voodoo women, but they know how to give blessings and curses. If you think that's foolishness, you're the ones who are fools."

While not giving full credence to their grandmother's words, the boys nevertheless felt a tiny seed of doubt begin to grow in their young minds. Later, discussing Rita's unexpected advice, they came to a mutual agreement. Maybe some girls were up to no good.

The list went on. But the story the kids liked best was that of the wailing woman. Having drowned her offspring in the river's marshy waters, she was doomed forever to wander the riverbanks, calling out for her lost babies. This wailing woman, called La Llorona, with her wretched, tormented soul, was rumored to ramble through the very streets of the Harbor, looking to grab children who had disobeyed their elders and remained outside after dark. Upon hearing this ghost story, the night would suddenly seem filled with screams and cries. The leaves of the trees seemed fraught with horror, trembling as the lady passed beneath them. Most times the younger Arredondo children took care to be securely behind closed doors as dusk fell to avoid falling prey to the unhappy woman.

As fall approached, the children prepared for school's reopening. When Ramón was first taken to kindergarten, his mother walked him into the school grounds and watched as he climbed the stairs to the main hall. Seeing him get into the line that marched two-by-two into each classroom, Maria turned and began her walk home.

Ramón, however, took an immediate dislike to the idea of his mother leaving him in this new environment. Spotting the school's large back door, he kept walking as his classmates turned into it and found their classrooms. He beat a rapid retreat back home and sat waiting on the steps as a startled Maria made her way along the sidewalk.

"What are you doing here? How did you get here?" She interrogated her son.

"I ran, Ma," Ray said proudly. "I don't like that place. I want to stay home with you and Lorry."

Exasperated, she made it clear to her boy that what he liked did not matter. School was where he must be. Grabbing his little hand once more, the two repeated the trip, this time with Maria seeing him into his classroom. Though Ray tried his tactic for nearly a week, he soon accepted his fate and trudged to school—though unwillingly.

As time went on, the children settled into a routine. After an unwelcome wakeup call from Maria, the youngsters lined up for the bathroom. The girls had first dibs on the bathroom, then moved into their bedrooms to dress and brush and braid their long, dark hair. The boys made shorter shrift of their toilette, washing up quickly with lye or Ivory soap, brushing their teeth, pulling on pants and shirts, and straightening their room, though Lorenzo often lingered a bit to be sure his swooping wave was combed to perfection. This small vanity did not go unnoticed by his siblings who teased him unmercifully.

The children then assembled at the kitchen table for their traditional toast and *atolé*, followed by the ubiquitous dose of cod liver oil, the aftertaste of which haunted them throughout the morning. Often, their meal was accompanied by radio programs on the local WJOB station or Chicago's WIND. Listening intently to the news and weather, the younger boys, Ramón and Lorenzo, spent many winter mornings eagerly awaiting an announcement of school closings. Sadly for the boys, such announcements virtually never materialized. Not the motivated, school-loving role models that their sister Jenny had been, the boys grudgingly pulled on jackets and resignedly marched off to school with their siblings. Often they picked up friends en route and chatted along the way to wait for the dreaded morning school bell to call them to class.

When the lunch bell rang, the Arredondos hurried home for beans and tortillas, sometimes accompanied with potatoes and eggs.

During the school hours, and especially after lunch when time seemed to pass in a tortoise-like manner, Ray had to fight to maintain his focus on the assignment at hand. How much more pleasant it was to stare out the large school windows and daydream of traveling to faraway places or playing baseball with a major league team. Though sometimes he worried that he had no real plan to achieve such dreams, he felt with great certainty that someday, somehow, such dreams would become reality.

When the last bell finally rang for dismissal, the girls would walk home to help their mother with household chores. The boys would often hang around the school grounds to play pickup basketball or baseball. Then Ray and Lorenzo would return home to flop on couches and nap until dinner was declared "ready."

Maria saw no disparity in her boys resting while the girls worked. Males were favored in the Mexican culture, and "that was that." Though the girls often voiced complaints over the unfairness of this arrangement, tradition trumped equality, as was usually the case in households where the children were first-generation Americans.

When supper ended and dishes were washed, the children gathered again at the table to complete their homework. This was a nonnegotiable item, and it was understood that the work would be done. Neither Maria nor Miguel could help, though the older siblings assisted the younger ones when they could. Growing up in a home that could not supply written nursery rhymes, fairy tales, or adventure stories was often difficult for the children. While in later years they had Spanish newspapers that taught them to read and write their native tongue, as youngsters they lacked study aids—as did children of many newly immigrated ethnic groups.

However, what they did have was an abundance of dedicated teachers who were available to tutor those who sought help. These outstanding educators were even more appreciated in later years when the Arredondo siblings came to value education; without the help of teachers such as theirs, it was a lesson they might not have learned.

18

Diet and Discipline

To counteract the influence of the street and to protect the family name, immigrant parents commonly held older siblings responsible for the behavior of younger brothers and sisters and were quick to resort to corporal punishment even at the risk of alienating their children. Years later, Chive recalled Maria telling him, "Don't embarrass me," adding, "I can still remember some of the times she hit me with the broom."

Though Maria continued to prefer that Miguel pay less attention to social issues and more to putting in hours at the mill for additional pay, the family managed to fall into a comfortable, if Spartan routine. Payday brought hundred-pound sacks of flour, potatoes, and beans. The daily diet was comprised primarily of these items supplemented with chicken soup on Sundays, some fresh fruits and vegetables (especially during summer when street vendors hawked their wares), eggs, and, on rare occasions, red meat. *Atolé*, a gruel-like combination of oats, milk, and chocolate, was often a breakfast item. Maria breast-fed her infants and religiously gave each child a teaspoon of cod liver oil each morning.

Cod liver oil had replaced Maria's early preventive medicine, Scott's Emulsion. This thick white liquid poured from a bottle labeled with a picture of a man holding at his side a huge fish on a string. Jenny and Jesse had spent their early years gulping and gagging on teaspoons of the nasty white stuff.

Another favorite antidote to "whatever ails you" was Pluto water, a curative bottled from a spring at French Lick in southern Indiana. Each Saturday Jenny was sent to the drugstore to buy a pint-size bottle of the highly touted elixir that Maria directed the kids to drink, saying, "How do I know what you've eaten when you're outside this house? This will give you a good cleaning out."

On that she was right.

For the most part the children escaped major diseases so prevalent during the era. Rickets, tuberculosis, and malnutrition were not factors in the Arredondo family, although that is not to say that food was rich or even plentiful. Maria's choice of menus, dictated solely by the money available for purchasing groceries, coupled with her curatives, somehow provided sufficient proteins and nutrients to stave off most illnesses.

Mealtimes were family times in that the children gathered at the table; it was not a time, however, for discussion. "The table is to eat," their father dictated, "talking is for later." The children followed this dictum, at least when their father was present. Of course the rule did not hinder Miguel's own conversation, and mealtime was his forum to expound on events of the day, offering his strong beliefs and values, which ran the gamut from the state of the world to his expectations for his children. These family dinners, though basic in food value, were supplemented by a rich daily diet of world events and political philosophies. The children were fed on a wide, if biased, scope of topics, which ranged far beyond anything the public schools offered. Understanding how the world worked was fed to the Arredondo children as pabulum was spooned up in other families.

What was not present at dinner was a traditional blessing of thanks for the food. Perhaps it was because the family ate in shifts; but, more likely, it was due to Miguel's disillusionment with the Church over some of the Church's views. As a child and young man, Miguel was a devout Catholic, who even served as an altar boy. When he grew older, he came to resent the Church for not assuming a significant role in helping the poor during and after the Mexican Revolution. Later, during World War II, the failure of the Church to address the plight of Jewish refugees deepened his disillusionment. Karl Marx and other communist philosophers seemed more in tune with his own belief that all mankind deserved equal and compassionate treatment. Jenny recalled later that her father's distrust of the Church grew as he read a novel that underscored the hypocrisy and corruption that Miguel felt was deeply ingrained within the Church's hierarchy.

———◆·◆·◆———

Running concurrent with political and sociological lessons learned by the Arredondo children was the "family first" mantra that served as the unifying theme in the family's value system. Both parents hammered home the necessity of family members taking care of each other at every opportunity. Added to this "golden rule" were other cardinal rules: "Never lie; never steal; always work hard; and above all, do nothing to sully the family name."

"Show me your friends, and I'll show you who you are" was Maria's version of "Birds of a feather flock together," intoned whenever she had misgivings about her children's choice of friends. She never held back her opinions regarding the children's companions. Her likes and dislikes were vocalized in detail and at length. Even physical characteristics were noted and classified as negative or positive indications of character. "Stay away from short, squat women with large breasts," she would warn her sons. Just why these particular traits were held to be so unfavorable was unknown, but Maria was strong in her conviction that the combination boded no good.

Maria was quite stingy with praise for her children; her goal was to keep her brood humble and grateful, not proud and full of themselves. Often friends would compliment her on the achievements, conduct, and character of her offspring. Her response was to shrug off accolades. Whether this was a knowledge that even the best of children could slip up or an innate fear of changing her good fortune by calling attention to it, the modern notion of building a child's self-esteem had no place in Maria's rules for child rearing.

On one occasion a young Lorenzo came home from school and, letting the screen door slam behind him, said, "Ma, guess what? I came in second in the spelling bee."

"Oh," said Maria. "And who was first?"

"Connie Villalpando."

"What?" shot back Maria. "You let a girl best you?"

Lorenzo's pride sufficiently quashed, he exited meekly to the bedroom. Years later, when he discovered his female competitor was older than he, he told Ray, "See? It wasn't fair. I could have beat her if we'd been the same age."

The sisters were painfully aware of Maria's adherence to traditional male-female roles not only in obvious examples such as "the men eat first" but also in the affection shown them.

A common term of endearment in the Spanish language was to refer to boys as *mijo*, meaning my son. For girls the equivalent term was *mija*. Maria often referred to the boys as *mijo* but virtually never called her girls *mija*, a fact not lost on them.

Jenny related that hugs, affection, and terms of love were simply not within Maria's range of emotions. "Ma just didn't display physical affection. Not that she didn't love us girls. It just wasn't part of the family culture. For the boys it was different, and we accepted it."

Jenny recalled, "I only remember one time I was called *mija* and that was by my dad. Sue was telling me a story about some girl saying something mean about me, and I was crying because it wasn't true. Dad walked in and asked what was wrong. When I told him, he said, 'Don't let that make you cry, *mija*. It's only words, and she can't hurt you unless you let her.' I never forgot that. Not only for what he said, but he called me *mija*."

Many of their friends turned to drugs and other vices plentiful in the environment of the mill town. Whatever their differences may have been on other issues, each parent held fiercely to the principle that the family honor must not suffer. On this at least, Miguel and Maria agreed wholeheartedly.

They stood shoulder to shoulder as to the consequences of bad behavior as well. Miguel would clearly outline the results of any actions that could bring disgrace upon the family. "If the police arrest you, don't bother to call me because I'll tell them I don't know you." Or, "If I find you've done something wrong, see that tree out there? I'll hang you from it myself!" Such pronouncements may sound like hyperboles, but each child firmly believed that their father spoke the truth and that his threats were not idle musings.

Though far more affectionate to the children than their reserved and demanding father, Maria brooked no arguments when it came to her children being obedient. If one child strayed, all were punished equally. It was not just the child who caused the situation who bore the consequences; the innocent siblings were along for the ride. Perhaps the couple were simply ahead of their times with their unique approach to "tough love"; whatever the case, the technique produced a family of motivated, productive, and strong individuals.

As with most kids, the Arredondo clan attempted to circumvent one parent's directive by appealing to the other. However, Miguel and Maria were wise to this ploy and when permission was asked for something, the standard response was, "What did your mother/father say?" If the reply of the other had been "No," the "no" stood.

Corporal punishment continued as a disciplinary option no matter how old the child was. "Never raise your voice to your parents" was an edict followed by a caveat: "No matter how old you are, I can still give you a good licking." Once, the usually obedient Mikey had committed a transgression. He and Pepé had been playing outside when a boy hit Pepé in the nose. Pepé came in the house crying.

"What's the matter?" demanded Maria.

"A boy hit me," Pepé answered. Without hesitation Maria turned on Mikey with her broom. His duty was to see that no harm came to his younger sibling; he had not fulfilled this requirement.

Grandma Rita tried to intervene on Mike's behalf.

"I'm the one who gave him birth; I'm the only one who can kill him," was Maria's quick and angry retort. She loved her children dearly, yes. But she was not about to let her concept of bad behavior go unpunished.

Everyone was a recipient of the Arredondo disciplinary code, though the older boys caught the brunt. One day, Pepé and a few friends were playing catch outside of Field School. After losing a few balls, the game was called due to lack of equipment. Bored, the boys began horsing around, eventually climbing to the roof of the small, wooden schoolhouse. Someone spotted the kids and called the police.

Thinking the boys were up to no good, the cops answered the call and shouted up to the boys, "All you guys get off that roof! What do you think you're doing?"

The boys scurried down and were confronted by a tall policeman who said, "OK, smart guys. You were trying to break in, weren't you? Don't lie to me. If you do, I'll throw you all in jail."

Each boy responded in turn, "No, officer, we didn't steal nothing. We were just fooling around."

The policeman finally came to Pepé, who was trembling with fear. This might be an offense punishable by death if his father found out. Going to jail was the worst offense, guaranteed to disgrace the family. Unforgivable.

As Pepé stood pondering the disastrous circumstances in which he found himself, the officer lost patience, saying, "Come on, kid. Speak up! Remember, you lie to me and you'll be in jail before you know what hit you."

Fear ran through Pepé's veins like a burning bolt of lightning. His mind flashed back to every sin he committed in his short life. Confession was the only course open to him.

"Well, I once stole some grapes, and once I took an orange," he stuttered. A list of food pilfering spilled from his lips. He had no control; he continued until he had recited every small sin he had committed in his short life.

The policeman looked down at him with amusement. Stifling his urge to laugh, he waved the boys away, saying, "Get out of here. And don't let me catch you hanging around again or the whole bunch of you will be sitting in a cell."

He did not have to repeat himself. The boys took off running. Of course news of the discovery of possible mischief at the local school inevitably made its way to Miguel. Just as inevitable was the swipe of his father's belt on Pepé's backside.

This was the era of "Spare the rod and spoil the child." Both parents agreed that strict child rearing was the best, indeed, the only way.

When Ray and Lorenzo were around five and six, they were playing outside when a group of buddies decided it would be fun to jump on a parked car to see what impact their large, heavy clodhopper shoes might have on the car's roof and hood.

Even at that young age the Arredondo boys knew better than to participate in any mischief, particularly anything in close proximity to their home. An angry Maria was a scary Maria; inciting her wrath was to be avoided.

Ray and Lorenzo huddled back against a building and watched as their friends jumped on the car. If they had hoped for a stunning result on the hapless vehicle, they were quickly rewarded with dents resembling a hammer attack. Ray and Lorenzo beat a hasty exit and were sent straight to the bathroom for baths upon entering the apartment.

While they were washing, the owner of the car came to Maria to tell her what had happened. "Mrs. Arredondo, I don't know if your boys were involved," he said, "but I was told they were with the kids who did it. I thought you'd want to know in case they're running with the wrong crowd."

Maria's mouth had tightened considerably as she listened to the story. "Thank you for telling me," she said. "Don't worry, we'll take care of the boys."

A somewhat hesitant neighbor turned to leave, his anger now tempered by the possibility he had gotten good kids into trouble.

"Innocent until proved guilty" didn't apply when Maria felt there had been a possible blot inflicted on the family's reputation. As the neighbor's footsteps faded down the staircase, Maria grabbed the dreaded belt and burst into the bathroom where she commenced to take the strap to the very surprised, naked, little boys.

"I don't know if you did anything or not," Maria punctuated each word with a slap of the belt. "But if you did, you deserve this. If you didn't, you never will!"

Lorenzo (left) and Ray, ca. 1947, wearing clodhopper shoes

The protesting and crying boys avoided many of the blows as they slipped around in the bathwater. But Maria was right. It was a lesson they never forgot.

———◆◦◆◦◆———

Chive spent more time out of the house than in it, so many of his transgressions escaped notice. One of his worst habits was his tendency to oversleep. Rousing him was a multi-wake-up-call effort. Once, when staying with his grandmother during Jenny's absence, Rita needed Chive to run an urgent errand.

After several attempts to awaken him failed, even her doting disposition was tested. Turning to a boarder, she vented her frustration, saying, "I'll lick him. That's the slowest child in the world! If he isn't out here in two minutes, I'll grab him by the neck and choke him. I swear it!"

Some minutes later Chive, having dawdled through dressing, walked non-chalantly into the kitchen. "I'm ready," he announced.

The boarder looked up from his cup of coffee and responded, "Why go? She's going to choke you to death anyway."

In this instance Chive knew he had nothing to fear from his beloved grandmother whose purpose, in the eyes of the Arredondo siblings, was to adore her grandchildren and shield them from life's unpleasant moments.

However, another situation truly put the fear of God (and Miguel) into Chive. One day as he was playing ball with some of his buddies, an unlucky hit sent the baseball through a window. The boys scattered, but Chive froze and was quickly collared by the building's owner who duly called the police. The result of the mishap was Chive's appearing in court with Miguel in attendance.

When the judge began to question him, Chive burst into tears. The judge felt sympathy for the young boy and attempted to soothe him. "Now, now, lad, I'm just trying to get to the bottom of this. What's the matter?"

"My dad will beat me," Chive managed between sniffles.

"No, he won't," the judge assured him. "Mr. Arredondo and I know you're a good boy. You just were hanging around with the wrong crowd. Right, Mr. Arredondo?"

Miguel nodded solemnly to the judge's query. The matter was settled with an admonishment from the bench for Chive to choose his friends more carefully. Miguel and Chive exited the courtroom and headed for home. No sooner did the door of their apartment close behind them than his father took off his belt and gave Chive the licking he knew was coming. Not even a judge could interfere with Miguel's child-rearing tenets.

———◆◆❉◆———

Jesse was often the recipient of his father's discipline. As the oldest boy, he, in many respects, had the toughest time. Not only was it his constant responsibility to act as his mother's "assistant" in the early years, a job which consisted of translating and stepping up as the man of the house in his father's absence, but also he bore the brunt of the sternest of punishments.

Once he questioned his father, "Dad, I remember you beating the hell out of me all the time."

"You deserved it," was the succinct reply.

"Yeah, but look at the young guys. What about them?"

"Oh, I'm getting too old to get up and beat them."

"So they can do what they want and get away with it?"

"Shut your mouth," was his father's quick retort. He glanced at Jesse and returned to the newspaper he was reading. The discussion was over. Such was the lot of the oldest son. As with most families, things tended to get a bit more lax as more kids came into the mix and the parents' time and energy became scattered.

Not *too* lax in the case of the Arredondos, however. If the parents mellowed somewhat with time, the older children were still very much at the ready to measure out discipline as needed.

19

The Haunting

Belief in magic, superstitions, and ghosts is not unusual in ethnic households but did not play a major role in the Arredondo home. Still, at times hard-to-explain events did occur.

Overall, life on Michigan Avenue was happy for the Arredondos. There was, however, one peculiarity about the apartment—it was rumored to be haunted. Before moving in, the children had heard stories about the old clinic and its spooky inhabitants. The ghosts of those poor souls who had died there were said to roam the rooms. What had caused these restless spirits to wander was not part of the tale, but just the suggestion was enough to give the place an ambience of mystery. In fact, there were several incidences during the Arredondos' stay where the pots and pans that hung on the kitchen wall had fallen with a clatter in the middle of the night. There seemed no logical explanation for this phenomenon since they fell out of the blue. No trains or storms could be cited as the cause for this puzzling occurrence. Strange, yes, but maybe not so much scary as annoying.

But there was one inexplicable happening that was far more disturbing than falling kitchen utensils. It became the stuff of legends. Late one night when Miguel and the older siblings had gone out to a dance, Maria was left at home with the four smaller children. As the hour grew late, Maria set about getting her young ones to sleep.

"Come to bed. The others are going to be late, and it's almost midnight. Come on, you can all sleep in my bed until your father and the rest of the children come home."

Mary, Camila, Ray, and Lorenzo were excited to have an unexpected chance to snuggle with their mother. It gave them special time alone with her, a rare and precious commodity. Just as they were dozing off, they heard a door open and close.

"Jesse?" Maria called, to ascertain which of the family had returned. There was no answer. "Miguel?" She tried again with the same result. She called in turn to the remaining children, "Jenny! Sue! Mike! Chive! Pepé!" All with the same result. No response.

Maria was losing patience. If this was a prank, she saw no humor in it. Someone had definitely opened the door, and they had all heard footfalls walking along the hall before another door closed. Maria called again with a harsher tone.

"Who is it? Answer me!" She was tired and had nearly succeeded in getting her little ones to sleep when this jokester disrupted them. When she found out which child was playing tricks, she planned to give him a good thrashing. Pepé was capable of a prank like that, or, for that matter, so was Chive, who loved to party and have a good time. Or perhaps it was Jesse. Maybe he'd had too much to drink and was trying to sneak in. Maria was sure Miguel would have answered, as would Mike who was too serious to risk scaring his mother and siblings. Surely neither Sue nor Jenny would be up to such foolery. As her mind completed its inventory of possible perpetrators, she became more annoyed.

Maria called out once more, this time louder and showing her anger. "Stop this at once! You're frightening the children. José! Jesus! Sylvester!" she called, using their full names to underscore her annoyance. "Come in here at once!"

Her calls were met with a dead silence. She knew her children would not continue with such a farce for this length of time. They knew better than to risk her anger, and they also knew they were never too old for her to punish them. No, if it had been a family member they had heard walking and opening and closing doors, he surely would have identified himself by now.

The children were beginning to whimper with fright. Each clutched their mother's nightgown and pressed as close to her as they could. Maria, too, became alarmed. Someone had come into her home and had not exited. Whoever it was still lurked within the shadows outside the bedroom door.

"I need to go see who came in," Maria whispered, trying to extricate herself from the eight little hands that gripped her. The children clutched even more tightly and pressed closer.

"No, Ma, don't go," begged Mary as she held back sobs.

Front, left to right: Ray, Camila, Pepé (José, Joe) and Mary; back, left to right: Cousin Lucy Perez, Jesse, Chive, Sue, Mike, and Jenny, in front of the Inland office building, July 1941

"No, Ma, please stay here with us. The ghost might get you if you go now," cried Lorenzo.

All the kids began to choke back sobs and continued to hold onto their mother with vice-like grips.

Just as Maria was about to make another effort to leave the bed and investigate, they heard the door open for a second time.

Each breathed a collective sigh of relief when Jesse's familiar voice rang out.

"Where is everybody? Ma, are you asleep?"

The five in the bedroom rushed for the living room.

"When did you get here?" Maria demanded of a surprised Jesse.

"I just walked in the door, Ma. You heard me hollering for you, didn't you? What's the matter? You all look scared to death."

"Jesse, listen to me. Somebody came in here before you got home. Did any of the others leave the dance before you?"

"Jeez, Ma. How should I know? Some of the guys and I left early and hung out. I figured the others would beat me home. Aren't they here?"

An exasperated Maria shook her son. She spoke rapidly, her voice ragged with anxiety.

"Listen to me. Someone is here. We all heard him. Get something to hit him with and go look. Find whoever it is. He is still here! We would have heard if he'd left. He must be hiding!" A frightened and flustered Maria paused to catch her breath.

Finally understanding that his mother's fear was real, Jesse yanked a heavy skillet from the kitchen wall and proceeded to search the house.

Maria and the kids stayed huddled together, not daring to move until the intruder was found.

Just when Jesse returned to report his search had yielded no results, voices sounded in the hall as Miguel, Jenny, and Sue tramped in. Moments later, Mike, Pepé, and Chive also returned. They looked at the frightened faces before them and then listened carefully as Maria tried to explain what happened. Each knew it was not like their mother to become alarmed easily. Her fear was real, but they could not find a logical explanation for it. A second search had yielded no more than the first. At last the family settled in for the night. Each slept fitfully with the four youngest refusing to leave their mother's side. The mystery of the ghostly spirit, if that, indeed, was what it had been, was never solved, but the five who were there continued to swear to its validity. Spirits of the dead were an accepted thing in old Mexico, and many looked to a deceased ancestor to watch over and guide them. Why would the ghostly walking and closing of doors not be real?

The world holds many unsolved mysteries. Certainly those who were in the apartment that night accepted a roving spirit as plausible an explanation as any.

20

Maria's "Confession"

In large ethnic households, the eldest children often acted as surrogate parents, as happened when Maria was in the hospital. Many ethnic families regarded hospitals with suspicion as places for the dying, so when one entered Saint Catherine Hospital, founded in 1928 by the Poor Handmaids of Jesus Christ, the family became quite alarmed.

In 1946 Maria became very ill and had to be hospitalized. The younger children were not told what the illness was, though in later years they learned she had undergone a hysterectomy.

Maria had been having "female trouble" for years. When Sue was around eight, she recalled coming home from school and finding her mother heaving on the bed, clutching the bedposts in agony.

"Ma, what's wrong?" she cried.

"Don't worry. Just get me some clean towels from that cupboard." In those days rags and old towels were often used as sanitary pads during women's monthly periods. Sue was puzzled and frightened to see blood as her mother made her way to the washroom. She later learned that the doctor had advised Maria to have a hysterectomy following Camila's birth, but she had put it off until she became so ill, she had no choice. This procrastination was not uncommon. A mother's first concern was for her family's welfare; her own health needs often had to wait, especially when there were children to care for.

Maria had not complained of feeling ill. She stoically continued in her usual routine until the pain and discomfort became too great to ignore. When at last she saw the doctor, he insisted on an immediate operation. Before entering the hospital, a priest was called to administer the Church's last rites and hear Maria's confession. This was a serious medical concern, and spiritual ministrations were considered as important as anything medical science might do. Maria was a devout Catholic even though she did not have time, for the most part, to attend church.

The priest approached Maria's bedside and began preparations for extreme unction, the deathbed rite designed to guarantee a pure soul at death.

"Now, Señora, I am prepared to hear your confession," the priest said in a solemn, gentle voice.

Maria sat straight up, leaned toward the priest and stared at him, her eyes blazing with indignation. The startled priest pulled back a bit as Maria began a harangue.

"Confession!" she snapped. "What do you mean confession? ¡*Dios mío*! What do you think I could possibly confess, Father? Do you know what my life is? Let me tell you!" She proceeded without pausing.

"I have ten children. My life is cooking, washing, cleaning, and taking care of the *niños* (children) and my husband!" She spat out the words, seething with frustration long suppressed. "Do you really think I've got time to sin? Why, I hardly leave the house except to buy groceries!"

Maria's face was flushed dark with ire. She made no move to apologize for her outburst; rather, she glowered at the shaken priest with a look so penetrating that he sat even further back in his chair. As he stared at this small woman whom he had assumed would display a meek gratitude at his coming, he noted her red face and chest heaving with each breath. His thoughts swirled. Was she preparing to leap from the bed and physically assault him, or was she so agitated that his question had pushed her to the brink of a stroke or heart attack?

"Dear God," he prayed. "Don't let this woman die! I only did my duty, Lord."

The priest, himself, felt almost breathless with the emotions running rampant within the room. A sense of lightheadedness caused him to become momentarily faint. Inhaling deeply and fumbling as he located the accoutrements required for the ceremony, he began to babble.

"Of course, Señora, of course I understand. I meant no disrespect. I understand, I understand."

Quickly, he gave the necessary blessing. Never had he encountered such a situation. Best to exit with as much haste as possible. As he turned to leave, he glanced at Sue standing stock-still in the corner. Her expression showed none of the incredulity he felt. Indeed, she seemed nonplussed.

"I should have warned you, Father," she spoke softly as they left Maria, now lying back on her pillows, eyes closed and breathing peacefully. "Ma is

COURTESY OF THE ARREDONDO FAMILY

Sue (left) and Jenny, late 1930s

a bit touchy on the subject of sin. She always tells us she's too busy to even think about sinning, much less commit any."

"Yes, yes," nodded the still shaken man. "Don't worry. I understand. I do." Still nodding and muttering unintelligible phrases, he backed out the door and fled.

Later, as Sue recounted the "confession" to Jenny, both girls broke into uncontrollable gales of laughter. When they had composed themselves, wiping their eyes to clear away tears of laughter, Jenny observed, "If Ma is that tough with the priest, she'll pull through this operation with flying colors. The doctor will be so intimidated, he wouldn't dare let her die!"

Little Mary, however, who was about ten at the time, took her mother's illness to heart. She was so overcome with worry about her mother that, while at catechism, her mind went blank. She simply could not think straight and had to ask a friend to sign her name for she could neither remember it nor how to spell it. A nun, knowing of her mother's health problems, hurried to reassure the distressed little girl.

"Go home," she told her kindly. "Try not to think about it. Your mother will be fine."

And so she was, to the great relief of all her children.

During Maria's hospital stay Jenny assumed the duty of surrogate mother and, only fifteen years younger than Maria, slipped into the part with a vengeance. After all, she had taken care of the kids since she was five, and her role model, her mother, had taught her the value of strong discipline as well as cleanliness, manners, and good behavior. She proved to have been a good pupil as she oversaw her younger siblings, emulating and surpassing her mother in the discipline area.

Ray and Lorenzo cringed at the thought of bath time when in Jenny's care. She bathed them with a scrub brush, making sure elbows, ears, and necks were clean.

"Ouch, Jenny, you're hurting me!" Lorenzo would wail as she scoured the boys from head to toe.

Should the boys be so careless as to drop their jackets on the couch as they came in from school, Jenny would pull their ear and direct them to hang them up. Chores were assigned, and the two brothers jumped to do them before Jenny's pinches caught them. With their mother, they could slough off to some small extent, but not with sister Jenny. "Make that bed and see your shoes are underneath it, *neatly*," she commanded. If they visited anyone, the boys were briefed on their behavior before arrival. No talking or playing. Sit quietly and behave! When asked if they wanted to go outside and play with the children, they shook their heads in unison "No." The dread of Jenny's wrath should they dirty their clothes or otherwise "break the rules" far overrode their longing for outdoor play. To those who only knew the boys from observing them while in Jenny's care, they appeared to be paragons of virtue. Indeed, under their sister's stern glance, they were just that.

In a brief moment of defiance, Lorenzo yelled the accusation heard by babysitters throughout the ages: "You're not my mother."

Jenny responded by grabbing an arm and reminding him, "I am for now!"

Lorenzo threatened her. "I'm telling my mother you mistreated us. As soon as she gets home, I'm gonna tell."

Jenny was well prepared for what she called Lorenzo's "ornery streak," a characteristic he had displayed on other occasions. Jenny vividly remembered the "streak" showing itself early on during Maria's hospitalization. She had decided she would hold a birthday party.

"I'm giving Ramón a party," she announced to the four youngest. "You kids are invited. Ray deserves a party because he minds me and tries to help."

Jenny had never given a party, so the kids were excited. The great day came. Jenny brought out a cake with candles flickering. After Ray blew them out, Jenny left the room, leaving Mary, Camila, Ray, and Lorenzo to enjoy the cake.

Not wishing his day in the spotlight to end so quickly, Ray grabbed two candles, lit them, and began marching around the room, his face beaming. Lorenzo followed suit, and the boys made several trips around the dining room. At one point Ray veered close to the window, stopping to display his candles in the hope that neighbors would notice. In doing so he managed to set the window shade alight.

"Jenny, Jenny, come quickly, the house is on fire," cried the girls as Ray and Lorenzo stood dumbfounded by the potentially tragic turn of events. Both boys thought that if they did not die in the fire, their parents would surely kill them. This revelation paralyzed them.

Jenny rushed to the kitchen and retrieved the pan from beneath the icebox that caught drippings from the melting ice. She quickly doused the flames with minimal damage resulting.

"OK," Jenny told the boys sternly when it was evident that all was well. "Now go into the kitchen and wash your plates while I clean up this mess."

Realizing that he was no longer in imminent danger, Lorenzo regained his bravado and responded, "No, I'm not washing no dishes! I'm a guest. You invited me."

"Well, you won't be invited next time," Jenny replied, glaring down on Lorenzo, hands on hips.

Shifting skillfully into a new argument, Lorenzo shot back, "Well, who cares? I'll come anyway. You don't have to invite me. I live here!"

Jenny grabbed both boys by the ear and led them to the sink. Seasoned as she was by this and other displays of stubbornness, she continued drilling the boys, as well as the younger girls, in manners, morals, cleanliness, and general straight-and-narrow behavior. Had she not excelled in the secretarial field, she could surely have found a career as a drill sergeant.

Upon return from the hospital, Maria quickly sent Jenny back to work; her paycheck was needed. She could recuperate on her own, she insisted, though she was weak and without pain medication. Rita pitched in as much as she could, though meals and clean clothes were still expected, and Maria had little time to rest.

21

Jesse Joins the Army, then the Union

*In the midst of World War II, Inland Steel signed its first union contract in
1942, culminating six years of effort by the Steelworkers Organizing Committee, the group that was involved in the Memorial Day Massacre at Republic Steel
as well as a simultaneous but peaceful strike at Inland Steel in East Chicago.
For the duration of the war, patriotism prevailed, and workers put thoughts of
strikes behind them, realizing steel was essential to the war effort. However,
workers found that work slowdowns and other tactics were also effective methods of getting resolutions from the company.*

*Though World War II had come to an end by the time Miguel's eldest son went
into military service in 1945, his subsequent experiences in occupied Germany
broadened his horizons much like happened to Mexican Americans who served
during the war. Meanwhile, as a shop steward in the transportation department
of Inland Steel, Miguel served as a liaison between workers, the union, and management and as the first line of defense for workers in the workplace. As such, he
was part of a militant union leadership that engaged in several "wildcat" strikes
(work stoppages without union authorization) beginning in 1945.*

Jesse, fast approaching manhood, had five close buddies with whom he
hung out, Paco, Danny, Jesse (Martinez), Keno, and Manuel. These boys got
into various kinds of trouble. Most of it was typical teenage shenanigans;
other situations were more serious. Church was a given activity on Sundays,
just as catechism was a required teaching when the children were younger,
and the nuns corralled the kids in as they left school, literally marching them
into the church basement for lessons. Despite knowing that church was

mandatory, Jesse and his friends unilaterally decided a Sunday of "bumming around" was often a better use of their time than attending Mass.

Church was not the only thing Jesse tired of. School, as well, held little interest for him. He much preferred being out and about to sitting in a classroom. He and his buddies took to playing hooky on a regular basis. One day Mr. Buzzy, a new truant officer at Washington High, rode up to the Arredondos' home on his bike. With a determined thrust of his heel he pushed down his kickstand and strode to the door.

"How come Jesse hasn't been in school?" he asked Maria when she answered his knock.

Shocked, Maria replied via her interpreter daughter, Mary, "What? Of course he goes to school. He comes home for lunch every day."

"Maybe so, but that doesn't mean he's been going to class. He hasn't shown up for three weeks!"

Jesse was met that afternoon by a very composed Maria, but a Maria whose anger churned just beneath the surface.

"How was school?" she queried, as her oldest son came in the door.

"Ah, you know, same as usual," Jesse nonchalantly flung his answer over his shoulder as he headed toward the kitchen.

Maria was too quick for him, stepping to block his way as he reached for a snack of tortillas and cheese.

"So what did you study today?" Maria persisted.

"Oh, something about Romans. Nothing that matters much," Jesse tried to reach for a plate, but once again Maria stopped him.

"I don't think Mr. Buzzy would agree with you," Maria said calmly.

Jesse knew in an overdue flash of insight that he had been nailed. He held his tongue as his mother looked steadily at him.

"He says you haven't been in school. He says you haven't gone in three weeks. Is that true?"

"Yeah, Ma," Jesse admitted, recognizing the uselessness of denial.

With that, the conversation ended. Time passed with agonizing slowness as Jesse waited for the other shoe to drop.

A few days later when he was beginning to believe all was well, Maria noticed how unruly Jesse's hair was and ran her fingers through it, demanding, "Why don't you comb your hair?"

The answer was simple, but one Jesse preferred not to explain. He had been in a car accident while out riding with friends. Dried blood from the injury was in his scalp. It was too painful to comb it. Maria felt the sticky mass.

"What *is* this?"

"Oh, I was at the show and tripped and fell. I hit my head on a chair's armrest." Jesse improvised glibly, hoping to stem her interest. In doing so he violated a cardinal rule of the family value structure: No lying!

Like most lies, it did not take long for his prevarication to be found out. Maria learned from the mother of one of his friends that the boys had been playing hooky, hanging out at Wolf Lake, a local fishing spot on the way to Chicago. Driving home from the lake, they had been involved in a minor traffic accident in which Jesse had injured his head. Maria was incensed by both the deed and the lie. Coming on the heels of the truant officer's visit, this latest infraction was one Maria could not overlook. His father learned of his son's transgression and lost no time in acting. He called Jesse to the table and directed him to sit.

"Okay," his father told him. "You don't want to go to school, then you can go to work."

This was not open to negotiation; neither was it a suggestion. It was a direct order. With that, Jesse's formal work life began.

———————

At the time, the only place hiring was the railroad. Jesse was only fifteen, and sixteen was the age limit for hiring. Jenny came to the "rescue" by forging a birth certificate showing him to be a year older. The honesty rule was temporarily suspended since it assisted in helping the family's financial situation and ensured Jesse would have no time to get into trouble. The ploy seemed a good idea at the time and worked well as far as gaining employment. But the forged certificate backfired later when the draft came into play, for it meant Jesse would be a year earlier in his eligibility. His father made a special trip to Blue Island to secure a copy of his original birth certificate to avoid an early forced enlistment.

Jesse worked on the railroad, bringing home his paycheck and considerably swelling the family's income. Always a generous son and brother, he bought special treats for his younger siblings. Top on the list of goodies were caramel candies and White Castle hamburgers. "Castles" were a midwestern delicacy, often referred to as "sliders" because of their greasy makeup. Small soft buns filled with square, flat hamburger meat mixed with chopped onions and topped with a pickle composed the makings of the much sought-after meal. They were cheap, so Jesse would bring home sacks of forty at a time.

After a year on the railroad, Jesse landed a job at Inland Steel where he labored for another year earning more money and receiving better benefits. After a long strenuous week, Jesse made the most of his weekends by partying in Calumet City, Illinois, a place famous, or infamous, for its clubs and strip joints. Jesse was happy; his parents were satisfied that he was not wasting his life or pulling stunts that could land him in jail or worse; and his younger siblings considered the addition of candy and sliders into their diet as a kind of culinary blessing.

On his eighteenth birthday, September 5, 1945, Jesse registered at the draft board office on the corner of Guthrie and Deodar. It was after this that his carefree attitude changed. He began to think, and thinking changed everything.

"I'm gonna get drafted and probably get killed," he convinced himself as he plunged into a fatalistic mindset. After a month of mulling over this unhappy scenario, his prophecy was fulfilled. His draft notice arrived.

"I think I'm gonna die," Jesse confided to his brother Mikey as he prepared to leave for processing at Camp Atterbury, south of Indianapolis.

"I actually believed this was it for me," Jesse remembered. "I figured I'd never see Ma and the family again. Maybe my body would rot overseas in some unmarked grave. I was scared. When I got on that bus to Atterbury, me and the other guys from the Region were pretty low, but we tried not to show it."

Following processing, Jesse took a troop train to Fort Belvoir, Virginia, for basic training, then on to New York for a thirteen-day ocean crossing, landing in Le Havre, France. Another train transported the troops to Bremerhaven, Germany, where he met three girls whose fathers were German but whose mothers were from Argentina. The families had lived in South America until the war broke out and Hitler ordered them to return to Germany.

Shortly after arriving in Germany Jesse arrived in a troop truck in Schweinfurt, which had been the location of a major ball-bearing factory during the war and the target of a devastating Allied bombing raid in 1943. Jesse recalled later that bombers had blown "that town all to hell. They had to. It was war."

Jesse in World War II uniform, 1945

The war in Europe and Asia had ended, and Jesse was not involved in actual combat, but his mother worried herself sick over her son's military service. This was the first of her children to leave home, and she prayed and wept daily while he was away. Every spare moment was spent looking out of the window, wondering when and if Jesse would return.

"He'll be okay, Ma," Mikey would tell his mother, hoping to alleviate her dread.

"You can't know that! He's my firstborn son, and he's suffered so much. He was just a baby when he started selling newspapers, and he's worked hard ever since. Why did he have to go into the army? I should have made him stay in school and never gone to work on the railroad. God is punishing me," she would cry.

"Ma, where's your faith? God will take care of Jesse. You'll see," Mikey told her as he tried to calm her fears.

But Maria could not take comfort in anything. She grew thin and went about her household duties as if in a daze, praying her rosary in a constant attempt to placate God for her shortcomings in raising her son. No sooner had World War II ended than the cold war with the Soviet Union took its place. Maria jumped whenever someone knocked on the door, fearing the dreaded Western Union telegram that announced losses on the battlefield. For an entire year Maria anguished over her son's fate.

The one thing that did brighten Maria's day was a letter from Jesse. She anxiously awaited the mailman's twice-daily stop. When the first letter arrived from her eldest son, Maria opened it with eager anticipation. Jenny had been dusting the furniture, a regular Saturday chore, and listened for her mother to share Jesse's news. After a few minutes of dead silence, Jenny turned from her work and asked in Spanish, "Ma, what does Jesse say? Is he doing all right?"

"I don't know," replied Maria. "This letter must be in English. I can't read it," she confessed, handing the thin sheets of paper over to her daughter.

Jenny glanced at her brother's bold writing and laughed. "Oh, Ma, Jesse thinks he can write Spanish because he went to school in Mexico those few months we lived there. He's got the words all misspelled and mixed up! This is what he's trying to say." Then Jenny proceeded to interpret her brother's poor attempt at written Spanish.

After reading the letter, which reassured her mother that Jesse was alive and well, Jenny sat down with pen and paper and made a list of all his errors as well as the proper Spanish he should have used. She slipped the list in with

Maria's return letter. This procedure continued for three more letters until one day Maria received a letter and said nothing to Jenny.

"Do you want me to read it to you, Ma?" inquired her daughter.

"No, no. It is fine. Jesse has learned how to write in Spanish. Maybe they give lessons in Germany."

When at last Jesse did return home in January 1947, his mother glimpsed him from the window as he stepped off the bus he had caught in Gary, Indiana, after a train trip from Fort Dix, New Jersey. Her happiness so overwhelmed her that she could not speak and could only throw her arms around her son and hold him close. His homecoming was joyous. His mother and sisters treated him as if he alone had won the war. His brothers welcomed him with bear hugs and questions about his stay in Germany. Ramón and Lorenzo clamored for him to tell the "war stories." Miguel welcomed his son, taking him around town to show him off to his friends. It was a grand celebration.

During his stint in the service, Jesse had dropped from 160 pounds to 120. He was handsome and fit, but far too thin to suit Maria. His mother set about fattening him up, feeding him all of her delicious Mexican dishes. Maria was determined to make up for the hardships her son had endured. Her way of doing so was as it had always been—through offerings of food. Jesse happily accepted his mother's kitchen tributes and lost no time in hooking up with his old buddies. Once more he hit the party circuit.

———————

Jesse's hedonistic life continued for nearly a month until one morning, coming in around five a.m., "half shot" from a night of drinking, Jesse ran into his father eating breakfast while Jenny was getting ready to go to work at her job at the union offices. Jenny regarded her brother's appearance with disdain.

"When are you going to get down to the picket line?" Jenny inquired in what Jesse always referred to as her "troublemaking" voice.

With the war's end the steelworkers were on strike, seeking the changes they had put on hold during the country's war effort. Miguel was preparing to join his fellow workers on the picket line. But as for Jesse, he was actually enjoying his respite from the army and work and said so.

"I don't mind not working," he replied to Jenny. Since he had been working since the age of four, it was understandable that he might wish for a bit of rest and recreation. His sister, however, viewed the situation quite differently.

"Don't mind!" Jenny shot back. "What do you mean, 'you don't mind?' We need money for groceries!"

Jesse, sleepy and emboldened by his earlier drinking, replied, "Money? Hell, I got money. Here, how much do you want?" With these words he produced a wad of bills from his pocket.

Maria, Miguel, and Jenny looked at each other in amazement.

"Are you all right?" asked Maria. "What have you been doing? Where did you get that money?"

"My girlfriend."

"Girlfriend? What girlfriend? Who is she, what is she? Is she a prostitute?" the horrified Maria cried out.

"Hell, I don't know what she is. She gave me some money. Who cares what she is?"

This brought an end to the handsome twenty-one-year-old's cockiness. His mother and Jenny "pitched a fit," according to Jesse's description of the scene that followed the disclosure of his newfound wealth. After the women completed their histrionics, all stared at him in disbelief. His father broke the silence.

"Well, whoever she is and wherever the money came from, it's time you take some responsibility." After he had summed up his son's situation, Miguel began lecturing him about the union, the strike, and the picket lines.

"We have to take a stand. The war is over, and there's no excuse for the steel companies to keep wages and benefits down. They've made themselves rich. The big shots always get their share. It's time for us to make sure we have our fair share, too. We need contracts that guarantee us a living wage and a decent pension. As things stand now, the company can fire you if they decide they don't like the way you wear your cap. It's time the working man had his due!"

The tirade on workers' rights continued, with Miguel becoming more adamant and eloquent as he spoke. This was the side of Miguel that so impressed his colleagues. He spoke with passion as he outlined what he believed to be a righteous cause for workers' rights. Jesse was moved by his father's words in spite of himself, though his courage was wearing thin and he longed for a soft bed in which to sleep off his hangover.

"Just to get him off my back, I said, 'Okay, tomorrow I'll go,'" Jesse later told Mikey.

That was the beginning of Jesse's work with the union. He found that many of the young men his age were very impressed by his father and, as he became more involved, Jesse's personal admiration for his father grew.

Everyone knew and liked Miguel, and each month he signed up more union recruits than anyone else. At that time, an individual needed a sponsor to become a union member, and Miguel was sponsor to many. While Miguel sincerely backed the union cause, the five dollars received for each new member recruited was a secondary, yet much welcomed, motivation.

Jesse began attending meetings with his father, entering more and more into union activities. At that time, he was much too young to be part of the union staff but, because of his father's reputation, he was singled out by a union leader, Jimmy Stolla, for a special position. Jimmy came to the house to talk to Jesse.

"I really need a man to help me investigate union members' claims for assistance," he explained. "You'll need to go to their homes and fill out a form to determine if they're eligible before the union can pick up the tab for their request for help."

Jesse eagerly accepted the offer and after a week of on-the-job training with Mr. Stolla, he was on his own.

"I made a lot of friends that way and met a lot of people. That helped me as I moved up the ranks," Jesse remarked in later years while reviewing his career's beginnings.

Like his father, Jesse became heavily involved in union activities. Workers had held off striking during the war, but when peace was declared it was time to address their long-simmering concerns. All of the past injustices resurfaced as discussions of present concerns grew passionate.

At last a strike was called to highlight various grievances, with pension benefits being the primary point of contention. At the end of the long, tough negotiations, every issue had been settled with the exception of pension benefits. Nevertheless, Phillip Murray, president of the AFL-CIO at the time, directed workers to go back to work. Local 1010, begun by Miguel and four other organizers, was now a strong chapter and refused to follow Murray's directive. The local held out for resolution on the pension issue.

Maria, whose goal never wavered—keep her family fed and secure— once again preached against Miguel's involvement, again to no avail. Tension mounted between labor and management, as well as between Maria and Miguel.

When a commotion beneath her window caught Maria's attention, she peered down to find out what was transpiring and was horrified to see her husband at the front of a line of marching workers waving signs for reform.

Miguel's mission for the betterment of the workingman overrode all other considerations; the immediate welfare of his family was not exempt. His vision was always broad and futuristic; the betterment of life tomorrow overrode the mundane needs of today.

"A farmer doesn't know when planting who's going to be able to reap that seed," he would say, secure in his belief that the union's actions of today would bear positive fruits in years and decades to come.

Maria did not have the luxury of "future think." Her dreams were founded in day-to-day needs. Once she had sat on the porch watching men going off to work, saying wistfully, "I wish I were a man. If I were, I could work hard and earn money." She understood the power of finance and certainly recognized that the role of women was severely limited by their housebound status. Though the war had moved other women into the dawn of a new era by opening the workplace, Maria, as a mother of ten, was not among the vanguard. She could envision both husband and son out of work due to unions.

"Talk all you want about your damned union," she would tell her husband. "All well and good for you to make your pretty speeches and play the big hero with your no-account buddies at the Hall. It's easy to be on the side of 'workers' rights' and helping 'the noble working man' when you have your gut full of beer and your head full of praises for your great leadership."

Maria was also aware that union activities could be dangerous. She remembered the incident at Republic Steel in South Chicago when union members from Inland went to support their union brothers. The fight that broke out resulted in a shooting that gravely wounded several men and killed ten others. Miguel had wanted to attend this show of solidarity but had been persuaded to stay home because of his family responsibilities. "There but for the grace of God," she thought.

"You better think of us, Miguel," Maria continued. "Your wife and kids who are sitting here with no money to pay the bills—no food to eat and a landlord knocking on the door for rent. You won't look like such a great man when your family is hungry! Or when you have a bullet in your head!"

"Let someone else lead this great cause of yours. Let the single guys who have no one depending on them march down the street. You keep your nose clean and your mouth shut, and maybe you can keep your job, and we won't starve!"

As events proved, Maria's fears were well-founded. During a lunch break Miguel was posting union flyers on boxcars when a company spy caught him. He was fired immediately.

This angry verbal battle between husband and wife continued as the labor troubles dragged on. Both had righteous causes; both saw no way to compromise. In this struggle, negotiations could not bring settlement.

--------◆-◆◆-◆◆--------

An initial problem for strikers was the return of soldiers. Soldiers had fought for their country and many of them had no intention of letting strikers keep them from jobs, money, and the opportunity to buy homes for their families.

"Hey, we fought, now we need to settle down and make a living. Don't rock the boat with strikes. We didn't fight to come home to this," these newly discharged soldiers declared.

This concern was addressed by other veterans who got in the forefront of the strikers, telling their comrades, "Look, these old-timers are doing something for all of us. We understand it. So before you make trouble, you'll have to deal with us first, not the old-timers. Think about it. If we have a good contract, we're all gonna benefit!"

Once the veterans gave their unreserved and outspoken support, "that was that," as Jesse said. He explained what happened then:

"Back in those days we had a lot of what they called 'commie guys.' You know, real radicals. They were determined, 'We're gonna strike. We're gonna hold out for the pension. Hell, we earned it!' Finally, the big guys had enough and said, 'We might as well agree to something for them.' Okay, so they gave our union, Local 1010, the pension. We were the leaders, the most progressive union in the country. When we went to conventions the other guys watched to see what 1010 would do—then they'd follow our lead. We proved we had the guts to stand up for what we deserved. In those days there were no workers' rights. We got them."

With the strike settled, Miguel got his job back. For the time being, all was running smoothly for the family.

22

"Happy Days" in the Harbor

The relative prosperity of the 1950s made home ownership a reality for a growing number of immigrant families. Indiana Harbor was a unique blend of Old World and Americana. Ethnic shops and department stores vied for customers, while kids of all nationalities cheered for the same heroes at the Saturday movie matinees.

It was with Jesse's help that the Arredondos were able to purchase their first house, located on Block Avenue. Jesse provided a large part of the down payment with money he had saved from his wages. Still four hundred dollars short, Maria was able to secure a loan from José Perez, a man who, in earlier days, had given Ray and Lorenzo World War I artifacts that the boys had used to play war games. Señor José was sweet on Jenny, though she had no interest in him whatsoever. Like her mother before her, Maria had little compunction about using her daughter's would-be suitor to further her own aims. She had never owned a house, and this opportunity would help her and her children move one step further up the ladder. She would have it by whatever means necessary. It had taken decades, but Maria finally obtained a vital part of the American dream. She had persevered and won.

⬥•✦•⬥

As Jesse advanced in the union and Maria wrangled the purchase of a home, the rest of the family moved forward as well. Sue added babysitting to her after-school tasks, earning enough for school shoes. Washing dishes at her grandmother's restaurant allowed her to buy clothes; a pink dress she purchased for 72 cents was a special favorite. Hand-me-down dresses were the usual attire for the girls, so anything new was a rare treat. Mary washed out her school dress each night to make sure it was clean for the next day. As for the boys, they wore hand-me-downs, which were always clean, though often patched. Baggy, knee-length trousers called knickerbockers or knickers and clodhopper shoes were the standard attire early on. Later, they were exchanged for jeans and flannel shirts. The jeans were as patched as the knickers, but as money became more abundant, there was enough for buying new clothes. Ray got his first new pair of jeans around the age of eight.

"Hey!" he thought, "Look at these, I'm the first one who's wearing them. They're new. Nobody's ever worn them before!" It really was a big deal for the young boy.

Chive took his mother to buy what the family needed.

"Come on," Maria would tell him, "You boys need shirts and underwear."

Chive would go with her to explain styles and sizes to the store clerks, while Maria pulled the necessary money from her small purse.

Strangely enough, as youngsters, the kids never realized they were lacking. They were together, fed, and had relatively happy childhoods, despite living in less than ideal circumstances. In reality, they were not unlike many of their schoolmates and neighbors, so they seldom compared themselves to others, but rather accepted life as it came. Not until they became older did the truth of their situation hit home. And yet, later on they remembered their school days as happy ones and realized their circumstances had improved over time.

The single exception to these positive feelings came from Camila. Far from recalling a happy childhood, she felt the "good old days," were hardly "good." One incident in particular caused her pain and anger. It was spring, and the family had settled into the newly purchased home on Block Avenue. Camila asked her mother for an Easter dress.

"No, there's no money. You can't have one."

The tenants, who were at the time renting a basement flat in the new home, had not paid the rent. On Easter Sunday the children of the renters came upstairs to show off their Easter dresses.

Camila was dumbfounded. Here these girls who owed her mother money were wearing the Easter dresses that were rightfully hers.

She turned to her mother as the girls went merrily off to church in their new frocks.

"Ma, that's not fair. I wanted a new Easter dress. You should have made them pay the rent so I could have one."

"Life's not fair, Camila," Maria answered wearily, "and you can't always have what you want. Stop your fussing and let me get dinner."

Camila's fury would not subside. She was too angry and too envious of the little girls who were wearing "her" dresses. She went to her bedroom and cried with frustration for the rest of the day.

⚫•✦•⚫

While Camila wished for clothes and resented the renters, Mary had a more optimistic attitude toward life. To her, childhood was a wonderful period filled with the excitement of living in the Harbor. She loved the constant ebb and flow of life around her.

The Harbor had many attractions that enlivened the area and gave it a kind of electricity. Main Street alone sported two dime stores, Newberry's and Woolworth's, whose lunch counter and soda fountain was a favorite with kids. Gould's Furniture Store tempted those who longed for pretty living rooms, and Mademoiselle's, with its window displays of exclusive women's apparel, acted as a temptress to passersby and sparked dreams of fashion heaven for the ladies of the town. People crowded the sidewalks, and the clang of street-cars was a sharp exclamation point that underscored the merger of commerce and pleasure.

Especially memorable were the townspeople turning out in holiday dress. Not only was a major holiday such as Christmas thrilling, so, also, was Easter. Newberry's sold baby chicks dyed every color of the rainbow. Also available was delicious beige Easter candy, hard on the outside and soft inside, which was a special seasonal treat that Mary coveted.

Halloween brought stage shows to the Indiana Theater, which featured Dracula, the Werewolf, and Frankenstein. In one show a prize of $100 was to be given to the first patron who would venture up to Frankenstein, but Maria refused to let the kids go to that one, saying it was too gruesome. A hypnotist dressed as Dracula, replete with slicked-back hair, penetrating dark eyes, and the ubiquitous cape, was another forbidden show, but Mary quickly learned the details of his performance from friends in attendance. Most macabre of all was the Halloween window display at Hurwich's Furniture Store.

"Mary," her best friend Frances told her, "you gotta come down to Hurwich's and see the man in the coffin." Frances shivered as she described the gruesome display.

"He's all laid out in a real coffin," Frances continued with a voice shaking with both excitement and fear. "Nobody knows who he is. And, Mary, guess what! His hair and fingernails are still growing! No kidding. You gotta come," she urged.

Lincoln Elementary, third grade class, 1948. Ray is on the far left in the front row.

Mary was both fascinated and repelled by the thought of a "real live" dead body displayed for all the world to see right in the front windows of Hurwich's store. Of course she had to go, even if it were scary. She had to see for herself.

"All right. Let's go then. But don't say anything to Ma, or she won't let me."

"Tell her we're gonna walk downtown," Frances offered.

"OK, wait here. I'll get my sweater."

The two girls went to visit the unknown cadaver (if indeed it was a "real" body). Other kids from school were gathered around the window, jockeying for a better view.

"Look at that guy," the boys teased, "I bet he jumps out of that coffin and sneaks into little girls' bedrooms at night and strangles them!" They ended with a roar of laughter.

"Don't be stupid!" A girl countered. "He's dead, and besides, if he creeps into anybody's room, it would be a stinky old boy's!"

"Yeah, and he'd strangle you with his wrinkly old hands!" giggled another girl.

This banter kept up for several minutes until Mary tugged at Frances' arm.

"Let's go home. This is spooky."

From the look on Frances's face, she was more than ready to leave as well. Visions of the ancient guy sneaking into their bedrooms were all too vivid. Halloween was full of gruesome props, but none quite like this. The two girls turned and ran down the sidewalk. That night Mary was happy that she shared a bed with her sister. Every creak and thud of the house as it settled during the night brought a little tickle of terror to her. She pulled her covers over her head and snuggled closer to Camila.

Yet, the next day, she and Frances could not resist one more look at the old man in the coffin.

⟐

Scary radio programs the Arredondo kids listened to at home also provided them with thrills and chills. With all the lights off, the only illumination being the orange light of the radio, the siblings stared at the large radio cabinet and prepared to be delightfully frightened out of their wits. Imagination came into play as the children visualized horrific tableaus as *The Shadow* stalked the "evil in men's hearts" or the squeaky door on *Inner Sanctum* promised more imaginary terror than any movie screen could provide.

When Mary grew older the movies offered more horror. In the 1950s 3-D had come into fashion along with the magic of air-conditioning. Sitting with huge eyes, the kids watched Vincent Price mug through scenes in the 3-D *House of Wax*. Other films were horrifying even without 3-D. In *The House on Haunted Hill*, horrible undulating acid pits swallowed a man who emerged as a skeleton. Everyone screamed as he shuffled his way seemingly out of the screen and toward the audience of spellbound watchers.

"Feelie" movies also made a lasting impression on Mary. *The Tingler* offered graphic depictions of a huge crawfish-like creature coming out of a body slithering along the floor like a snake. Prior to the movie's beginning an announcement was made to all viewers advising them that they were watching history in the making. Never before had a "feelie" been shown. Only those "sensitive people" in the audience would experience the actual tingling sensation. Most important, the fear such a thing might induce could actually lead to death unless people screamed. Such screaming would give "immediate relief" from the terror. Moviegoers were only too happy to comply.

Unaware that some seats had been equipped with buzzers that produced the tingling sensation, kids screamed to one another, "You feel it? Oh! Do you feel it?"

"Yeah, yeah, I feel it," was the answer. As the strange reverberation made its way along the theater seats, the screams rose to higher decibels.

———————

As for Maria, she loved baseball. Ted Williams was her favorite player, and thus, the Red Sox was her favorite team. Chive, Mike, and Joe (Pepé) would sometimes take her to Comiskey Park when the Red Sox came to Chicago. They sat in the cheap seats in the leftfield bleachers watching the game and munching on the lunch Maria packed for these occasions.

———————

While Maria was savoring baseball games with her older sons, Ray was soaring toward stardom. He sang in the elementary school choir, which had been chosen to perform on the local radio station. How thrilling. His voice would travel the airwaves for all to hear. When the big day arrived, Ray was overflowing with excitement. The show was to be aired after school, so he and his family could savor his rise to fame together. Thrill of thrills. The announcer introduced the choir, and young voices began to sing.

Ray sang especially loud; in fact, the whole choir followed their teacher's instruction not to be shy. They were not. Each boomed out carefully rehearsed words to the accompaniment of an upright piano. The overall effect was one of, well, enthusiasm.

"Listen, Ma. Hear that. That's me. Can't you tell? Listen right after this line. See, it's me again."

Maria smiled and nodded.

"How can you tell it's you?" asked Lorenzo skeptically.

"Listen. It's him. I can tell," countered Mary. Camila agreed.

"Oh, yeah, I hear you now. Hey, that's pretty good," said Lorenzo, falling in with the prevailing sentiment.

The show proved nothing if not memorable, though the music instructor may have regretted her urging the students to "sing loudly." Next day Ray and his fellow choir members were the toast of the school. By Friday their notoriety had faded, and kids moved on to other topics. Fleeting or not, however, Ray relished his time in the limelight.

———————

Never a limelight seeker, Mary was a happy girl, who enjoyed every bit of the busy atmosphere the Harbor presented. Though she was not particularly fond of school, she did well enough. The school population was a learning experience in itself with Mexicans, Poles, African Americans, Romanians,

Serbs, Greeks, Irish, Chinese, and Gypsies all attending and getting along well. Together they lent a cosmopolitan, international flavor to what was a very midwestern working-class community.

Mary was creative. Her art teacher, Miss Carter, noted her artistic abilities.

"Why did you draw this?" she asked Mary during one class period, pointing out a picture of a woman with strange, haunting eyes.

"I don't know," replied Mary. "I just grab a pencil, and the pictures come to me."

"Well, I notice that when you draw, you make the eyes like the ancient Egyptians."

Mary had never seen ancient Egyptian art and had no idea where the inspiration might have come from.

"Well," Miss Carter continued, "when you're ready to graduate, come to see me, and I'll get you into an art school."

Mary knew her mother would never agree to further school. The idea of higher education lost out to the practicality of earning a living and contributing to the family. Nevertheless, Mary was pleased that someone had noticed her talent. She did not dwell on what seemed out of reach; instead she concentrated on what was at hand.

Even the seamier side of the Harbor appealed to her eager mind; her sense of optimism turned any event into an adventure or at the very least into an interesting diversion. When the family lived on Block Avenue, a sailor knocked on the door, mistaking their house for a place of ill repute. Maria answered, but was unable to understand what he wanted.

"Mary, come here and see what this man wants," she called from the doorway.

Mary began translating to her mother the sailor's request, too young to understand the implications of what the man was asking.

"Go!" her mother suddenly shouted. Then in Spanish she commanded, "Mary, tell him he's lost. Send him over to the corner to the black guy."

Mary did as she was told. As soon as the sailor left, Maria began shouting at Mary.

"He wanted the red light district! How dare he come here!"

Mary gazed at her mother in puzzlement. What was causing her such consternation?

"Jay Jay," a black man who lived on the corner and sported a tee shirt and black pants, ran dope dealing and prostitution out of his establishment. He had erected a red light next to his place of business, a not-so-subtle signal to those searching for his "merchandise."

Mary was aware of this "business" but had no true understanding of it. She was aware, also, of the men who came in from Whiting, Munster, and Hammond and stopped at Jay Jay's. She had a vague idea these men were lost, but only in later years did she realize they came for drugs and women. When the sailor had knocked, she was too naïve to have recognized the purpose of the house with the red light. She was merely puzzled by her mother's dramatic reaction to his visit and thought the whole episode "interesting" in the same way she found the electric trolleys interesting as they criss-crossed the town dropping off and picking up throngs of people at each stop, taking them to destinations she could only guess at.

In those days the town was full of first-class clothing and millinery shops, which attracted the rich, famous, and infamous of Chicago. There were furniture stores, retail high-end jewelry stores, expensive clothing stores for both men and women, groceries and meat markets, dime stores, five movie theaters, after-hour joints, bars, and restaurants. It was where the action was. Mary could not imagine why anyone would ever want to leave the Harbor.

23

Love Calls—"California Here We Come"

America has always been a land of much social mobility compared to other nations, and inevitably this affected ethnic families as well. In Indiana Harbor, while the first generation remained near the vicinity of the mills around Block and Pennsylvania avenues, their children and grandchildren often fanned out beyond la colonia. *Still, when the first son or daughter moved away, it caused anguish and often consternation.*

After graduation Sue, like Jenny before her, went to work at Local 1010. As with Jenny, her father was instrumental in securing this job, and she proved herself to be an excellent secretary. Her paycheck was added to the family income. Like all the siblings she would put her check on the table each payday, and her mother would use it to help with the bills. Maria gave back whatever she thought her children might need for themselves. There was never any hesitation on the part of the kids to contribute or on Maria's part to take any or all of the money that she deemed necessary for family needs.

Jenny and Sue would socialize together with Sue being her chaperone. Jenny was rankled at never being allowed to be alone and once told Sue that "people think you're my maid." Not surprisingly, Sue was not delighted by the arrangement or Jenny's comment, but it was a requirement for girls to be accompanied, and their father would not hear of any exceptions.

It was, of course, inevitable, that the two girls would eventually have suitors. As it happened, the men who were to become their lifelong partners were best friends. Originally from Mexico, the two, Manuel Fernandez and Guadalupe (Lupe) Sanchez, met at Inland Steel in the fall of 1947. Alone in a new environment, they sought out companionship and soon spent their free time together.

Manuel had a cousin in the Harbor, Tony Fernandez, who knew the Arredondo family. One day in 1949, after the Arredondos had enjoyed another milestone in their lives via the installation of a phone in their home, Tony called to talk to Jenny. "There's someone I want you to meet," he told her, "my cousin Manuel."

Handing the phone to Manuel, the two talked at length, with Manuel ending the conversation saying "one of these days we'll have to meet in person."

That day came as Lupe and Manuel were walking back from an afternoon at the beach. Crossing the railroad tracks, they saw two girls strolling in front of them.

Lupe told Manuel, "That's Juanita Arredondo." He recognized her as the Queen of the Mexican Independence Day Parade, a huge event in the Mexican community. During the festival, streets were blocked and traffic was replaced with food stands and dancing to mariachi bands. Motorcycle groups from

Manuel Fernandez (left) and Guadalupe (Lupe) Sanchez crossing railroad tracks in Indiana Harbor, late 1940s

Monterrey, Mexico, came to the Harbor to perform during the celebration, doing fancy tricks during the gala parade. The year Jenny was queen, she sat on a float and waved to the crowd. She looked lovely with her hair pinned up, displaying a posture of untouchable regality.

Jenny had earned the queen title by selling tickets for ten cents apiece; the girl selling the most tickets was crowned. Because of Miguel's being so popular, she won easily.

Jenny's attending page boy was her little brother Lorenzo. The day before the parade Miguel took him to get a haircut. While Lorenzo sat in the barber's chair,

Miguel and "Maestro" José Lopez, the barber, embarked on an intense discussion about a keynote speech for next day's event. Both interjected ideas and emphasized points with wide-flung hand gestures. Shots of whiskey quickly appeared. Within minutes the entire barbershop was involved in making suggestions for the speech. The result was evident in Lorenzo's haircut. Señor Lopez had underscored each point with a quick swipe of the clippers. Lorenzo sported a distinctive sidewall cut as he left the shop, as portions of his cheeks and neck had been newly uncovered and were noticeably less tan than the rest of his head.

From the day of the parade, Jenny remembered a handsome man had called up to her as she passed and asked if he might take her picture. Lupe was that man. As Juanita sat on the float with head high and an expression of a haughty and aloof queen, she was touched in a way she had never before felt by the man calling to her. Though she had only had a glimpse, she often recalled the man's face and romanticized him in her fantasies; he became an integral part of her imaginings, and she had not forgotten him.

As the girls strolled, Jenny recognized one of the voices behind her as the voice from the phone call. Just before the men caught up with her and Sue, Jenny turned and said, "You're Manuel Fernandez."

"Yes, I am," he confirmed as they approached the girls. Manuel introduced his friend Lupe to Jenny and Sue.

Jenny was startled to recognize the young man standing next to Manuel. He was the man who had asked for her photo, the man of her dreams. This chance official meeting confirmed the strong attraction between Jenny and Lupe. Manuel's cousin had originally thought to set up Jenny and Manuel, but for Jenny, meeting Lupe ruled out any thoughts of another man. The two began seeing each other.

There was no way that Jenny and Lupe could be alone under the "chaperones until married" rule. Lupe cajoled Manuel into escorting Sue, forming a double-date approach, which would fulfill the necessary chaperone clause in the family's code of social conduct. With Jenny and Lupe happily in love, it would have been in keeping with fairy-tale romances if Sue and Manuel had shared the same feelings for each other. But this was real life; there was no spark between them initially.

However, the relationship between Sue and Manuel gradually moved from instant dislike to an affable friendship. The two were thrown together as chaperones for the courting couple and, as they grew to know each other better,

As Jenny is crowned queen in September 1947, her youngest brother Lorenzo, a page boy for the Mexican Independence Day Parade, holds up a corner of her robe.

the beginnings of romance slowly crept into the relationship. But for Jenny and Lupe the attraction evolved much more rapidly. Before long they were inseparable.

As the couple became an obvious item, the family's scrutiny of Lupe Sanchez increased. Jenny's father knew Manuel because he, too, was involved in the union. Often the two of them would sit at the bars and debate history, philosophy, and strategy for advancement of the local unions. As the relationship between Manuel's friend Lupe and Miguel's daughter Jenny progressed, Miguel began to question Manuel.

"What part of Mexico did this Lupe Sanchez come from?" he asked. "What did he do there? Is he a worker or a slacker?"

Manuel was well aware that his friend was under close inspection. He answered Miguel with vagaries and tried to move the subject away from his friend as quickly as he could. Miguel much preferred intellectual subjects to complex emotional ones and was easily persuaded to return to broader topics of world affairs. These he found more manageable than personal dilemmas. Besides, Juanita knew better than to do anything without his permission.

The couple's courtship continued.

One night Lupe dropped Jenny home after work. As she walked in the door, she passed her parents as they were leaving for a movie, an unusual event, for Miguel usually went out while Maria stayed at home.

Rita was there and about to serve dinner as the phone rang. Rita picked up the telephone and mumbled a few words, then called to Jenny.

"It's that guy Lupe, again," she said with an edge in her voice.

Jenny was surprised.

"Lupe? He just dropped me off. What does he want?"

"Humph! Why don't you just take the phone and ask him?" her grandmother responded, thrusting the phone in Jenny's direction.

"Hey, Juanita. There's a good show on at the Paramount in Hammond. It's called *Battleground*. Wanna go? I'll wait for you outside the theater."

"Well, okay, I guess," she responded. Her parents were not there to ask, but she had taken the bus to the movies many times. She quickly ate and grabbed up her purse, calling to her grandmother that she was going out as she closed the door. She did not want to listen to Rita grumble. She knew that her grandmother did not like Lupe, but Jenny was too much in love to care what others thought, even her beloved grandmother.

She caught the 8:00 p.m. bus, and the couple enjoyed the war movie in the company of a group of friends. After it ended, Lupe walked her to the bus stop, and she boarded the 10:30 p.m. bus for home. When she got there, the whole family was sitting in the living room. They were obviously awaiting her return.

"Where have you been?" demanded her father, so angry that his ears were red.

"To the movies. I caught the bus to Hammond," Jenny answered.

"To be with that Lupe guy, no doubt."

"Yes, Pa. He asked me to go. It was a good movie. Our friends were there, too."

"I don't care if the movie was good or not. I don't care who was there with you. You have no business going without asking!"

"But you weren't here. You and Ma were leaving when I came in. I didn't know I was going then. He didn't call until you'd already left."

"Then you should have stayed home! What kind of self-respecting girl is on the streets after ten o'clock?"

Her father was shouting now. The rest of the family sat holding their breath, waiting for Jenny to reply. Maria and Rita were stony faced. The smaller kids were openly curious to see what the results of this showdown between father and daughter would be.

"I wasn't 'on the streets.' I was taking the bus home. It was just a movie with a lot of other people around. Not like some secret rendezvous," Jenny justified her actions, so angry she was on the verge of tears.

Miguel ignored her protests.

"Next time you do something like that, your suitcase will be waiting for you. No daughter of mine will disgrace this family. Do you hear me?" Miguel shouted.

Jenny nodded and stormed to her room. She was caught between her family and the man she knew she wanted to spend the rest of her life with. Whatever she did, she would hurt somebody she loved. She resolved then and there that she would not give up Lupe. She would continue to see him. When her parents and Grandmother Rita saw how she cared for him, they would learn to accept him. It was just because they did not know Lupe that they hated him so. It would work out, she was sure of that. Like women in love throughout the ages, Jenny chose to believe that love truly would conquer all. It was just a matter of time.

What Jenny had failed to factor into her reasoning was her grandmother. The years had done nothing to diminish Rita's belief that she must step into any situation that adversely affected her family. She knew what was best for them, even if they did not always know themselves. Rita was fiercely protective of her first grandchild. She would not stand by and see Jenny ruin her life. Her Juanita would get over this man; Rita just needed to get him out of the picture for a while.

Rita had heard rumors of Lupe's life in Mexico that had greatly disturbed her. She had not been able to verify them, but she was determined to shield her granddaughter from the pain she was sure this man would bring to her. She set about devising a scheme that would save Jenny from herself.

She confronted Lupe on her own, telling no one her plan.

"I don't want you seeing my granddaughter any longer. You aren't worthy of her. Leave her alone."

Lupe looked down at Rita who had accosted him as he left the gates of Inland Steel. He saw a small, aging woman who wore an apron over her dress and glared at him from a still-handsome face. His first instinct was to laugh at such an unlikely combatant, but this was Jenny's grandmother and he knew he must respect that.

"Señora," Lupe addressed Rita politely, bowing slightly as he did so. "I can see you are upset. But you must understand that I cannot do as you wish. I love your granddaughter, Señora, and she loves me. I'm afraid I cannot stop seeing her," Lupe smiled, thinking his handsome face and charming manner could help reassure Rita that he was not the monster she had made him out to be. As others before him, Lupe had gravely underestimated his adversary.

Rita was silent a moment, then spoke in a steely voice, locking her eyes with Lupe's.

"I was afraid you might feel that way, Señor Sanchez. I regret I have no choice since you fail to listen to my request. I will report you to immigration."

With that Rita turned her back and walked quickly away.

Lupe was stunned. He knew the old lady was not bluffing. He also knew that he could not stay and risk being deported. His future lay in the United States; he would let no one change that. He knew California was full of Mexicans. Friends had told him of the state's beauty and the opportunities that awaited anyone who was willing to work. He was confident that he could blend in. It was his only choice; he packed immediately and headed west, leaving word for Jenny that he had to leave and would contact her when he could.

———————◆◆◆◆◆———————

When Jenny learned of Lupe's departure, she was inconsolable. Lupe communicated by sending letters to her at work, afraid to risk their interception if delivered to her home. When Lupe told her she could join him if that was her wish, she did not hesitate. Calling her sister, Sue, she asked her to meet for lunch.

"I have something to tell you," Jenny said.

As Sue slid into the restaurant booth across from Jenny, she looked closely at her sister. It was obvious that she had been crying.

"Why are your eyes red?" demanded Sue.

"I have to tell you something," Jenny repeated.

"You said that before," said Sue, becoming impatient. "So what is it that is so important?"

"I'm leaving."

"Leaving! What are you talking about? Where are you going?"

"I'm gonna follow Lupe. I'm going to California."

"What?" Sue exclaimed, aghast at such an unthinkable explanation. Sue was rendered nearly speechless by this sudden declaration.

Jenny continued. "Yeah, I've got my plane ticket. My boss, Les Thorton, is taking me to the airport. I've already packed my stuff."

Sue gazed at Jenny with huge incredulous eyes.

"You packed? When could you pack? How could you do that and nobody noticed?"

"I packed a few clothes in a bag every day as I went to work." Jenny explained.

"But do you know what you're gonna do? You don't just follow a guy! Dad will kill you!" Sue was beginning to realize the implications of Jenny's plan and the havoc such action would wreak within the family. No child had ever dared display such audacious disregard for the "Arredondo Rules."

"Well, I have to," Jenny interrupted as Sue continued her protest.

"But what are you going to do, Jenny? California is a long way off. You'll be leaving your job and all of us! You'll be out in the middle of nowhere with no family, no job! What are you going to do?"

"I don't know, but I love him."

No matter how hard Sue pleaded, Jenny remained adamant. She loved Lupe. She was going to him in California. Nothing and no one could change her mind.

The year was 1950. Jenny was nearly twenty-seven, hardly a child, but the magnitude of her proposed action was not in any way lessened by her age. Family rules forbade anything but a traditional courtship and marriage. Jenny knew that her family disapproved of Lupe primarily because of the rumors about his past. She also knew that, despite the often tense relationship she had with her father, he viewed her as the apple of his eye, and there was no way he would ever agree to her marrying Lupe, much less running away to California to be with him. She was in love, and that love was stronger than ties with her family. Perhaps the years of rigid obedience added to her determination to leave and begin her own life. Whatever the motivation, there was no turning back.

"I'm going, Sue," Jenny repeated. "I've already sent a telegram to mother."

Jenny Arredondo, Queen of the Mexican Independence Day Parade, September 1947

With that pronouncement, Sue's concern for her sister shifted to fear for herself.

"What!" she cried as she stared at her sister. "You mean they'll get your telegram at the house before I get home?"

"Yeah."

"So I'm gonna get it. What you're going to do, I'll pay for!" Sue told Jenny angrily. Her anger was all the greater because Jenny had been given advantages the others had not: beauty school, secretarial school, modeling school, and she was the only one to go to the prom! Jenny was tall and attractive and her father's firstborn daughter. Through the years she had advantages the others had not shared. Though theirs had been a love-hate relationship, Jenny, too, realized that her father had treated her as special.

"You can't do this, Jenny. You can't leave me with this mess! It's not fair!"

"Well, I'm going! I love him." Jenny stated with determination. There was nothing left to say. Still bound by tradition, Jenny had waited to leave for California until the forty days of Lent were over. That year, it ended early. Jenny would delay no longer. Today she would leave. On March 30, 1950, Jenny boarded a TWA plane to join her love.

Sue went back to work, though she could do little but sit behind her desk in shock. At quitting time, she reluctantly headed for home where she found her mother crying.

"Did you know anything?" demanded Maria as soon as Sue walked through the doorway. She wiped her tears away with an angry gesture as she faced her daughter.

"No, Ma, I didn't."

"Here's the telegram we got when she took off." Maria waved the offending paper in Sue's face as if it offered proof of conspiracy.

"Ma, I didn't know," Sue repeated, knowing there was nothing she could do or say to redeem herself. Though she was innocent of any knowledge, she would bear the brunt of Jenny's actions for she was here, and Jenny was gone. Her anger and resentment toward her sister grew.

"You're not going out of this house," shouted a furious Maria, apropos of nothing. She was hurt, fearing for her daughter's future in California while, at the same time, angered by such a break in the family unity. What would people say? How could Jenny disgrace the family's good name? With Jenny out of reach, Sue became the obvious scapegoat.

"You're not leaving this house for two weeks, not until I go and bring your sister back!" she shouted at Sue again. She might not be able to reach Juanita, but she surely could vent her ire on her sister.

Maria had been planning ways to retrieve Jenny from this disastrous adventure ever since the telegram was delivered. Sue was not surprised that she was the one being punished for her sister's actions. It was in keeping with the traditions of the family; all suffered if one misstepped. It was just in this case, she would suffer the most.

"Fine," answered a resigned Sue, realizing her mother was ready to board a plane, kill Lupe, and drag Jenny home. But Sue was wise enough to know that there was no changing the situation. Jenny was gone and, despite her mother's anger and the raging of her father, which was bound to come as soon as he learned what had happened, Jenny was not coming back.

24

Jesse Takes a Wife—and More

Miguel's long history of union activism facilitated Jesse's rise in union politics.
In 1952 he was elected treasurer of Local 1010, the largest chapter in the
USWA—United Steelworkers of America—with approximately 18,000 members.

The reverberations from Jenny's leaving rippled throughout the family.
Miguel was devastated at his firstborn's defying his teachings and, to his mind,
sullying the family's honor. That Jenny was a grown woman, hardly a child
who had been led astray by a predatory adult, was of no matter. To Miguel she
was his little girl, the lovely daughter who had brought honor to the family
as the Queen of Mexican Independence Day. Now she had broken his heart,
and he would sit, quite literally, crying into his beer, as he commiserated with
friends about his loss. His initial anger metamorphosed into grief as real as if
Jenny had died.

The siblings reacted with varying degrees of concern. Jesse, as the oldest,
tried to soothe his mother, although there was little he could do to assuage her
sense of outrage. He was relatively calm compared to Mike, who was furious.

"We'll call the police. I'll contact them in California and have them arrest
Lupe and throw him in jail until they can deport him! We'll go bring Jenny
back! Hell, I'll kill Lupe if that's the only way!" Mike fumed.

Like his mother, Mike was all for immediate action to put the family back
together as quickly as possible while seeking an Old Testament revenge for
Lupe, the perceived villain of the situation.

Chive, who had quit school shortly after Jesse, was too caught up in his
work at the railroad and later at Inland, to become ensnarled in family crises.
Chive was what Chive always had been: a happy, carefree soul whose greatest
love was dancing and a good party. Of all the older siblings he was the least

affected by his sister's defection. It saddened him, but he accepted it as part of life, Jenny's life for that matter.

Pepé was busy in high school where he had become interested in sports. Jenny's defection was a shock, but nothing that he was going to allow to deflect his goals.

The younger children were bewildered by the intense emotion and drama surrounding their sister's flight. Understanding their sister was gone, they were curious as to whether they would ever see Jenny again and what exactly her leaving meant to the family. Her "running away" was both scary and exciting.

"Do you think she'll come back?" wondered Camila.

"Who knows?" Mary replied. "I sure wouldn't if I'd made Ma and Pa that mad. I'd stay away forever!"

"Yeah," mused Lorenzo. "We probably won't see her ever again."

"We might," Ray contradicted. "You can't tell. She might come back. Don't you think she'll miss us?"

"No," said Mary. "She doesn't care about us. She cares about Lupe. That's why she left."

"That's right," Lorenzo responded. "We won't see her again . . . unless maybe it's when she dies. I guess maybe Ma and Pa might forgive her if she's dead!" The four giggled at that ridiculous scenario.

The older siblings dwelled on more practical implications. They understood that her leaving would shrink the family income. Harder to calculate was the impact her defiance of tradition would have on the family's standing in the community. This was the first major breech in the family's strongly founded nucleus, and it shook them to the core. No longer could Maria and Miguel count on the established mores that had, until now, ensured family interdependence and loyalty that was so ingrained as to be unquestioned.

<hr />

Though Maria eventually reconciled herself to the situation, and Mike finally realized there was little to be done legally regarding a grown woman's decision to move to California, Jenny's departure remained something of an open wound within a family unused to internal "betrayals." Nevertheless, the family gradually settled back into the daily routine, minus their older daughter and sibling.

Jesse continued to move up the ranks within the union. In 1952 he had campaigned for and won the office of treasurer. He worked to earn a high school GED and began studies at Roosevelt University in Chicago. He loved the excitement the union work afforded him. The rough-and-tumble world of the down-and-dirty negotiations and strategy sessions suited him to a tee. His brash comments and outspoken honesty won him respect even when others disagreed with him.

Jesse's earnings increased, and he became the primary source of income for the family. It was his savings that had allowed him to front the down payment on the family's Block Avenue home. He also was generous with his father, giving him pocket money that Miguel used to go drinking. Although he felt great regret for this practice in later years as he watched his father slip further and further into alcoholism and depression, at the time his gesture was done with the thought of supplying his father with a little happiness and recreation.

In the early 1950s, while returning from his night shift at the mill, Jesse had noticed an attractive young woman waiting to catch a bus. Each morning as he returned home, the same young lady caught his eye. After some weeks Jesse's curiosity got the best of him, and he strode up to the girl.

"I'm Jesse Arredondo," he announced loudly. He would have preferred to meet her through a third party, but since none ever seemed available, he decided to take the introduction upon himself.

"I'm Eva Navarette," she responded a bit startled by this bold young man's forwardness. But Jesse was handsome and had his own brand of charm. Though a bit rough around the edges, Eva could see that Jesse was a smart, likable young man, and she was attracted to him.

They began dating. Jesse learned that she was working in the main office of Inland Steel. Jesse shared with Eva stories of his union involvement and confided that some day he hoped to become president of the local branch of the steelworkers.

Eva's mother had died when she was a child, and her father, a chef, had given her to her Aunt Herlinda to raise while he continued with his career in New York. Eva was a pretty, practical woman who wore lovely clothes. Both she and Jesse enjoyed dancing, and their courtship went smoothly. She laughed off Jesse's sometimes gruff manners and took his teasing sense of humor in stride.

When Jesse brought her home to meet Maria and Miguel, she was well-received by both parents. "Papa Pancho and Mama Quita," as the children called the Arredondos' longtime friends Frank and Maria Ramirez,

Eva Navarette and Jesse on their wedding day, October 1953

vouched for her proper upbringing. When Jesse announced that the two were going to marry, he received the blessings of his parents with no reservations whatsoever.

Jesse and Eva were married in October 1953 in a large Catholic wedding held at Our Lady of Guadalupe Church on Deodar Street in East Chicago. Both Maria and Miguel attended the wedding, along with family friends and the rest of the Arredondo family, with the exception of Jenny who remained in California. Councilman George Lamb, a well-known politician, gave the newlyweds a glass lamp filled with money. This made a lasting impression on Camila, who had felt so deprived about not having a new Easter dress years before. To her the lamp seemed a marvelous symbol of wealth. Though still very young, she longed for a beautiful wedding of her own.

Jesse and Eva honeymooned in Mexico, returning to take up residence in the basement apartment of the family home on Block Avenue. They remained there as they saved to buy a home of their own. Eva, who handled their finances, kept twenty-nine dollars each week for household expenses and placed the rest of their earnings in savings.

Eva and Jesse continued to enjoy their social life, going to dances and nightclubs on weekends. They established a routine. Each Friday after work Jesse and Eva would eat supper at Taco Joe's restaurant on Pennsylvania Avenue. Then they would return home to rest awhile and dress for the evening. They would climb into Jesse's car, pick up a couple named Leo and Ida Arreguin, and the foursome would head into Chicago and nightclub at Matt Ziegler's, the Heidelberg, the Arabian nightclub, or Riverview Park. Chicago offered a never-ending array of places to enjoy a night out, and the couple took advantage of all its many attractions.

The younger children were happy that Jesse, though married, was still at home and looked forward to the candy, ice cream, and hamburger treats he brought them. Maria was glad to have her son still with her and assisting with household costs. Miguel approved of Eva, although he seldom saw her except for the occasional meals she and Jesse took with the family. Usually, Eva left for work and returned to cook delicious meals for Jesse in their basement apartment. All in all, the match seemed a happy one.

In 1954 Jesse decided to continue his climb up the ranks of union politics by placing his name in the ring for financial secretary of Local 1010. Once Jesse had made the decision to enter the union race, the gears of the

Left to right: Eva's Dad, Joseph Navarette, Eva, Jesse, Maria, and Miguel, October 1953

Arredondo campaign machine went into action, using the lessons learned from Jesse's first campaign, Miguel's advice on strategy and organization, and most of all, leveraging the "who you know" factor from Miguel's past union activities. Jesse's campaign became the focus of the whole family.

Jesse and Eva's basement apartment became the headquarters for the effort; it was turned into a minifactory designed to produce and distribute campaign literature by an assembly line of workers grouped around the dining table. Campaign literature was written and typed by Sue. Friends, both personal and from the union, helped set up workstations for folding, stuffing, stamping, and bundling letters that were sent to voting union members. Ray and Lorenzo, though young, worked with the team. It was exciting for them to be exposed to the frantic world of political campaigning. Maria, with the help of Mary and Camila, kept the troops fed with sandwiches and tacos.

Eva kept a large coffeepot going at all times and learned to plan her tasks around the timetable of the campaign. She knew that each day as she returned from work, her home would be a hub of activity. Fortunately, her easygoing demeanor allowed her to accept the upheaval with little complaint, even when planning sessions went far into the night. She would refill the coffeepot and seek the relative peace of her bedroom as the campaign staff worked.

Jesse went out and sought union workers virtually anywhere they were to be found. He regularly made the rounds of union halls, taverns, social clubs, and billiard halls. Many of the workers knew him or at least the Arredondo name because of the years his father had been active in the cause. He introduced himself, shaking hands and expounding on his platform whenever possible.

Flyers were printed up, and he and union friends stood by the factory gates at each shift change to pass them out. Ray and Lorenzo were drafted to help in this activity; they stood handing out sheafs of flyers while asking the recipients to "vote for Arredondo."

The whole family was soon caught up in the fever that is an inevitable part of any political endeavor. The roller-coaster twists and turns of the campaign had a contagion that was unavoidable.

"Numbers are looking shitty," a worker would report one day as the inner group met for updates and strategy planning.

"What are you talkin' about?" another would butt in. "We got it in the bag. Everybody I talked to is for Jesse."

"Talk," spoke up a third tough-looking union guy, a cigarette dangling out of the side of his mouth. "Hell, talk is cheap. The vote is what counts, and that's anybody's guess."

Every day brought new rumors.

"They gonna try to steal it from you Jesse," were some reports that circulated. "You gotta have somebody watching the count like a hawk!"

"They got more signs than we do," offered another worried supporter.

"So what," countered his buddy, "signs don't vote."

So went the weeks that led up to the actual election day. A tired candidate watched as the votes were tallied. His family and campaign workers were almost too exhausted to take in the final count.

"You won!" a friend yelled as the voting trend became evident. "God dammit, Jesse won!"

Tiredness suddenly fell away. Supporters were ecstatic, and drinks appeared for toasts. The battle for politics is truly its own genre of warfare, and the war had been won. Jesse's buddies began fantasizing as to how they might benefit from their friend's victory. Jesse himself was flushed with the high that comes with winning. The family, especially the younger ones, were in awe that their older brother was now a "big shot."

Most of all, Miguel was proud—proud that his son had accomplished that which he had been denied. The seeds he had planted had indeed come to fruition. If there were regrets that it was his son and not he who was receiving toasts of glory, he did not betray it. His expression held only pride and happiness as he lifted his beer to toast the new financial secretary of Local 1010.

"I won because of you, Dad," Jesse broke in as the toasts were being raised. "They knew the Arredondo name and voted for me because of that. Thanks, Dad." With that, Jesse raised his glass to his father.

When the celebration had ended and the revelers had gone home to their beds, the women set about cleaning up the remains of the campaign and the celebration that had followed. The table was cleared, dishes washed, and trash collected and set out in the alley.

As Maria settled into her bed for the night, her spirit was not as buoyant as those of the others. The last one awake, she found the house unusually quiet and still. She said her prayers, thanking God for her family's blessings, although even as she recited her rosary, she felt a small twinge of foreboding. Gaining recognition was one thing, but she had no illusions. Fame exacted its own price from the recipient. She suspected this political arena would be anything but a walk in the park. At last she slipped into a troubled sleep, arising next morning to greet the new dawn.

25

Maria Battles the "Commies"

A succession of events in which the federal government interfered with steel-worker union members heightened fears about the "Red Scare" in the Harbor area after World War II. As early as 1943 the FBI had urged Inland to fire several Mexican workers due to their alleged radical views, but the union forced the company to back down. After the war, however, several Local 1010 union leaders with socialist leanings, whom Miguel was close to, including Nick Migas, John Sargent, and Jim Balanoff, were driven out of leadership positions due to pressure from the United Steelworkers of America president, Philip Murray, who held more conservative views. Also, the House Un-American Activities Committee had hearings in northwest Indiana to investigate communist influence in the mill. Thus, in 1954 when the McCarthy hearings were being televised, many Harbor residents, including Maria, became very worried.

Having long recognized the deplorable working conditions at the mills and having fought for workers' rights, Miguel had a positive attitude toward the communist idea of workers "uniting for the betterment of all." These ideas flourished strongly in his mind as he read literature of Bolshevik philosophers, causing him to champion justice for the common man and to admire aspects of collectivism.

"Stalin knows what he's doing with the working class," he would thunder after reading the daily paper. "Listen to this! He knows the laborers are being exploited. That's what we need here, in this country! Somebody who cares about the working class!"

"Miguel!" Maria would interject. "Don't talk like that. Someone will hear you! They'll think you're a communist!"

"Let them think what they like!" Miguel would counter. "What do I care? A man has to stand up for his rights, doesn't he? Look how those foremen treat us at the mill! 'Scum' they call us. If you don't move fast enough to suit them, they kick you in the behind and curse you for being a lazy Mexican! No, I don't give a damn who hears me. I'm right! Workers need to unite, or we'll never have the respect we deserve!"

Such talk terrified Maria. She knew the sentiment against the "Reds" was growing, and she was fearful Miguel would be branded a communist.

———◆•✦•◆———

As World War II ended, and Korea became the first "military action" of the cold war, Maria once again fell to worrying about the survival of her family. Meanwhile, Miguel focused on larger issues, a luxury he could afford only because Maria kept the home fires burning and the tortillas at the ready. First there was the war. Maria wondered if her middle sons might be drafted. And then there was the threat of nuclear attack. Nuclear power had become a reality that hung like a mushroom cloud over the world's population. The younger Arredondo children were taught to "duck and cover" under classroom desks in preparation for an attack, which seemed a strong likelihood as former allies became enemies.

The "communist threat" became a permeating theme, which tainted America's collective conscience. What kind of dastardly plots were being hatched in the Soviet Union? Had communism infiltrated our country? Was a governmental overthrow just a matter of time? Senator Joseph McCarthy thought so, and his hearings on potential "Reds" within the ranks of all segments of society brought Maria more unease. Miguel was as adamant as ever in his defense of workers' rights, and Maria feared he would be singled out for his socialist leanings and, perhaps, deported.

Miguel's oratorical skills were great, and he found a useful platform for his views on communism in the Mexican societal organizations that had formed alongside union halls, such as the Benito Juarez Mutual Aid Society. He soon had a wide range of friends, acquaintances, and admirers who sought his help and advice about everything from political concerns to what doctor to visit when children grew ill. Miguel spoke mainly to men, however. Although there had been an effort to form organizations for Mexican women, such as the Society for Mexican Women, many, like Maria, simply had neither the time nor the energy to attend. In many cases, the women so often sent their husbands to represent them that the women's groups became all male.

Maria heard plenty about communism without leaving home. In the first years of the cold war, television became a household staple. Even the Arredondo household had traded radio for television, thanks to Jesse's generosity. Miguel watched McCarthy's Senate hearings on communism and vocalized his disdain.

"It's a witch hunt, that's what it is. Look at him. He's attacking that guy sitting there just 'cause he speaks his mind. Those senators think anybody who supports unions is a commie. And so is anybody who stands up for his friends. Look at how that committee browbeats the movie stars! I thought America was all about free speech!"

With each of Miguel's blunt pronouncements the fears of being deported for Miguel's Red leanings surfaced for Maria. So great became her agitation that Maria's mind fixated on a need to protect her family from the government's "witch hunt." She envisioned squads of FBI agents swarming into her home as they searched for subversive materials. She imagined the heartwrenching scene as she and her children were led off onto the next train to Mexico as Miguel, shackled and in handcuffs, went to prison, never to return. All would be lost—her home, her friends, her hopes for the future. In her mind she cursed Miguel's collection of books and pamphlets about communism, which mocked her with their presence. At night, as she lay awake filled with dread, a thought became clearer and clearer: she must be rid of the silent enemy whose pages seemed to her a nemesis, laughing at her anguish. The books and pamphlets had to go, and she must be the one to banish them.

For Maria, the threat was personal and impossible to put into a perspective of relative importance. Maria was convinced that her husband's rash behavior had put them on a collision course with tragedy. It was her duty to step in and take action.

As the hearings droned on, her obsession strengthened. At first she was content to gather up the offending tomes and hide them from curious eyes. Into closets, under beds, and behind wardrobes Maria found dark caches for her identified contraband. Then she waited. And waited. When the explosive reaction from Miguel did not materialize, her thoughts took a more treacherous turn: why not destroy these repositories of evil and be done with them once and for all?

For days she watched Miguel until she was certain he was too engrossed in matters of the moment to revisit objects from the past. This revelation led her

Maria and Jesse, ca. 1947

to plot the most brazen deed of all. She set about retrieving her hidden stash and hauling the poisonous literature into the alleyway.

Deliberately dropping a few books into the large steel barrel that was used for burning refuse, Maria struck a long wooden kitchen match and dropped it into the pile. The first match flickered and died. So, too, did the second. But with the third match, the pages of one book caught fire, and soon a blaze grew.

———————

"Ma, what in the world are you doing?" Sue cried out. She had a rare afternoon off and had come by for lunch. Now she spied Maria from the kitchen window as she prepared to wash dishes. She was not sure what was taking place in the alleyway, which was deserted save for her mother, but the expression on Maria's face was enough to frighten her.

Sue ran out the back door and saw the stacks of books. In an instant she took in the situation.

"¡Dios mío, Ma! Those are Dad's books. He'll be furious! Have you lost your mind?"

Maria's audacity stunned Sue. She stood in shocked silence as she waited for her mother's reply.

"Have *I* lost *my* mind? Have *I* lost *my* mind?" Maria repeated, each word spat at Sue in fury.

"No, my mind is the only one working around this house! It is your father who has gone *loco*. It is he who places his whole family in peril with this commie stuff!

"I am destroying them before we are deported and your father locked away! There will be no evidence left for the FBI!"

More frightened than ever, the dumbfounded Sue gazed with horror at her mother, whose eyes gleamed with madness through the smoky haze of the fire. As the flames' glow lit Maria's face with dancing shadows, she came to resemble the pictures Sue had seen of avenging angels.

"Ma, what are you talking about? Who's being deported? What FBI? Are they taking Dad away? What's happened?"

Now both women were crying hysterically as the smoke nearly obliterated Maria's face, which was set in a rigidly determined mask of rage and desperation.

"Oh, God," thought Sue. "My mother has gone mad. She's insane! What should I do? Call Dad? Call the police?" There was no family she could turn to as everyone else was at school or work.

Sue quickly discarded such ideas. Who knew what repercussions might come from her mother's unbalanced actions? Getting anyone else involved might only make things worse. No, Sue decided, far better to humor her and try to get her back inside. As it was, some neighbor would show up soon enough.

As if reading her thoughts, Maria hissed, "Don't say one word to your father!"

Sue nodded mutely. She was not about to play the messenger on this one! Maria had no worries on that score.

"OK, Ma. Don't worry. I won't tell anyone," she tried to calm Maria. Sue held her hands in front of her as if warding off an evil spirit. She backed slowly away and waited as her mother threw the last of the books into her improvised witch's cauldron.

When her mother was satisfied that only smoldering ashes remained, Sue gently took her by the arm.

"Come on, Ma. Let's go inside. I hear Señora Martinez coming. She will wonder what is happening."

Maria came quietly. Now that she had accomplished her mission, she seemed drained. Her face, which just moments before had been filled with purpose, fell into an expression of bewilderment as she meekly allowed Sue to lead her inside.

Following what Sue thought of as her mother's temporary insanity, the two women awaited discovery. But, again, the drama in the alley faded quietly away until Maria's book-burning event hardly seemed real. To Sue, the wild woman so caught up in the violence of her one-woman rebellion became a sur-real memory.

Maria, however, felt not a moment of remorse for the actions she had taken. To the contrary, her memory held only feelings of pride and freedom—her soul as free and pure as the ashes that had drifted on the breeze.

26

No Good Solutions

*In 1949 the state of Indiana opened a mental hospital in Westville called the
Norman M. Beatty Memorial Hospital, which began admitting mentally ill patients
from northern Indiana counties in 1951. In 1954 the hospital added a maximum
security division for criminally insane patients from across the state. Eventually, the hospital housed approximately two thousand patients from the age of six
through adults. Before the hospital was converted to the Westville Correctional
Center in 1979 it played an important role in the life of the Arredondo family.*

Life became increasingly difficult for Miguel as his union activities caused
him to be fired twice. He had been a major player in the organizing of workers, a bright, self-educated man who was well-known for his abilities as an
orator and because of his strong influence within the union. He had become
a prominent member of the community, while at the same time he counseled
and mentored individual workers. In his work situation, however, there was
little reward for his efforts. The management saw him as a troublemaker and
agitator. Since he was not a citizen, nor fluent in English, after he was fired
the second time, he was finally rehired but in a much lower position. From his
menial standing as a janitor, he watched firsthand as others gained promo-
tions and status. His years on the front line of the workers' cause had helped
to advance his son, Jesse, and daughters, Jenny and Sue, but his personal lot
was one of deep disappointment and bitterness.

From a young man who never touched a drink, Miguel slipped further and
further into alcoholism, depression, and despair. In spite of his being proud of
the accomplishments of his children, their growing up and establishing lives
of their own gave him a sense of further loss. His strict discipline and control
had lessened. He felt useless and defeated. His firstborn daughter, Jenny, had

eloped to California, defying his wishes and leaving a hole in the fabric of the family. Jesse was married and busy with union activities. His other children had grown further from him as they grew up and found their own paths.

Maria became increasingly frantic as Miguel slipped down into the black hole of alcoholism.

"For the sake of God, stop this drinking! Get out and work. Do you want to disgrace this family? Do you want us to starve?" Maria lashed out at her husband as her despair at his condition deepened. She felt Miguel must be pushed. Helpless and frustrated, she berated Miguel's lethargy. It was all she knew to do.

Miguel had developed diabetes, an illness he had always feared, the illness that in earlier days he had cautioned his children about. "Don't eat candy. It will give you diabetes. It is a terrible thing; you never, never want to get it."

Now, he himself was afflicted. His heavy drinking exacerbated the illness, and his fluctuating blood sugar only caused his moods to swing more radically. He was caught in a vicious circle, not wholly of his own making.

Mike was particularly distressed by his father's condition. As the drinking increased, Miguel would often be unable to make his way home from the bars. He would stumble and fall, lying on the sidewalk until Mike would learn his whereabouts, pick him up, and bring him home. Mary, who was always close to her father, would meet Miguel and Mike at the door and help put their father to bed. This behavior escalated at an alarming rate. His children watched and suffered to see their father's deterioration. Their feelings ran the gamut from sadness, to anger, to disgust, to love, and back again.

Miguel became more and more despondent. He had lost his years of seniority and was working as a janitor after enjoying so many years of prestige and respect from his fellow workers. As his drinking increased, he seldom made it to work, and only by the kindness of his foreman and good friend, Willie Vega, was he holding on to any job at all. Maria, fearing for her family, continued to badger him to go back to work. This was a time when depression and alcoholism were viewed as character weaknesses, not as illnesses. Those with a dependency problem were treated with scorn, not sympathy. For Miguel, treatment was virtually unavailable; he felt inundated with the losses and failures both at work and at home.

Relief was only to be gained from drinking, an escape that allowed him to forget the hateful disappointments of his life, if only briefly. His medicine

COURTESY OF THE ARREDONDO FAMILY

Miguel Arredondo, ca. 1940s

was a bottle of Jim Beam whiskey or cheap wine in which he could literally drown his sorrows.

To Maria, he had become almost unreachable. She worried that he was spending the little money they had on liquor instead of caring for his children. Jesse had realized that giving his father pocket money only fed his habit, and he had quit supplying him with funds. As for the other children, the older ones had moved on with their lives, though they still faithfully contributed to the household.

The four younger siblings were at a loss to help their father. Ray and Lorenzo, particularly, felt the lack of communication and affection. The older siblings had known their father at a different stage of life; for the two youngest boys, there had been little interaction, and his alcohol dependency had lessened even that. They fluctuated between worry and denial. Mary remained the closest. She would sit with her father when he was lucid, and he would converse with her on "life lessons," which she took to heart and for which she felt grateful. There were still times when Miguel would regale the family at the dinner table with talk of world affairs, but as his alcoholism progressed even dinners with him dwindled. He preferred his wine to food.

Mike took on the role of father to his younger siblings while he watched his father sink deeper into his addiction. He graduated high school and, like his brothers, went to work in the steel mill. Also, both Mike and Chive joined the National Guard, training as "weekend warriors." The cold war escalated, and these home-based troops were considered crucial as a crisis in Korea developed and worsened.

Maria came to depend more and more on Mike to care for her, the children, and his father. Mike actually became like a father to his father. He shouldered the role without complaints. He had always been the most responsible of the boys, the one who worried about all of them and tried to keep the family on a stable course.

There came a time when everyone recognized that things could not continue as they were. Miguel had lost track of his days and had begun hallucinating. Maria could no longer deal with him, and the children became fearful that their dad would lash out at them in his befuddled state.

Mike took Jesse and Chive aside.

"Dad can't go on like this. If we don't do something, he'll end up dying," he told his brothers.

"What can we do?" asked Chive. "You know he won't listen to anything we say."

"You're right," Jesse agreed. "He won't listen to Ma either. But he's got to get help. We'll have to commit him."

"Commit him?" Chive echoed. "Commit him where?"

"Westville," Mike said gravely, referring to the state mental institution located in a small town about forty miles from East Chicago.

"We've got to." Jesse nodded. "He won't go on his own. It's the only way."

"Who's gonna do it?" asked Chive, still stunned at the idea of his father being placed in a mental institution against his will.

Miguel had always been so strong and in command. His children had been in awe of him. Like all children who watch the painful process of parents losing the characteristics that make them who they are, Chive was in denial.

"Don't worry," Mike answered, "I'll do it. I'll have the papers drawn up, and Ma and I will take him. The sooner he goes, the sooner they can get him better."

Mike felt his stomach knot as he spoke. Saying what was going to happen made it real somehow. Up until then, the idea of committing his father had been merely a concept, a possibility that could be explored and acted upon or rejected. Now the decision was made. He felt sick with apprehension.

"Yeah, yeah," Chive agreed, relieved that Mike was taking the lead once again. Chive would do what he could to help, but he could not handle the thought of checking his dad into a mental institution.

"Let me know what you need me to do," Jesse said, his voice tight. "I'll do whatever."

With that, it was settled. Maria, at her wit's end, was ready to agree to anything that might alleviate the state of affairs she had lived with for years. She was grateful to turn the matter of Miguel's problem over to her son.

By the end of the week, Mike had arranged for the proper papers to be signed by his mother. The next Monday, Mike, Maria, and Miguel made the drive to Westville, and Miguel was institutionalized.

"How could you?" Miguel turned to his namesake with hurt and anger in his eyes. He understood what was taking place and was thunderstruck that his wife and son had conspired against him.

"How could you do such a thing to your own father? I hate you for this. I promise you, I won't forget the harm you've done."

Mike led his mother from the halls of the intimidating institution. As they climbed into the car, Mike's heart was heaving and his ears were ringing with his father's words. The imposing red-brick buildings of the hospital disappeared in the rearview mirror, but his father's words haunted Mike from that day forward.

———◆•※•◆———

The Arredondos became accustomed to life without Miguel, but there was a pall over their days. Each handled it in his or her own way. The older siblings had their jobs, the younger their schoolwork. Chive and Jesse took turns driving their mother to visit Miguel on weekends. Maria reported his progress upon her return, but otherwise, by an unspoken agreement, everyone did their best to avoid the topic. The whole situation was too painful to be pulled out and examined, even if only among the family. Best for one to process the horrific turn of events in the privacy of one's own mind and soul. The family was forged in the "one for all and all for one" mentality. Yet this circumstance closed communication to a great extent. For the most part, the Arredondos kept their thoughts and fears to themselves.

Months passed. Miguel's hallucinations became more pronounced, and at times he "spoke" to his mother in Mexico. On other occasions he conversed with the famous Yankee players, Mickey Mantle and Whitey Ford. The doctors in the hospital administered drugs and later electrical shock treatment as they sought to ease his tortured mind. These methods were the standards of the time.

Sometimes Ray and Lorenzo would accompany their mother and brother to Westville. The drive seemed very long as the car made its way down Ridge Road from East Chicago to the rural setting of Westville. Maria made sandwiches, putting rice and mole sauce between slices of white bread. For the boys this was a treat that they ate as the fields of cows and corn passed by the car window.

Although they were allowed to go to the hospital, Ray and Lorenzo were never allowed to visit their dad. Whether that was because of the institution's rules, as they were told, or because Maria wished to spare her younger children the heartbreak of seeing their father so broken was not clear. Whatever the cause, the boys remained outside on the grounds, which had been fitted for patients' recreation. They passed the time by playing games of horseshoes, the actual shoes being made of rubber for the safety of the staff and patients should a resident become violent. They also played basketball, focusing on getting the ball into the hoop as they tried to ignore their reason for being there. Time seemed to crawl by as the family waited for Miguel to return.

Several months slipped away as late summer gave way to fall. Miguel remained hospitalized, the visits to Westville continued, and the silence in the family deepened. When questioned as to how Dad was, Maria's response seldom varied. "He's fine," she would say and the topic was closed. Neighbors and friends would inquire about him in a discrete way. They, too, got only a "He's doing better" or "He's fine" to which they would nod and change the conversation to another subject. They empathized with the Arredondos and respected their desire to bear their sorrows stoically.

At last in the deep cold of winter the doctors determined that Miguel was ready to return home. The final diagnosis was that the combination of drinking and diabetes was the cause of what was then termed a "nervous breakdown." The emotional stresses that he had suffered were barely recognized, much less acknowledged. Follow-up counseling or other kinds of psychological assistance were not even considered.

Jesse drove his mother to the hospital and announced at the front office that they were there to pick up his father, Miguel. After signing a few papers, his father was released, free to leave. It was as simple as that to end one of the most difficult phases in the life of a family that had continually faced challenges. The only instructions given were for Miguel to "take his insulin," something he had not been doing prior to being institutionalized.

On the way back from the hospital the roads were treacherous and coated here and there with thin, invisible ice. Hitting a particularly slick spot, Jesse almost lost control of the car as it fishtailed along Ridge Road, stopping on the shoulder.

"Goddamn it, Jesse! Watch your driving. If we wreck, people will say it was my fault!" shouted Miguel.

Jesse eased the car back onto the road and grinned. Dad was back and seemed his old self again.

Homecoming was as if he had never been gone. "Glad to see you, Dad," the kids said matter-of-factly as the family sat down for dinner. With that, the family was once again whole.

27

Love and Uncle Sam

*In 1951 while the cold war was in progress, Congress passed the Universal
Military Training and Services Act that conscripted men into the service for up
to twenty-four months of active duty.*

It was around this time that Mike met the woman who would become his
wife, Eugenia Gonzales. Eugenia had come to the United States from Mexico
City. She had ambitions to become a dress designer and was a talented seam-
stress. Her sister, Angela, and her brother, David, had already been living in
East Chicago when Eugenia moved in with them. She found a job in Plant 4,
one of the steel mill factories of Inland Steel that manufactured armor for
tanks. Here she made a friend of Gloria Delgado, a girl Chive was dating at
the time.

The two girlfriends were coming out of the plant one evening after work
when Chive came by to pick up Gloria.

"Get in, girls," called Chive.

The girls climbed into the backseat of Chive's old blue Plymouth. Sitting in
the front was Mike. Eugenia got a quick glimpse of him as he glanced around
during their introduction. She was impressed by his handsome face, which
bore a striking resemblance to Glenn Ford, a well-known movie actor.

Mike was smitten by the pretty girl who spoke little English and intrigued
by the fact she came from a big city. Her mother had died when she was
young, and her father had raised her. Now it was her brother who looked after
her well-being. Mike approached him to request permission to date Eugenia.

David agreed to Mike's proposition, but put restrictions on the arrangement.
Eugenia was to be home by ten o'clock each night. Like the Arredondo daughters,
Eugenia's family required strict regulations when it came to courtship.

Some months after the couple began dating, two events moved the relationship forward. Eugenia made plans to return with her sister to Mexico, and Mike and Chive were called up from the National Guard to active duty.

Mike was forced to act quickly. He had made up his mind to make Eugenia his wife, and he was determined that he would do so before leaving for active duty. Being both romantic and possessive of his chosen wife-to-be, he wasted no time. One night Mike went to Eugenia's home and, in front of her sister, bent on one knee and asked for her hand in marriage.

When David learned of this, he wanted the couple to slow up a bit.

"Go to Mexico," he counseled his sister. "When you come back here, then you can decide. You'll have a chance to see if he's serious and to decide if you really want to spend your life with this man."

Although David gave good and sensible advice, Mike was having none of it. His mind was made up, and his determined nature thrust him forward. He wanted to get married quickly, before the army could ship him off—perhaps overseas. Eugenia would come and live with his mother. That way he would know she was safe. In his mind, the matter was settled.

Chive wanted to marry Gloria as well, but she was not so sure she wanted to live in her mother-in-law's house. She was a beautiful girl and enjoyed her freedom. She had heard how dominating Señora Arredondo could be and had seen for herself how completely devoted her sons were to her. The thought of sharing a husband with a strong mother-in-law did not appeal to her. She chose not to make the commitment.

In the end, Eugenia agreed to Mike's wishes, and in 1953, while Mike was on a seven-day furlough, the two were married in a civil ceremony in Crown Point. The wedding party was small with Eugenia's brother, David, and Mike's sister, Sue, and brother, Chive, as witnesses.

Mike had arranged for the two to be married by the Catholic Church the next day, having persuaded the priest to forego the usual months of prenuptial instructions because of his army obligations. Eugenia spent the night in between civil and religious ceremonies in her mother-in-law's home. She slept with Camila, and the two girls talked late into the night.

The ceremony was scheduled early the next morning because Mike was understandably anxious to be with his wife. Eugenia, tired from the events of the previous day and her late-night chat with her new sister-in-law, was roused from sleep by frantic knocking on the bedroom door. She had overslept!

Left to right: David Gonzalez, bride's brother, Chive, Sue, Eugenia, and Mike, November 28, 1953

She quickly dressed in her long Spanish-style wedding dress. It was full skirted, white, and adorned with a seemingly endless row of tiny buttons. She struggled to fasten them and just made the ceremony in time. This time the guests included the witnesses of the day before as well as Maria and Lucy. After returning home for a meal, Mike and Eugenia honeymooned at a small motel called the White Owl. Only seven days later, Mike left for the army, and Eugenia moved in with his mother.

This was the arrangement for eighteen months while Mike completed his service obligations. It worked because Eugenia had been motherless since the age of seven. She had longed for a mother and viewed Maria as her mother's surrogate, even calling her "Mommy."

Mike and Chive trained in the military together, taking the bus with other troops to report for physicals in Chicago. Mike was in great shape, having been an outstanding athlete in high school. He had won second in the state swimming competitions, being one of the many young Harbor boys who had "trained" in the water of Lake Michigan.

Mike was so good at baseball that scouts had begged him to play in the minor leagues; as a hitter he had few equals. He always refused. He was a shy young man despite his strong personality. The thought of playing with hundreds or even thousands of spectators watching was intimidating to him. In addition, he wanted to be with his family. The Harbor was his home, and he planned to stay there. Chive was more a party guy than an athlete, but both brothers passed the army physical with no problem.

From Chicago the two young men went to Fort Sheridan, Illinois, for a week of processing. Here, they were issued their gear. Their next stop was basic training at Camp Chaffee, Arkansas, via a troop train.

Each brother viewed the experience differently. For Chive it was the beginning of an adventure. He was young and excited to see new things. Each weekend Chive would go into town and visit the nightclubs and bars.

"Come on, man," he would urge his brother. "Don't stay cooped up here in the barracks. Let's have some fun!"

No amount of persuasion could convince Mike. He stayed in the barracks, worried about his family at home, and wrote letters to his new wife and mother.

"OK," Chive would say when he gave up trying to get Mike to join him and the other soldiers for a night on the town. "Say 'hi' to Ma when you write."

With that Chive would head out for his party night, leaving Mike to his correspondence.

Army life was not all partying for Chive. The basic training was hard, hot, and physical work, but both Chive and Mike were unperturbed by that. After all, each had done their time in the mill and understood manual labor. What Chive was not prepared for was the blatant discrimination faced by African Americans.

One night Chive and a black buddy named Al Williams were on their way back to the barracks. They had hitched a ride into town but had been separated from the friend with the car. It seemed a simple thing to board a bus, so the two soldiers waited at a bus stop and began to enter the first bus that was headed their way.

"Hey," the driver barked when Al stepped aboard. "No colored on this bus. Whites only!"

Totally surprised, Al shrugged and disembarked.

"You mean my friend can't ride?" Chive asked, still not sure he had heard right.

"Yeah, whites only. Your buddy is colored, ain't he? He can't ride. Now sit down, I've got a run to make."

"No, thanks," replied Chive. "I'll walk with my buddy."

"Suit yourself," said the driver as Chive jumped down the steps to the road. Soon Chive and Al were walking back to camp, watching the bus speed away in a swirl of dust.

—————◆◆◆◆◆—————

Mike and Chive spent sixteen weeks together as they trained in infantry and artillery. Then they received their orders: Chive was to go to Camp Kilmer, New Jersey, to ship out to Europe; Mike's port of debarkation was Fort Lewis in Washington state. He was headed for Korea. Both brothers wished to remain together, Chive for the comfort of having his brother with him, Mike because he worried his happy-go-lucky sibling would never be able to get out of bed in the morning without his prodding. But joint assignments of siblings to the same units had been discouraged since three brothers had been killed on a U.S. naval vessel during the Japanese attack on Pearl Harbor. After a two-week furlough, Mike and Chive set off for an eighteen-month tour of duty at their respective posts.

28

Forgiveness and Reconciliation

Accustomed to their word being law, immigrant parents had difficulty giving up that control as their children grew into adulthood. Nothing had more potential for straining relationships between the generations than matters of selecting a spouse. In the Arredondo family, potential spouses required approval from both Miguel and Maria in order to be welcomed wholeheartedly into the family. This was difficult to achieve. Maria regretted losing the help of her girls at home, worried about losing the income each child provided, and felt she was losing her boys altogether. Most of all, as each child married, Maria felt more and more alone.

While her brothers were overseas, Jenny asked to return to the family for a Thanksgiving visit. There was much discussion as to whether the prodigal child should be allowed to come home at all. She had defied her parents and caused them great anguish. In her mind she had done what she had to do. In the family's opinion, she had broken with the sacred creed of family honor.

Her request to visit was weighed carefully. On one hand, there was an instinctive urge to banish her forever as punishment for her misdeeds. On the other hand, she was a beloved daughter, granddaughter, and sister. No one really wanted to cut her out of their lives permanently. The younger children eavesdropped as the arguments on both sides were examined.

"Betcha' they won't let her come back," Mary said. "Dad was too mad at her. He said he never wanted to see her again."

"I think they'll say it's OK," Camila countered. "She's their daughter. I think Sue is talking to Ma about how the Bible says to forgive."

"It will take more than the Bible," Lorenzo chimed in. "Don't you remember how Ma wanted to go and kill Lupe?"

"Yeah, but that was then, this is now," Ray offered. "Don't you think they'd forgive one of us if we did something they thought was wrong?"

This caused the siblings to pause for thought. Each of them knew they could easily take some kind of misstep that would anger their parents. They knew if they were in Jenny's shoes, they would want forgiveness. The thought of being banished from the family was a thought none of them could bear to contemplate.

In the end, a compromise was reached. Jenny could return to the fold on the condition that she literally got on her knees and begged forgiveness. While this may sound a bit dramatic, it was in keeping with the traditions of the culture and the family. Jenny must show contrition for her "sins." What more appropriate method than to humble herself in this manner?

Jenny complied with this requirement and, after proving her contriteness in a somewhat archaic manner, the family celebrated the holiday together. Lupe did not accompany Jenny on the trip back home.

———•◆◆◆•———

Jenny's flight to California had not put an end to the relationship that had begun between Sue and Manuel. They had continued seeing one another, and in between happy times and stormy ones, their feelings for each other grew. Manuel was a smart, ambitious, and hardworking man. He had struggled to educate himself in the most difficult of conditions, at one time being so poor that he could not afford shoes, which almost prevented him from going to school.

Like Sue's father, Manuel pursued intellectual ideas. He had worked at Inland Steel and seen for himself the shameful way in which workers were treated. He abhorred the humiliation men had to endure just to earn a living and was a strong union supporter. He, like Miguel, was a man of strong opinions and stubborn ways. Once he made up his mind on a subject, it was highly unlikely that he could be persuaded to change it. He had an aura of determination about him and showed signs of becoming successful in his career.

Sue was not anxious to jump into a permanent relationship, particularly with the sting of Jenny's abrupt departure still very much in the forefront of the family's psyche. Manuel was headstrong and determined to make Sue his wife. Sue was equally strong willed and refused to make any rash decisions. For what she believed to be good reasons, for a while she ignored his attempts to contact her.

Manuel had been married before in Mexico. It was an unfortunate match, and he had filed for divorce soon after. He knew Sue would never entertain his becoming her husband unless he was free. He did his best to persuade her that he was sincere and was putting things right as far as ending his previous marriage. At last she consented to marry him, but with the usual caveat: Manuel must ask permission of her family.

Manuel approached Sue's father after he had gone to Mexico to handle the legal aspects of his first marriage.

"I want to marry your daughter," he said. "Here are the divorce papers that prove I am a free man." He held the documents out for Miguel to review.

Miguel liked Manuel and respected his views on politics and world affairs. During their talks over beer, Miguel had been impressed with the intelligence of the young man who wished to be his son-in-law. He willingly gave his permission, but Maria, on hearing the proposal, turned on her heel and left the room. She had "lost" one daughter to marriage and was anything but eager to let go of another.

"How can you even think of marrying that man?" she railed at Sue. "Can't you see he's no good? He had one wife in Mexico. What makes you think he won't have another? Didn't you learn anything from your sister Juanita! You think she's happy out there, far away from her family?"

"I love him, Ma. We're gonna get married," Sue responded. She had little hope her feelings would soften her mother's opinion, but she felt compelled to express them.

"Love!" Maria spat out. "Love! Do you really think love is the answer to all life's problems? Look at me. I love your father and what has it brought me? Ten kids to raise and a man who hardly knows I'm around except when he wants me to make him something to eat! I have put up with his women and his drink and stayed with him because I must. But you, you've got a job. You don't have to listen to any man. What do you want to mess up your life for? Love, huh! It won't keep you fed or warm at night!"

The years of hurt and frustration spewed from Maria's lips. She had watched Jenny let go of her life for a man. Now a second daughter proposed to do the same. It seemed more than she could accept.

The day Sue was getting ready to go to the county seat to marry, her mother was beside herself. She cursed her daughter, calling her names and warning her that if she went through with the marriage, she would put herself in disgrace.

Maria's entire life was built around her children. Theirs was a mutual dependency that she both nourished and manipulated to her advantage. The love and affection so seldom shown by her husband, Maria claimed from her children. After the hardships she had suffered, it was not surprising that she saw her daughter's leaving as another frightening betrayal.

"Don't talk to her like that," Grandmother Rita scolded her daughter. "Those curses you're hurling may come true. You're ruining her life!"

Maria brooked no interference. She turned to her mother and threatened, "If she leaves, she's never to return."

Sue left the house. She had no family in attendance because Maria forbade the siblings to attend. This upset Camila, who cried at what she considered an unfair edict. She loved the romance of a wedding and felt cheated that she was not allowed to attend, but in the end no one in the family dared disobey their mother's wishes. Sue was married in a quiet ceremony in the lovely old brick courthouse in the center of Crown Point's main square. She might have preferred a formal wedding, but she had no illusions on the matter. Her mother would have foiled any plans she might have made. Her only course was to marry Manuel as quickly and quietly as she could.

The couple moved into an apartment on Main Street. Sue continued working at Local 1010, and Manuel began a career, which included a stint in the Korean War, earning a college degree, and eventually becoming a federal mediator. For a poor farm boy who came to this country at age sixteen without a high school education, his achievements were remarkable, but this was in the future. For the present, the couple started their lives together in the Harbor under a cloud. It hurt Sue to be cut off from the family she loved.

Because she was banned from returning to the family home, Sue did not see her parents, but her sisters and brothers often dropped by on their way home from school. She became pregnant, and in 1954 she delivered a baby girl named Rita in honor of her grandmother. Throughout the pregnancy, Sue was still estranged from her parents, but after her child was born, she decided to make an overture at reconciliation. It would be up to her mother as to whether or not she accepted the gesture.

"Go tell my mother I had a girl," she directed Manuel. "If she throws you out, that's OK. At least she can't say I didn't let her know."

Manuel dropped by the Arredondos on his way to work. Maria answered the door. Before she could speak, he said simply, "I came to tell you your daughter had a girl." After that straightforward message he turned and left.

Left to right: Jenny's husband, Lupe Sanchez, Ray, Lorenzo, and Jesse, Los Angeles, 1953

Eventually, Maria's resentment at not being able to control her daughter's life gave way to the natural desire of a grandmother to see her grandchild. She made the short trip to Sue's apartment, and the new granddaughter healed the breech between mother and daughter. From that point forward, Sue and her family were welcomed back into the bosom of the Arredondo family. Baby Rita was a regular visitor as Rita, Maria, and Sue's younger sisters bickered over the privilege of babysitting the new arrival.

—◆◆◆◆◆—

Prior to her sister Sue's giving birth, Jenny had had a son, Juan Miguel, who was born in California in November 1952. Jenny became very ill after his birth and was unable to care for the baby and her husband.

After long-distance calls related the gravity of the situation, it was decided that Rita would go to California to care for Jenny and her family during Jenny's recuperative period.

Jesse was tapped for the job of making the long road trip west, driving Rita to minister to her granddaughter. It was summertime, so Camila, Ray, and Lorenzo went along for the ride. Climbing into Jesse's silver grey Hudson that he had purchased from "Jim Moran the Courtesy Man," a well-known car salesman from Chicago, they were off. Mary remained with her mother to assist with the housework.

For Jenny, the decision for Rita to come was a relief. She was ill, and the thought of having her grandmother with her was an answer to her prayers. She could stop worrying about the care of her child and her husband, and she would have her grandmother as a welcome companion. It would be like the old days when she was a girl and lived with Rita.

For Jesse, the trip was not such a bed of roses. The 1950s were presuperhighway years. Lodging and restaurants were few and far between on the long trek between East Chicago and East Los Angeles. Most of the meals consisted of food from hamburger and hotdog stands or milk, bread, and donuts purchased from local grocery stores. Sleeping was often in the car with Grandma Rita in the back seat, Camila in front, Jesse on the hood, and the boys across the roof. The trip west was an adventure for the children; indeed, Camila had the time of her life. Friendly truckers handled mishaps such as blown tires. Their jaunt through Wyoming was memorable because it was so cold in the middle of July; Arizona was equally hot day and night. They had to close the car windows to keep the heat out. For the three children it was a marvelous vacation. Never having left the Harbor, each turn of the road brought with it a new and fascinating sight.

For Jesse, it seemed more like a journey from hell. He worried about finding gas stations along the long stretches of highway. At times the chatting of the kids in the back seat nearly drove him mad. The weather was either too hot or too cold, and he had to watch his money as he doled out cash for food and drink. What was a grand tour for the kids was a worrisome chore for Jesse.

When they arrived in California, Lupe showed the ragtag group around the big city. Lorenzo and Ray had begged to accompany Jesse on the long excursion, and the trip surpassed their wildest dreams. The boys stayed awake as much as possible so as not to miss anything. Los Angeles was a paradise in their eyes; they were truly awed by the sights, sounds, and smells of the city.

Jenny and the new baby were wonderful "attractions" as well. Jenny and Juan Miguel were in a small hospital where visiting children were technically not allowed. Jesse explained to the nurses that the kids had not seen their sister in years, and he charmed them enough to sneak the three into Jenny's room. They fell in love with their beautiful little nephew.

When it was time to return home, Rita and Camila remained to help Jenny. Jesse and the boys piled into the car for the long journey home. Unfortunately, the return trip was severely marred by Lorenzo's violent attack of homesickness. Deprived of Rita's comforting presence, Lorenzo began an

Rita with granddaughters Camila (left) and Jenny, holding her great-grandson, Juan Miguel Sanchez, in Los Angeles, 1953

endless wailing for his mother. The magic of new sights was dulled by the absence of a mother figure, and Lorenzo was vocal in his distress. Jesse assumed that he would cry himself out eventually, but he was wrong. Lorenzo's crying only increased in volume as the car covered the miles.

Finally, Jesse reached the end of his rope as the threesome entered Arizona. He found a phone booth and put in a long distance call to Maria. True to his reputation for straight talk, he barked into the receiver when his mother answered, "You better talk to this guy. If you can't shut the kid up, I'm going to kill him and bury him in the desert! I can't drive with him crying all the time!"

On hearing this threat, Maria had no difficulty in recognizing Jesse's patience had been severely tried. She talked to the sniffling Lorenzo and calmed him down. When the phone receiver was returned to Jesse, she said simply, "Just bring him home."

Jesse needed no prompting. The group made its way back as quickly as possible. When they stopped in Saint Louis, they had no money for a hotel so they parked near a church by the waterfront and slept there, unmolested. Grand as the trip had been, all were delighted to return home to Block Avenue, perhaps none so grateful as the long-suffering Jesse.

———◆◆◆◆◆———

Mary's time at home with her parents was almost like a vacation for her. She did her chores, listened to Miguel's dinner talk, and realized how much less work there was with her three brothers on the road. Sure, she missed them, but it was nice being an "only child" for a time. She helped Maria in the kitchen, and the two chatted like friends, not like mother and daughter.

After several days this routine felt pleasant and relaxed. Mary enjoyed watching Maria break eggs directly on the griddle and flip them effortlessly so both sides cooked evenly. Mary had been helping with preparation work like peeling potatoes or chopping onions until her tears flowed but had not graduated to the actual cooking stage. She watched her mother carefully as she poured, pinched, and stirred ingredients with no recipe or measuring utensils.

Maria sighed heavily as she lifted a large bowl, preparing to make tortillas, and said: "Too bad you're too young to cook, *hija* (daughter). You could make the next batch and surprise your brothers and Camila when they come home."

"Too young? Gosh, Ma, how can you say that? I'm already cleaning and washing and making beds. I can cook tortillas, too. I know how!"

"Oh, you do," answered Maria. "Now how could you know that?"

"I watched you, Ma. I know what you put in them."

"Hmmm, you do, huh? Well, OK, then. Give it a try."

Mary quickly began to assemble ingredients, put flour and lard into a bowl, and using the "pinch" method added salt and baking soda. She stirred them together, added water, and stirred again. When the consistency was right, she rolled little balls of dough, then rolled them with the piece of pipe that Maria used for a rolling pin until flat, round tortillas took shape. All the while Maria watched silently.

"How's that, Ma?" a very proud Mary asked.

"Well, they look pretty good. Let's see what your father says when you cook them tonight."

Mary could hardly contain her excitement. She was going to serve her father her very own tortillas.

"How do you like the tortillas, Miguel?" Maria asked at dinner.

"How do I like them? Fine. Why are you asking me? They're the same every night."

"I made them Dad," interrupted his happy daughter. "Are they as good as Ma's?"

"Sure," Miguel looked at her. "Every bit as good. I couldn't tell the difference."

Mary was overjoyed to have pleased her father. She received the same accolades from her siblings when they returned.

"Thanks, Ma, for letting me make them. I knew I could."

"*De nada*, you're welcome, *hija*. You did well."

It was not until two weeks later that Mary realized her eagerness to prove herself had resulted in a permanent extra duty.

"I should have kept my mouth shut," she confided to Camila. "I forgot Ma always does things for a reason."

Camila laughed, vowing to herself to avoid volunteering at all costs. Tom Sawyer had nothing on Maria.

29

The Value of Education

*Coach Johnnie Baratto arrived at East Chicago Washington High School in
1944. During his career, he not only became a legend, he also helped many
high school basketball players go on to college. Despite walking with a limp and
talking out of the side of his face as a result of contracting polio as a child, he
demanded respect and took his team to the Final Four in 1947 and won a state
championship thirteen years later.*

While his brothers and sisters were marrying, shipping off to combat, or
taking road trips west, Pepé continued his studies. When he was a young boy,
Mike and Sue had taken him to a basketball game to see East Chicago Washington High School play Lafayette Jefferson High School. The atmosphere of
the game immediately captivated him. The music of the band, the energy of
the cheerleaders, and the excitement of the crowds rooting for their teams
mesmerized him. Most of all, the players seemed like special beings as they
ran up and down the court. To Pepé, they were superheroes with sweaty shirts
and flying sneakers. There was no doubt—this was the biggest event in his life.
Then and there he knew he must play basketball.

Pepé set about achieving his goal with determination and a focus unusual
for one so young. Knowing good grades were a determining factor in becoming a team member, he studied hard. The Arredondo home on Block Avenue
offered little in the way of peace and quiet so Joe, as he had become known at
school, studied at the library, often staying until it closed at nine o'clock. In the
relatively quiet library he could focus on his lessons.

When he reached ninth grade, Joe showed up at basketball tryouts and
made the team. John Baratto, the coach, became a role model and mentor
to him and, in later years, to his younger brother, Ramón. Joe's spare time

East Chicago Washington High School basketball team, 1952. Joe is standing in the back on the right, next to Coach Johnnie Baratto

was consumed with practice and, under Baratto's tutelage, he flourished. The coach was extremely dedicated to his players and made it a special point to go to their family's homes and meet their parents. Baratto believed his personal relationship with the Arredondos would help secure family support for Joe. As the season progressed, the upper stands would often be filled with his mother, brothers, and sisters cheering Joe along. Once, even his father attended the game. His teammates were his special comrades, and Joe was in his element on the court.

Though Rita did not attend the matches, she was very aware of her grandson's every game. She lit candles and prayed that East Chicago Washington would win against whatever opponent was scheduled.

On one occasion Rita had missed the scheduling of a game. She walked over to Maria's and, after settling into a comfortable chair, inquired, "Where's Pepé?"

Maria was in the kitchen getting coffee for her mother. The weather was frigid, and the walk to her daughter's had chilled Rita.

"Oh, he and the team went over to Jasper. They had a game there," called Maria as she poured the steaming beverage.

"What! I didn't know he was playing today. I didn't light a candle!"

With that, Rita jumped up from the chair and hastened to put on her heavy coat. Before Maria could stop her, she had fled the house, trudging the snow-covered sidewalks to return home where she would light a candle and pray for Joe's victory.

Meanwhile, tired from their trip to the small Indiana town of Jasper, the East Chicago Washington team was making a terrible showing. Suddenly their school's luck seemed to change, and the team miraculously snatched victory from their opponents.

When Joe arrived home, he described the sudden change in fortune to his mother.

"No, kidding, Ma. It was like a miracle or something. They were beating the heck out of us, and then the whole game turned around. These guys didn't know what to think. It was like we couldn't miss a basket," the exuberant Joe concluded, his eyes sparkling from the unexpected win.

Maria then told him of Rita's rush home to light the candle.

"Wow!" Joe exclaimed, hearing the tale. "She went home at 4:30? That's amazing, Ma. That's exactly when we started shooting right."

Telling his teammates of his grandmother's lighting of the votive candle, he swore it was the charm that changed the game's outcome. While some of the teammembers looked at him with skeptical eyes, Joe never doubted the power of Rita's prayers.

To keep in form, Joe also played with neighborhood teams composed of groups of boys in the area. When the teams had actual games, the kids in Joe's group had no uniforms and no money to get them. The team turned to a local "business" man to solve the problem.

A gambling house known to locals as the "Big House" was in the area by the tracks. The "Boss," who ran the gambling establishment, was called Peck Gardner. His bodyguard, Bruno, would buy milkshakes for the local kids in exchange for information.

"Let us know if you ever see people on the roofs around the house," Bruno instructed the kids.

The boys figured out that the gambling ring was worried about cops, cheaters, or competitors trying to horn in on their operation. The boys had no problem acting as extra eyes and ears for Bruno; after all, everyone accepted that gambling was an integral part of the city. Besides, the milkshakes Bruno handed out to keep the boys on board were delicious.

The girls had an interest in the "Big House" as well, though in a more indirect way. The glamour of the place lured throngs of people from Chicago to indulge in slots, roulette, and card games. The Arredondo sisters loved watching the beautifully dressed women and their escorts alight from buses chartered for the occasion. To the girls, the silks and satins, furs and jewels were as exciting as any red carpet parade in Hollywood.

When the lack of uniforms became a handicap to Joe's team, the group pondered the problem. They knew Gardner was the most prominent "businessman" around. After a bit of discussion, they hit on a plan.

"Let's ask Peck for a donation," the members suggested, quickly following up the idea by appointing Joe as the designated "ask man." After all, who better to approach the Boss than a guy who was noted for his gift of gab.

With some trepidation, Joe approached the Big House, timidly knocking on the door.

"Yeah?" asked Bruno, deliberately opening the door just a crack to check out the visitor.

"Could I see Mr. Gardner?" Joe replied, rallying his courage.

"Why?" replied Bruno, puzzled as to why a teenager would come asking for the Boss.

"Well, my buddies and I are forming a basketball team, and we wondered if Mr. Gardner would donate for uniforms?"

"Wait here, kid," Bruno said, having satisfied himself that Joe was neither hit man nor cop.

Gardner was summoned.

"How much ya need?" Gardner asked Joe, coming directly to the point when he arrived at the door. Gardner was not a man to waste time on the niceties of small talk.

"Its forty-nine dollars for ten uniforms," answered Joe who had prepared for the meeting by checking out the cost of the clothing needed.

"OK, kid. Here's $50.00—go get your uniforms."

Joe stuttered a shaky "thank you," then beat a path back to his buddies.

"Wow, Joe, you did it! You went right up there and asked old Peck for the dough!" cried one of his teammates.

"Yeah, he did," chimed in the others. "Great going, Joe!"

Joe was flattered by the praise and still a little startled that his mission had succeeded so easily.

Flushed with success, Joe shouted, "Come on, guys! Let's go spend this money before he changes his mind!"

Thrilled, the boys rushed to the sports shop and bought ten black and orange uniforms that transformed the group into a real neighborhood team.

Unfortunately, all neighborhood groups were not focused on such innocuous activities as basketball. Some older boys would use Saturday nights not for games, but for fighting. Gangs would square off against one another at the railroad tracks after attending local dances.

The Watling Trojans, Blockbusters, and Deodar Boys were all rougher versions of Joe's basketball friends. But even within these groups, there were specific codes. The fights were fair, and no weapons were used. Once one side was declared victor, everyone simply quit and left. The only exception was the "Wino" gang from South Chicago. These were a far more aggressive bunch, often having attended reform school. They strutted down the streets of the Harbor in their signature white sweaters and maroon pants, their expressions warning passersby that they were itching for a brawl. Often the excuse for a fight was that guys were going with girls who were "not in their territory."

After some really violent brawls, primarily instigated by the Winos or others of the same ilk, the parish priests and parents organized to provide a healthier atmosphere for the area's young people to get together. Our Lady of Guadalupe Church was instrumental in securing a recreation area that provided kids with ping-pong, a boxing program, and a black-and-white television where the boys watched sports. Football was played outside. This gave the local youths an area to gather and participate in directed activities. The community effort went a long way to keep neighborhood youngsters out of trouble.

As for Joe, his love of basketball served him well. Following a pep talk by Coach Baratto on the advantages of higher education, Joe set his cap on a college education. Unfortunately, his aspirations ran headlong into a brick wall when Joe broached his idea to the family. Miguel was firmly against any thoughts of higher education. The family did not have the finances, and, despite Miguel's personal love of learning, college was not in the mindset of a man who had struggled for his family's survival. There were no role models within the Arredondos' circle of friends and acquaintances who had even

entertained such a wild idea. As far as Miguel was concerned, Joe might as
well aspire to being King of England—it was as much within the realm of
possibility as college.

"We don't have money. That's why we're in the mill. It's a good, steady
living. Why do you think we worked so hard for the unions? So you could have
a decent life, that's why! Appreciate what you've got!" Miguel told Joe, closing
further discussion.

Joe knew better than to plead his case with his mother. Maria had
expressed her opinions often enough in the past.

"Stick to the mills," she preached. "It pays good money, and it's steady
work. Why would you want to spend more time in school when you could have
a good job here? Stay, *hijo*."

Higher education was a foreign matter to her—a mysterious enterprise
that stole years from a wage earner's life, and, in her opinion, offered no surety
of a more prosperous future. No, for her part, she wanted her children to get
to work, do their share to help the family, and be grateful for the privilege.

"Look, Dad, I'm going to college, and that's it. I'm going to make something of myself," Joe persisted.

"Make something of yourself! What do you think, I haven't made anything
of myself? Look, boy. I helped start the union. That's a big deal whether you
think so or not. You think your precious basketball is going to make you somebody? Well, think again. Most of these athletes end up with nothing but a lot
of memories!" Miguel shouted as his anger grew. He resented Joe's continuing
to argue when he had made it clear the subject was closed.

Maria spoke, "José, look at your brother Jesse. Look how well he's done
in the mill. You could do that. You could be somebody if you wanted. And you
could stay here and help out the family. With Juanita gone, we need the extra
money. Why can't you settle for a steady job like your brother?"

Joe was not persuaded. He had enjoyed a taste of fame on the basketball
court, and he did not want to get stuck in a mill job. His brother Chive had quit
school and gone from a railroad job to a position at Inland. He seemed happy,
as did Jesse and Mike, but Joe was sure it was not the future he wanted.

Joe refused to be deterred and pursued his dream of continuing school.
A buddy, Ray Dahlin, talked continually about San Diego State and a basketball coach there who would tutor them and get them jobs. Baratto continued
to encourage him, offering to work on securing a basketball scholarship for
Joe. Jenny, living in California with her family, further inspired Joe to make

the move, despite their father's strong objections. With eighty dollars in his pocket, he and his friend set off for California after high school graduation. It was a scary decision but one Joe was determined to make work.

Joe's determination paid off. His basketball scholarship materialized as he had hoped, and he quickly adapted to college life. He also worked hard at his job in the college cafeteria.

When he returned home at Christmas break, he was more certain than ever that he had made the right decision. At the end of the holiday, as he was preparing to leave, Miguel, who had said little during his stay, stopped him as he packed.

"Here, boy, take this." He handed Joe a twenty-dollar bill.

It was not much, but the gesture meant a great deal to Joe. He viewed it as his father's way of saying he had reconciled himself to his son's choice, and maybe that decision was not so bad after all.

Joe left feeling relieved. Though he knew his father could never bring himself to tell Joe he was happy for him, his action had been good enough. As he knelt to get a "blessing" from his grandmother, he prayed to himself as his grandmother intoned her own prayers to protect her grandson on his journey.

"Thank you, God," Joe thought. "Thank you for helping Pa to see I'm doing the right thing."

30

In the Blink of an Eye

Railroad accidents were all too common in northwest Indiana, both within the mills and outside the gates. Trains were such a familiar sight that it was easy to underestimate their danger.

About a month after the 1954 Christmas holidays, the Arredondos were preparing to begin a typical day. It had been a cold and blustery January, and the four youngest children gratefully ate the hot breakfast Maria set before them. They chatted among themselves about the usual school topics: how some teachers were too difficult, what the basketball team was doing, and how far away spring break seemed. Miguel was still asleep as his children prepared to leave for school, grabbing their books and bundling up against the bitter cold of the Harbor winter.

"Bye, Ma," they each called as they tumbled out the front door and down the steps to the sidewalk. Along the way to Washington High School they hooked up with friends who were headed to school as well. It was a routine morning, giving no hint of anything to come.

At lunch Camila, Mary, Lorenzo, and Ramón, whose friends called him Ray, walked home for the meal they knew would be waiting. As with the older siblings, coming home for lunch was a long-standing tradition. Something about eating their mother's delicious cooking strengthened the kids both physically and psychologically. The warm house, the familiar surroundings, the surety that their mother would always be there to greet them brought a sameness and security to their lives that helped them face the world outside with courage and confidence. Home and family were a touchstone for each, reassuring them that, no matter what difficulties life might throw their way, unconditional love was always awaiting them here.

As was his usual habit, Lorenzo dawdled after lunch as his brother and sisters left to return to school. He preened his hair one last time at the mirror that hung on the living room wall. He was vain about his hair and had actually dropped out of band when he realized that marching in the wind disturbed the carefully combed wave that dipped along his forehead.

Satisfied that his hair was perfect, he turned to follow his siblings when he heard his Dad's request that he change the television channel. Miguel's curiosity about world events had not faded completely. Watching the news was one of the few interests he maintained.

"Sure, Dad," responded Lorenzo, flicking the channel knobs, and adding, "Bye, I'm going back to school now."

"Bye," answered his father, not taking his eyes from the screen.

Sue had come home from her secretarial job at Local 1010 to have lunch as well. Her mother was babysitting her new daughter, and Sue noticed her father staring at her little girl.

"Look how nice she is," he said, admiring his granddaughter as Sue held her. "She's the little *generala*," he continued, using his pet name for baby Rita. "Yes, the little *generala*," he repeated, nodding to himself.

Before Sue returned to work, her father asked, "Would you give me a dollar?" Maria had warned the children against giving Miguel money, fearing he would use it for drink. Sue was caught in a dilemma, for she had also been instructed to always obey her father. Reluctantly, she handed him a bill. How could she refuse her father? Hopefully, her mother would not learn of the incident.

As she left the house, she heard her mother urging Miguel to come eat.

He responded, "I'll be back, I'm going out."

"Where?" insisted Maria.

"Just going out for a while, I'll be back."

Later that afternoon as Sue sat working in the union office, the phone rang. The lady on the other end was calling to report a tragedy greater than any the Arredondo family could have imagined. The woman, unaware that she was breaking such horrific news to a family member, blurted out, "I'm calling to say that a train just killed Mr. Arredondo."

Sue screamed, dropping the phone and causing the other girls in the office to look up sharply.

"What's wrong? What's wrong?" they cried.

At that very moment Jesse and two detectives entered the room. The police had come to inform Jesse of his father's death, and Jesse had rushed immediately to Sue, worried about what her response would be.

"Take her home," he told the police.

"No, no," Sue protested, "I got my car." She wanted only to go to her apartment on Main Street and get her husband, Manuel. Asleep, having worked the night shift, Manuel was slow in answering her frantic knocks.

Finally, coming down the stairs to let Sue in, he took one look at her distraught face and asked, "What's wrong?"

Sue was too shaken to respond, crying uncontrollably and unable to utter the terrible truth.

Manuel sat her down and gave her a drink, calming her enough to get the facts she hesitated to utter, for in doing so she must acknowledge their reality. Manuel dressed hurriedly, and they went to Maria's. There they found her crying and surrounded by her women friends.

While Sue was learning the details of the tragedy, Lorenzo was running home from school, cutting through open land filled with weeds and through alleyways to go to the little general store called Micus. It was his habit to buy a coke and donut each day after classes. His route took him down Pennsylvania Avenue, only half a block from the railroad crossing where his father had been struck by the train. People were milling around the site, but Lorenzo did not turn in that direction and never noticed the crowd. A classmate was also running home. He heard her call to another girl, "Did you see that accident?" She may have added the name "Arredondo," but if so, the information failed to register with the teen. He continued home, entering the house through the back stairs. It was then he heard the cries of the women and saw his brother, Jesse, accompanied by a police officer named Machuca, trying to quiet his mother.

Someone turned to Lorenzo. "A train just killed your father." Lorenzo turned and shut himself in the bedroom, staying there for hours before anyone missed him.

Like Lorenzo, Mary and Camila were also making their way home from school with a cluster of girls. As they were chatting, they noticed one of the other girls coming up to her sister and whispering something. Then all their companions turned to stare. Mary and Camila looked at each other, wondering what was going on, but no one was forthcoming.

"What's their problem?" Camila asked.

At first, Mary just shrugged. She never wasted energy trying to figure out other girls. But, as everyone continued walking toward their respective homes, the other girls continued glancing back toward Mary and Camila. Suddenly, the Arredondo sisters were overcome with a feeling of foreboding. They began to run. When they reached home, they saw their mother crying and learned the sorrowful news.

Ray was the last of the children to reach home, having had a late basketball practice. He walked home alone, pulling his jacket closer around his neck to ward off the howling wind. Just as he reached the railroad tracks a strange calm overtook him. The wind stopped completely, and everything appeared clearer and brighter than it had just moments before. He thought how very strange the atmosphere around him felt and was puzzled that the persistent wind had stopped so suddenly and in such an unexpected manner. The experience was unusual and disconcerting, but he felt no sense of dread. Instead, peacefulness seemed to surround him.

Ray continued to make his way home. Upon opening the door, he walked into a scene that was almost surreal: women crying, his mother totally overcome with grief, and his sisters sitting in stunned silence. When Sue told him what had happened, it was too much for him to comprehend. He walked to the kitchen in a daze and began to fix himself something to eat. This denial lasted for months with Ray thinking that each time he turned a corner he would see his dad just up ahead. He could not cry or grieve because he could not process the magnitude of the tragedy. There was no grief counseling in those days, no one to help the children understand what had occurred and how to deal with the loss. Ray and his siblings simply coped as best they could.

The other siblings were contacted. Neither Mike nor Chive could get leave to come home from the army because "emergency" or "hardship leave" was given only in cases of critical health matters. A priest took Chive aside to explain the situation. Death was finality. There was nothing anyone could do about it. Thoughts of the need for closure or family support were not part of the military's policy. The two young soldiers were left to grieve for their father on their own.

Jenny was called in California. Lupe answered the call; after picking Jenny up from work and arriving back at the house, he told her she needed to call home.

"Why, what's wrong?" she asked.

"Your Pa's been hurt," was Lupe's succinct reply.

When Jenny telephoned, her expectation was that there had been an accident and her father had been hospitalized.

"How bad is Dad hurt?" she asked before even saying hello.

"Jenny? Is that you?" came the voice on the other end. "Didn't Lupe tell you? He's dead."

At that Jenny threw down the phone and railed at Lupe. "Why didn't you tell me?" she cried hysterically.

"Because I thought your family should be the ones to do that," he answered quietly.

After resuming the phone conversation and composing herself, Jenny in turn contacted Joe at college, giving him the news and saying she had reservations for them on a TWA flight at 2:00 a.m. The young men in Joe's dorm all chipped in to pay for his train ticket to Los Angeles where he was to meet up with Jenny. It was Joe's first plane ride. When he saw the aircraft he was about to board, he was fearful that it would not get them to their destination. These fears were only exacerbated as the plane bounced across the Rocky Mountains in turbulent January weather.

Grief for Miguel found its way to Mexico. Camila, his mother, was discovered by her son, José, early on the morning after Miguel's death, sitting silently in her chair. It was apparent that she had not slept.

"Ma, what is wrong?" he asked.

"Miguel is dead."

"Dead? How do you know?"

"I know," she answered in a flat voice. "He is gone. A mother knows."

Alarmed by his mother's strange behavior, José called the family in the Harbor, a call that confirmed Camila's pronouncement. Miguel was dead. A mother does know.

After what seemed forever to the family engulfed in grief, the Arredondos, with the exception of the two brothers overseas, gathered for the ritual "viewing." The coffin was closed, and friends and acquaintances filed past in a long, slow show of respect. The room at the funeral home was packed.

The wake was attended by political officials, neighbors, friends, all the kids' teachers, union men, and many who had known Miguel simply as one who could be counted on to help those in need; a man who stood up for the rights of the average guy and was not afraid to put himself at risk in the process.

Miguel was the leader whose eloquent speeches inspired and comforted. His friendly chats on the streets or in the taverns gave insight on issues others had found confusing or too removed from their everyday struggle to sort out.

The old-timers, the ones who remembered conditions during the Depression, knew what it had cost to form the union. They were the ones who had lined up at mill gates in the mornings, hoping to be picked to work, hoping to bring home a few dollars to feed the kids and pay the rent—a few bucks to survive another day. They remembered, too, how those chosen to work earned their money: shoveling in the open hearth or rolling the huge steel coils in the rolling mills—doing the hardest, dirtiest jobs in the mill. Anyone who fell behind or did anything to upset the foremen could forget further work, so the men pushed themselves beyond endurance in the hellish environment. But in those days, no one complained. They were too poor, too hungry, and too tired to even consider protesting.

Then Miguel and a handful of others started forming a union. Somehow, when Miguel spoke of how things could be—with decent wages, bathrooms, time to eat and, most of all, the security of knowing that if you worked and followed the rules, you would keep your job despite the nasty foremen—somehow, he made it all seem possible.

As they grieved, the mourners recalled with regret that Miguel had never received the recognition he deserved as one of the union founders; his lack of citizenship and fluency in English were two major obstacles precluding such acknowledgements. But the old guys knew his worth.

Yes, the guys who had been around for a while knew what Miguel had done for them and what it had cost him. A few of the younger ones may have seen him as a has-been who drank too much, but that was because they did not know the history and could not imagine the sacrifice and suffering that had gone before.

"He talked to everyone and helped so many," a lady told Maria. "That's why you see so many people here. Everybody wants to say good-bye."

Maria nodded, but was too numb to answer. Her black veil hid the shock in her eyes. Friends and acquaintances rallied around Maria to give aid and support, but nothing could bring back the head of the family.

The funeral was marred by the priest's refusal to say Mass, citing Miguel's lack of participation in the Catholic Church's rituals and holy days. Had it not been for a close friend (whom the family called "Aunt Mary") seeking out

Mike Arredondo (left) and Chive Arredondo in military uniform for Korean conflict, ca. 1954

the priest and giving a contribution to the parish, the former altar boy might have been buried without the blessing of the Church. As it turned out, the priest offered a graveside service. The family never quite forgot the treatment they received at the hands of the Church during this most traumatic chapter in their history. Mike was particularly angry; it was many years before he returned to the Church that had once been such an integral part of his life.

Despite these undercurrents, the funeral was one of the largest the town had ever seen. There was no disputing its size as the procession wound around the city streets before making its way to the Ridge Lawn Cemetery in Calumet Township. A hundred and fifty or more cars crept slowly along, passing the UBM (*Unión Benéfica Mexicana*), the union hall, and the house on Block Avenue. It was Miguel's last journey, and the long black hearse was honoring him by passing those places that had held such meaning in his life.

Maria was hardly aware of any of this as she sat in her widow's weeds, the black veil covering her beautifully chiseled face, her long hair coiled in a bun, the large brown eyes no longer wet with tears. As the shock of Miguel's death set in, the tears had been replaced with an expression of resignation and fear. What was she to do now? Life had been difficult enough when she had a husband. How would she manage with children to raise and no man as her protector, her provider? She nodded mechanically as condolences were offered, but her mind was elsewhere. She was a young girl again, living with her mother in Mexico, afraid of what the next day might bring.

Hundreds of mourners crowded around the gravesite and watched as the coffin was slowly lowered into the hard, frozen earth. Jenny wailed loudly, regretting the way she had hurt her father when she left for California.

Sue sobbed softly, thinking of the hundreds of times she had taken her father's presence for granted. As all people do when they lose a loved one unexpectedly, she wondered, what if she had talked to her father more that last day at lunch? Could that have delayed his leaving long enough to avoid the oncoming train? Witnesses to the accident said that Miguel seemed oblivious to the noise of the engine and their shouts warning him to move. Had her dad been drinking, or was he simply so distressed by the sadness of his life that he lost touch with the reality around him? What if his sugar level had clouded his mind—could the diabetes have so debilitated and confused him that he no longer functioned in his surroundings, no longer heard or saw what was around him? All these thoughts flew through Sue's mind as the coffin was lowered. Then Sue shook off the useless speculations of "what ifs" and took comfort that her father had lived to know and love her daughter, his grandchild. She would hold that thought as she and the rest of the family went through the burial procedures.

Jesse and Joe stood silently at the gravesite, trying to hold back their grief. Jesse kept his arm tightly around Maria. Mike and Chive, thousands of miles away, grieved silently at the thought of the final good-bye ritual they were unable to attend. Each longed to be there with the family on this sorrowful day. All they could do was pray that their grief and that of their family would be healed with time.

Ray, Lorenzo, and Camila stood in shocked silence. The past few days had passed in a blur of grief. It was as if they were viewing the scene from above, detached and uninvolved in the horrific happenings that surrounded them. As to Mary, she had refused to attend the ceremony. From a child she had been a private person. She had no intention of witnessing this final chapter in the life of the father she had so dearly loved. She preferred to bear her burden of sorrow alone, away from curious onlookers—no matter how kind their glances were meant to be.

Much changed after the family's loss. In some ways they were drawn more closely together. The absence of their father brought home to the children the importance of staying close to one another. It was comforting to all of them to know that they had family on whom they could depend. The older children supplied their mother with emotional as well as financial support to assist in the raising of the four dependent children still at home.

Jenny went back to California and resumed her life there. Joe returned to San Diego and college, supporting himself as a busboy for Sigma Chi fraternity. Mike and Chive returned from the army in the spring. Mike joined the police force, fulfilling a lifelong dream, and he continued in his role as father figure, watching over and advising his siblings.

Chive met and married Carol Gibbons, an Irish girl who shared his love of fun and dancing. Sue continued her job as union secretary. Jesse resumed his role in union activities, working to climb further in the ranks. Ray, Lorenzo, Mary, and Camila returned to Washington High School.

Life took on a new rhythm, one without the unifying beat of a father figure. Gone were the worries that Miguel was not working or was drinking too much, but gone, too, were the lively dinner discussions of world events. Gone were the strong convictions and unwavering expectations that Miguel had brought to his children's lives. They were gone, but not forgotten. The lessons learned remained in the hearts of the Arredondo children to carry throughout their lives.

31

The Vision Revealed

Located on Chicago's southwest side, the Shrine of Saint Jude Thaddeus is run by the Dominican Friars of the Province of Saint Albert the Great. To date, it has attracted more than a million visitors.

A few months following Miguel's death, Maria expressed a desire to go into Chicago to visit the Shrine of Saint Jude as this saint was one of several to whom the family prayed. Jude was known as "the saint of cases despaired of," and Maria was feeling a pressing need for his comfort as she adjusted to the loss of her husband.

Chive drove his mother and two youngest brothers into the city. He parked on Ashland Avenue, and the group ascended the steps leading to the massive front doors of the Church of Saint Pius V. They knelt as they faced the altar and then made their way to a niche on the left-hand side where the statue of Saint Jude stood.

It was a Saturday morning, and the church was quiet. Sun shone in through its stained-glass windows and dappled the worn wooden floors with dollops of color. A huge crucifix hung at the rear of the altar with a figure of Christ hanging in the last throes of his terrible and wondrous agony. The Arredondos knelt on the padded bench before the saint's statue and kissed, in turn, the glass globe that offered indulgences for sin.

As he knelt next to his mother, Ray's eyes looked up and met those of Saint Jude's for the first time. He was startled by what he saw.

"Ma," he whispered urgently into the stillness of the sanctuary. "That's him, that's the guy!"

Maria glanced over to her son. She had been preparing to offer up her prayers, to ask for Saint Jude's help as she struggled to continue raising her

Shrine of Saint Jude in Chicago

COURTESY OF THE ARREDONDO FAMILY

family. Ray's interruption was both a surprise and an annoyance. It was not like this son to intrude on another's privacy. Ray had always been her most considerate child, careful to assess the feelings of others before voicing his own.

"What guy? What are you talking about, *mijo?* You're supposed to be praying for your father's soul."

"I know, Ma," answered the teenage boy, disturbed by his mother's sharp tone, but eager to explain himself. He had often seen the small statuette of Saint Jude on his mother's and grandmother's dressers. Lit by flickering candles, these likenesses depicted a youthful saint, with dark hair and a boyish face. The large statue in the church was that of a much older man with graying hair and a piercing glance that seemed to follow Ray as he moved. He recognized the saint immediately upon setting his eyes on him.

"Ma, you've got to listen to me. That's the old guy I saw sitting on the bench. You know, the day I fainted when I was just a little kid. That's him, Ma! You've got to believe me."

It was Maria's turn to be startled. Of course, she remembered that day so many years ago when her young son had seen the "vision" of an unknown stranger. She had often thought back to that day and the peculiar reaction of her son. She looked at Ray and then up to the statue, which stood above them. Saint Jude seemed to be looking at her and her children while the marble figures of worshippers knelt at his feet. She felt a strange sense of peace descend over her as she gazed into his piercing eyes.

"I believe you, *mijo.* I believe you," she murmured softly to Ray as he awaited her response.

"He says everything will be OK, Ma. I heard him. I really did. He says we'll be fine."

And they were.

Maria (Perez) Arredondo, 1950s

Epilogue

Maria (Perez) Arredondo

Maria remained in the Harbor for the rest of her life, becoming both father and mother to her children at the death of her husband, Miguel, in 1955. At the age of seventy, she became a naturalized United States citizen. In 1990 she was awarded the Sagamore of the Wabash, the highest civilian honor in the state of Indiana.

Maria's gratitude for the opportunities that the United States afforded her and her children was a consistent thread that ran throughout her life. Her personal faith and value system inspired her children to become active community servants. She passed away in her home in 2004 at the age of ninety-seven.

Rita Batalla Perez

Grandmother Rita, too, lived out her days in East Chicago and continued to be the foundation of the Arredondo family until her death in 1977 at the age of ninety-four.

Francisco Perez

Uncle Frank led a full life until his death in 1978. He continued to live with his mother and Maria's family. He never remarried. For a time the Arredondo family lost contact with his son, Robert (Bobby) Pochinskas but have since been reunited. Bobby lives with his wife, Arlene, near Indianapolis.

MARIA AND MIGUEL'S CHILDREN

Juanita (Arredondo) Sanchez

Jenny was the first Hispanic secretary to work at District 31 of United Steel Workers of America. After her move, she remained in California for nearly forty years until the death of her husband, Guadalupe. She returned to the Harbor where she resides, volunteering at a local hospital and participating in various organizations and societies. Her son, Juan, lives in Illinois with his family.

Clockwise from bottom, left: Jesse and Sue, 2006; Maria becomes United States citizen, April 1978; Chive, Maria, and Mike, ca. 1970s

Jesus Arredondo

Jesse was elected first Hispanic financial secretary and, later, first Hispanic president of the largest steelworkers' chapter in the nation, Local 1010. He also served as an international representative for the AFL-CIO and as an auditor for the United Steelworkers of America. He attended Roosevelt University, studying labor and history during his career. He and his wife, Eva, have one son, Jesse Jr. They reside in Granger, Indiana, with their son and his family.

Socorro (Arredondo) Fernandez

Sue continued as secretary for Local 1010 for more than eighteen years. She then traveled throughout the country with her husband, Manuel, as his career advanced within local and international unions and culminated in the position of federal mediator. They moved to Ohio to be near their daughter, Rita, and her husband. Sue passed away in 2008.

Sylvester Arredondo

Chive remained at Inland Steel where he worked as craneman, shop steward, and vice chair of the union's Safety Committee. He was precinct committeeman in Merrillville, Indiana, where he and his wife Carol, who passed away in 2004, resided. He has two daughters, Christine and Mary Ann.

Maria preparing a few dozen tamales for a Christmas feast, ca. 1990s

Miguel Arredondo Jr.

Mike remained in the Harbor where he became the first Hispanic chief of detectives of the East Chicago, Indiana, Police Department and, later, first Hispanic chief of the Lake County Sheriff's Department. He was considered a "policeman's policeman" and received numerous awards in law enforcement. He and his wife, Eugenia, had five children, Theresa, Miguel, Mark, Susie, and Gina. Mike passed away in 1993.

José Arredondo

Joe (Pepé) completed his education, eventually earning a doctorate degree. He entered politics, and was elected as the first Hispanic state representative, county auditor, and sheriff in the state of Indiana. Presently, he is an assistant professor at Valparaiso University in Valparaiso, Indiana. He has written on the topics of education and diversity. He and his wife, Delores, live in Merrill-ville, Indiana, and have three children, Felice, Monica, and Joe Jr.

Marie Arredondo

Mary lived in the Harbor all her life and became the communication hub for the family, keeping each sibling updated on family matters. She was also the unofficial surrogate mother to all her nieces and nephews, babysitting at

Left to right: Mary cooking in kitchen; Left to right: Jenny, Joe, Lorenzo, Maria, Camila, and Mary leaning on Ray, 2001

one time or another for each and every one of them. She kept the family home and prepared weekly Saturday lunches, which served as forums for family discussions. In later years she was a faithful caregiver to Maria. She never married. Mary died in 2005.

Camila (Arredondo) Trevino

'Mila never left the Region, living in the upstairs apartment of the family home for decades. She worked in a secretarial capacity for numerous local government offices. She achieved her dream of a beautiful wedding with her marriage to Rolando Trevino. 'Mila has two children, Juanita and Camila.

Ramón Arredondo

Ray completed his bachelors and masters degrees in public policy at the University of Central Florida, becoming the first Hispanic graduating the MPP program. He worked in the criminal justice system at local, state, and federal levels and was the first Hispanic in the East Central Florida Regional Planning Counsel office and was clerk's office chief deputy in Lake County, Indiana. Ray served as district director for an Indiana congressman and was governmental affairs adviser to the chairman of a Fortune 500 Company, from which he retired. He now serves as a commissioner of the Ports of Indiana. He and his wife, Trisha, reside in Crown Point, Indiana, and Redington Shores, Florida. They have two children, Kenneth and Kristen.

Lorenzo Arredondo

After teaching high school in the Region, Lorenzo moved to San Francisco where he received his law degree at the University of San Francisco. He returned to the Harbor to practice law. He became an assistant county attorney and deputy prosecutor. Later, he ran for and won the office of judge of the small claims court and went on to become judge of the circuit court. He is the longest-serving elected Hispanic state trial judge in the entire country, holding the office of circuit court judge for more than thirty years. He is divorced and resides in Crown Point, Indiana. He is active in numerous local, state, and national legal organizations, receiving many honors for his achievements.

Afterword

This book has been long in the making. More than thirty years ago, a friend and colleague, Sandy Appleby, approached us about participating in a project in which she was involved at Tri-City Mental Health Center called "Pass the Culture, Please." The concept was to "capture" the culture of ethnic groups within the area through personal interviews; from this a slide show would be made portraying the beliefs, customs, and values of each—a sort of low-tech version of present-day reality television shows. Ray checked with his mother and siblings, who supported the idea, and production started.

Initially, James Lane, Indiana University (IU) Northwest history professor and oral historian for the project, spent many hours (with Ray as interpreter) taping Maria as she shared her remembrances of her childhood in Mexico and the Arredondos' immigration and life as they settled in the United States. Though the family had a long history of oral storytelling, Ray was astounded by much new information gleaned in these directed interviews.

The second step in the project was to interview Maria's children. Sandy and Jim were invited to the family home in Indiana Harbor for talk and a traditional Mexican breakfast, which included eggs, beans, tortillas, a soup called *menudo*, and the ubiquitous chili.

Normally, conversation at these family meals consisted of politics, sports, and family happenings. This time, however, discussion focused on growing up in the Harbor, family values and anecdotes, as well as the siblings' views on the present and future of Mexican culture in the United States.

After meeting with the Arredondo children, Sandy and Jim finished the slide show. It was shown at local venues and then stored in the IU Northwest's historical archives.

Those of us who participated in that breakfast went on with our lives. As for ourselves, we raised our two children, Ken and Kris, continued our education, climbed our respective career ladders, traveled, and did the million and one things that families do in their younger years. Among these activities was Trisha's interest in tracing her family's roots as they emigrated from Europe to the southeast United States. She took multitudes of notes and recorded wonderful family stories, which were stored in a drawer where they languished for two decades until she "had time."

Then we became grandparents, a life-changing event that motivates a shift in priorities and a desire to leave a history for the next generations. Eventually,

Maria with her ten children at the Arredondo family reunion in August 1975, left to right: Chive, Jesse, Camila, Mary, Lorenzo, Maria, Ray, Sue, Mike, Jenny, and Joe

Trisha had two "books" that related the history of her paternal and maternal ancestors. It was not until we saw the interest and pleasure that these brought to Trisha's relatives that we began discussing a similar "book" for Ray's family. After a long series of interviews (there are ten siblings!) Trisha compiled numerous family stories. By this time another of life's milestones had been reached; we had retired! There was more time for grandchildren, gardening, traveling, reading, and "real writing."

We set about turning the little narrative into a full-fledged book. As we tried and rejected a number of approaches, Ray recalled he had once heard President Richard Nixon lament the fact that no one had ever written a book about his mother. Ray had always considered Maria to be the dominant guiding force in his life; telling her story seemed a natural. After much more research and several rewrites later, we felt we had accomplished our task. The majority of dialogues of persons living were taken directly from interviews. The others were based on the recollections of these relatives.

In May 2008 we caught up with Jim Lane, asking him to review the product of our labor and give an honest appraisal as to whether it merited publication. Frankly, we vacillated between wild hope and nagging dread as to what his reaction might be. We had asked that he be honest and spare no criticism, but what author really wants to be told his or her efforts are in vain? To our great joy, he gave a thumbs up. With his excellent suggestions, much appreciated encouragement, and formidable editing skills, *Maria's Journey* was readied for publishers' eyes. Our good fortune continued when editors of the Indiana Historical Society Press accepted the manuscript with enthusiasm and made suggestions on how it might be improved. We hope readers will be moved and inspired by this wonderful woman's story.

While our story ends in the mid-1950s, Maria's life continued to be one of wide-ranging experiences. She lived to see her family grow through five generations with her first great-great-grandchild being born shortly before her death in November 2004. Through the years her children, instilled with the values of hard work and family solidarity, had established successful lives of their own.

Maria's love of America only strengthened with time. Though she never spoke English, she certainly understood it. Watching newscasts, she expressed strong opinions with her trademark honesty and bluntness. Incensed by stories that she felt unfairly criticized America, she believed that all people, especially immigrants, needed to take active roles in forging their destinies and not to rely on others to make their way for them. She never hesitated to admonish her own grandchildren or great-grandchildren if they crossed what she considered the line of proper decorum in any aspect of life, whether being disrespectful of elders or dressing too skimpily for her taste. At the age of seventy she became a naturalized citizen, and at the age of eighty-three she received Indiana's highest award, the Sagamore of the Wabash.

To the end of Maria's days, her home on the Harbor's Euclid Avenue remained the family gathering place for holiday get-togethers and Saturday lunches. No matter how far her children strayed to pursue their education or careers, they returned home whenever possible. Her "boys" remained the center of her universe, and she continued to cater to them, somehow managing to convey that each was her favorite. She cooked them special dishes, and their sisters continued in their role as "servers" to the males.

Maria herself seldom, if ever, sat at the table with her children. When not in the kitchen, she preferred to position herself on a living room couch, still wearing her apron, listening to the lively talk about sports, the heated debate about politics, and the good-natured ribbing and laughter interposed between calls for more tortillas and chili. Her expression was usually one of joy and

*Maria surrounded by her children, grandchildren, and other family members at the
Arredondo family reunion, August 1975*

pride beyond description though if she disapproved of something one of her
family members said, she remained quick to scold them in no uncertain terms.

When Maria grew unable to cook the meals, Mary took over for her. She
served delicious food but was less indulgent toward her brothers. "The boys"
soon learned better than to question why an entree was slow in arriving from
the kitchen or to complain if a certain item was not forthcoming. Placing her
hands on her hips and giving them "the look," she reduced her brothers to
meek, obedient "little boys" again. Mary became Maria's caregiver and the
family's communications center, keeping all posted on the happenings within
the Arredondo clan. Her sudden death at sixty-nine, almost a year to the day
after Maria's passing, was a loss almost as devastating as that of Maria's.

Sadly, before this book went to print, the Arredondo family lost two other
members. Cousin Lucy Del Rio, affectionately called "Aunt Lucy," passed away
in 2009 at the age of ninety-one, and Socorro (Sue), who was also Trisha's godmother, passed away in 2008, but not before we were able to share portions of
Maria's Journey with her. Both are sorely missed.

Nevertheless, the family refuses to let their tradition of togetherness fade.
Gatherings at siblings' homes or favorite restaurants continue to perpetuate
the tradition. At the same time, Maria's beliefs and values continue through
the generations who are coming behind her. Her legacy is alive and well.

Acknowledgments

There are many people whose help and support contributed to the making of this book. First, thank you to all of Ramón's siblings: Juanita, Jesus, Socorro, Sylvester, Miguel Jr., José, Marie, Camila, and Lorenzo. Their shared memories helped to make the story come alive. We are also grateful to other family members, especially "Aunt" Lucy Del Rio, cousin Robert Pochinskas, and sister-in-law Eugenia Arredondo for adding their remembrances to the story.

Thanks also to Betsy Kraft, Connie McCormick, Kathy Hoess, Bruce and Kathie Mole, and family members Bob and Jan (Hull) Groome, Kenneth and Karen Arredondo, and Kristen and Chris Danikolas for their feedback and encouragement; to Peter and Patti Fazio who provided inspiration by example; to Gary and Shar Miller, Gary and Sandy Neale, Joe and Pat Turner, and Becky Sczudio, Ed Pease, and the Indiana Society of Washington, D.C., whose support will never be forgotten. Also, much appreciation to Professor Larry Okamura in whose class we learned much more than Oriental Art History; to Steve McShane of the Indiana University (IU) Northwest Calumet Regional Archives and Ray Acevedo for their help with the photographs; and to our special slayer of the dragons lurking within the legal maze, David Milberg. Thanks, Dave. Rock on!

Kudos to Nancy Blair, longtime friend and colleague, whose ability to produce legible manuscripts from piles of scrambled pages is phenomenal, and to Sandy Appleby for inviting us to participate in a project thirty years ago, sparking the idea for *Maria's Journey*. There are not enough words to thank Teresa Baer, Kathy Breen, and Rachel Popma, our publishing editors at the Indiana Historical Society (IHS) Press, whose knowledge, expertise, and unwavering belief in the value of *Maria's Journey* have guided this book to publication and brought us, intact and mostly sane, through the process. The editors, along with interns Karen Wood and Melinda Weaver, worked tirelessly to accomplish our purpose of telling Maria's story within the high standards of the IHS Press.

To Professor John Bodnar, Department of History, Indiana University, Bloomington, who lent his historical knowledge and summarized Maria's life and character so beautifully, we are grateful. And to James B. Lane, professor emeritus of history at IU Northwest, a very special thank-you. His enormous historical knowledge of Northwest Indiana coupled with his enthusiasm, encouragement, and editorial expertise assisted us through the final pain of "birthing" *Maria's Journey*. Jimbo, the time and patience that you so generously gave resulted not only in a better book, but also transformed an old acquaintance into a valued friend.

To the members of the clergy who have assisted us, may God bless you! We also cannot forget the many dedicated teachers, both in the Harbor and in the colleges and universities, who encouraged and enabled the Arredondos and untold others to persevere in their learning and goals—a heartfelt thank you goes to each of you. And to all—friends and strangers alike—whose kindness and generosity helped Maria along the way of her journey—many thanks. May the blessings of God and Saint Jude help you throughout your own special journeys.